The Political Sociology of the English Language

Contributions to the Sociology of Language

7

Editor

Joshua A. Fishman

MOUTON · THE HAGUE · PARIS

The Political Sociology
of the English Language

An African Perspective

Ali A. Mazrui

MOUTON · THE HAGUE · PARIS

Cover design by Jurriaan Schrofer

ISBN 90 279 7821 2

Printed in The Netherlands by Mouton & Co., The Hague

Acknowledgments

This book brings together ideas of mine that have developed over a number of years concerning the sociological and political significance of the English language in Africa. I am greatly indebted to a number of journals and books for permission to use within these covers ideas which I first discussed in their own pages. Appendix C of this book gives more precise references to those original essays.

I am also indebted to Professor Joshua Fishman for his advice and support. He encouraged me to bring together in this manner my scattered ideas and general interpretations of the language situation in Africa, with special reference to the role and impact of English.

To the Rockefeller Foundation I am grateful for sustained research support over the years in this and other areas of social investigation. Aspects of my language research also benefited from the generous support I received from the World Order Models Project, whose African section was financed by the World Law Fund and the Carnegie Endowment for International Peace.

My wife, Molly, is co-author of the last two chapters. But as a linguist her contribution to the other chapters has also been significant, and often vital.

To former President A. Milton Obote of Uganda and Professor Chinua Achebe of the University of Nigeria at Nsukka, I owe the enrichment afforded to this book by the inclusion of their excellent essays.

Mrs. Anna Gourlay, Mrs. Winifred da Silva and Mrs. Jane Hartley gave to these essays over the years the services of informed and committed stenography. Mrs. Karen Primack provided further editorial and stylistic help with characteristic thoroughness.

To my academic colleagues at Makerere's Department of Political Science I am indebted not only for the infrastructure of academic stimulation which their very presence afforded me, but also for general administrative support in running the Department. Both forms of support have been vital to my career as a writer.

Finally, I am grateful to the Center for Advanced Study in the Behavioral Sciences, Stanford, for facilitating the final stages of preparing the manuscript for publication.

As for the faults in this book, those I must obstinately refuse to share.

June 1973   ALI A. MAZRUI

Contents

WHO ARE THE AFRO-SAXONS?

AN INTRODUCTION

By the year 2000 there will probably be more black people in the world who speak English as their *native tongue* than there will be British people. This is quite apart from the millions more who will speak English as a second language. Already black Americans alone who speak the language as their mother tongue are nearly the equivalent of half the population of Great Britain. And then there are a few more million black speakers of the language scattered around the Caribbean and the northern fringes of South America.

Within the African continent the only black native speakers of the language who are politically significant are the ruling community of Liberia descended from black Americans. There are also a few black native speakers of English in places like Sierra Leone. But at least as important a phenomenon is the growing number of educated African families that are using English as the language of the home. A number of African children, especially in West Africa but also increasingly in East and Central Africa, are growing up bilingual in English and their own African language because their parents are highly educated and speak English to each other.

It is these considerations which make it likely that by the end of the twentieth century there will be more black native speakers of English than there are speakers of it in Great Britain. And the speakers of it in Great Britain itself should, by the end of the century, include a few million black Englishmen.

Dr. Tom Soper of the Overseas Development Institute, London, once estimated that two-thirds of black Africa was in the process of becoming English-speaking. These Commonwealth Africans may well be joined by the inhabitants of what is now Portuguese Africa. It is possible that Angola and Mozambique, following the precedent of Indonesia, might decide that there is a case for changing their metropolitan language from Portuguese to either French or English. The idea that Portuguese and French are both Latin languages may tend to pull Angolans and the people of Mozambique towards French. On the other hand, if a decision as momentous as discarding the inherited language of Portuguese colonialism was being taken in any case, the people of Angola and Mozambique might as easily shift towards English. After all, they have many more neighbours who are English-speaking than French-speaking. And many of the top leaders of the Liberation Movements have acquired English as an additional language, partly because of their work in Dar es Salaam at the headquarters of liberation movements, in Addis Ababa at the headquarters of the Organization of African Unity, and in New York in the venue of the United Nations.

Yet it is feasible for all the inhabitants of the continent of Africa to become speakers of English, and yet for English to remain a foreign language. What then would make English indigenous to Africa?

One criterion is when a substantial number of indigenous Africans, placed in positions of policy makers, acquire the language as their first language.

But what is a "first" language? Is this a chronological "first" – the language one spoke as a baby? Or is it a functional primacy, "the first in importance" in the total life of the individual – the language that comes to dominate one's life?

English is already becoming the first language in the functional sense of dominating the lives of many Africans. Significant sectors of the ruling elites of African states conduct much of their public thinking, and in some cases, much of their private lives, in the English language.

It seems possible that English will continue to be the first language functionally of large numbers of Africans critically placed in the destinies of their nations, for the rest of this century. But in addition it looks feasible that English will become increasingly also the first language chronologically of many African children. One sense of "first" tends to lead on to the second sense of "first" in the succeeding generations. For me English is my first language in terms of dominating my life, both public and private, but it is not my mother-tongue chronologically. For my children on the other hand, English is the native language.

My own case is complicated by the fact that the mother of my children speaks English as a native language, and not simply as a first language functionally. But the home of my old neighbours in Kampala, Dr. and Mrs. Sekabunga, is bi-lingual because both English and Luganda are used. Moreover there are signs that, in the case of their children, English is gaining the upper hand. This is partly because at school they get only English, while at home they get both English and Luganda. The children are indeed growing up bi-lingual, but functionally the English language seems to be gaining the upper hand. The functional primacy of English among the parents leads on to the chronological primacy of English among the children.

Then there is a third category of parents in Africa, growing in number – the category of "inter-tribal marriages" among the educated. As the father and mother come from different African linguistic groups, they resort to English as the language of the home. English thus becomes the mother tongue of their children, with a clear ascendancy over the indigenous languages of both the father and the mother.

This emergence of black people who speak English as a native language chronologically is what we have termed the emergence of Afro-Saxons in the world.

For a number of historical and cultural reasons, Africa was more exposed than Asia to both Christian and linguistic penetration from the West. It is not of course true that African societies constituted a *tabula rasa,* a blank slate, on which a new mission from the West was to be impressed. The French policy of assimilation certainly assumed a kind of cultural blankness in Africa, for which French culture could be substituted. It is true that this kind of reasoning was false to its very roots. And yet the smallness of African cultural groups, and the degree to which these cultures were often pre-literate, made them more vulnerable to the Western impact than were the larger and more militantly traditionalist communities of Asia.

On the religious front, Africa as a continent did have Christian nations even before Christianity conquered the bulk of the European continent. Egypt was a Christian country before the Muslim conquest in the seventh century. And in black Africa, Ethiopia has been a bastion of Christianity from the days when much of the British Isles was inhabited by "heathens".

But apart from these few Christian nations, the African continent was a "fertile ground for the seeds of Christian salvation". Missionary activity in Africa was on a scale quite unprecedented in modern history; and the power of the missionaries in African countries bore no comparison to their influence in Asian countries under colonial rule. Christion missionaries were much more influential and more powerful among black populations than they were in India, Burma, China or Indonesia.

Christianity in Asia has basically remained a religion of minority groups, overshadowed by millions of others belonging to religions which were older on the Asian continent. Christianity in Africa, on the other hand, is the religion of the power elite in the majority of countries south of the Sahara. In some sense there are indeed Christian nations or Christian states in Africa, just as there are Christian states in Europe – but apart from the Philippines, there are no Christian states in Asia. The Christian nations of the world are either white nations or black nations – there are almost no Christian nations in the intermediate colours of Asia.

Similarly with linguistic penetration. We may be moving towards a situation where English-speaking nations are either white or black – but with virtually no English-speaking nations in Asia in the sense of nations under the control of people to whom English is the mother-tongue. At the moment we do have English-speaking nations among black populations in the Caribbean and in Liberia. As the elite of former British Africa pass on their English in the home to their children and convert their children into genuine black Afro-Saxons, we may expect more nations in Africa that have not only adopted English as the language of government and business, but where English is the language of the home within the ruling elites.

In Asia outside the Philippines, the English language is likely to continue indefinitely as a language understood only by a minority of the population in each country. In India, the proportion of those who understand English has not been increasing since independence. The quality of English among large sections of Indians who enter university has in fact declined. The competition of Hindi is one basic factor behind the deterioration of Indian English. In Africa, on the other hand, English is still in the ascendant. It is conceivable that a majority of people in each so-called English-speaking African country will be able to conduct a conversation in English by the end of the century. Of course, the populations of African countries are much smaller than those of Asian countries. But combined with a demographic resistance to the total Western impact has been the phenomenon of depth among Eastern religions and cultures, and the resultant cultural impermeability among the larger Asian communities.

If then significant numbers of black countries are going to be breeding grounds for Afro-Saxons, the English language itself must sustain closer scrutiny. Is it a language that can be made to bear the experiences of the black man? Is it a language that does justice to that experience, and is it compatible with the dignity of the new races which are adopting it?

SHOULD ENGLISH BE DE-ANGLICIZED?

Because of these issues, a number of ambitions have arisen concerning the reform of the English language. The most ambitious of the proposals for reform would amount to the *de-Anglicization of the English language*. The reasoning involved in this aspiration is to the effect that the logic of the universalization of English must lead to its de-Anglicization.

As we shall see later in this book, a similar dilemma once agitated James Baldwin, the black American novelist and one of the most gifted black users of the English language living today. We shall relate how Baldwin rebelled against Shakespeare as a symbol of the linguistic oppression of the black man in North America, and how Baldwin was later reconciled to the bard and his significance.

A more modest ambition among linguistic reformers is not the de-Anglicization of English, but the de-racialization. The language's own adoption as the official language of black states is certainly one step in the direction of de-racializing it. But that is by no means enough, as we shall indicate later. The English language, because of its origins as a language of white-skinned people, has accumulated a heritage of imagery which invested the word "black" with negative connotations. The "black market" was a market of illicit merchandise; "blackmail" was an exercise in the exploitation of fear; the "blackleg" was an adventurer who betrayed collective bargaining by the workers; the "Black Hole of Calcutta" was a miserable instance of the agony of suffocation.

If the English language is now to mature into a language of black people, can the black users of the language afford to be complacent about the cumulative negativeness of the concept of blackness in English imagery? Of course, users of phrases like "blackmail", "blackheart", "black mark on the record of an individual", are not always conscious of the neo-racialistic implications of their usage. But it is arguable that unconscious self-denigration is even more alarming than purposeful self-devaluation.

But can the English language help it if the night is dark? Yet the night is dark in tropical Africa too – and yet African languages do not always associate *blackness* with evil, with sinister forces, with death. We shall discuss this more fully later.

The third process that flows on logically from the partial de-Anglicization and de-racialization of the English language is the more positive aspiration to Africanize it. African writers have a special role to play in experimenting with usages more appropriate to the African experience. Those of their books which find their way into the new systems of education in African countries may help the trend towards the Africanization of English. African fiction in English produced in West Africa is already well on the way towards this kind of commitment. The characters in the novels of Chinua Achebe do not use the Queen's English. They use more credible English in the African context. As a conscious artist Achebe has himself illustrated how he has sought artistic credibility by maintaining contact with the world of simile and metaphor in West Africa. In his novel, *Arrow of God*, the Chief Priest is telling one of his sons why it is necessary to send him to the mission school:

I want one of my sons to join these people and be my eyes there. If there is nothing in it you will come back. But if there is something there you will bring home my share. The world is like a Mask, dancing. If you want to see it well you do not stand in one place. My spirit tells me that those who do not befriend the white man today will be saying *had we known* tomorrow.

In an article published later Achebe pauses to suggest the following alternative way in which he might have expressed the same little speech:

I am sending you as my representative among these people – just to be on the safe side in case the new religion develops. One has to move with the times or else one is left behind. I have a hunch that those who fail to come to terms with the white man may well regret their lack of foresight.

The author goes on to say that these two speeches have the same material. "But the form of the one is *in character* and the other is not."

Achebe himself revels not only in the distinctiveness of West African English, but also in the very fact that writers like him are not native to the language. He feels inclined to the view that this very fact of not being native to the language, at least for the time being, would put the stamp of distinctiveness on African usage.

So my answer to the question, Can an African ever learn English well enough to be able to use it effectively in creative writing? is certainly yes. If on the other hand you ask: Can he ever learn to use it like a native speaker? I should say, I hope not. It is neither necessary nor desirable for him to be able to do so.

And then Achebe captures the essence of combining the Africanization of the English language with a continuing commitment to the role of English as a world language. Achebe's formulation would be well within our conception of a sub-federation of Anglophone cultures, each sector of the English-speaking world maintaining its own dictinctiveness without departing so far from mutual intelligibility as to render the language no longer useful as a universal currency. To use Achebe's words again:

The price a world language must be prepared to pay is submission to many different kinds of use. The African writer should aim to use English in a way that brings out his message best without altering the language to the extent that its value as a medium of international exchange will be lost. He should aim at fashioning out an English which is at once universal and able to carry his own experience. . . . But it will have to be a new English, still in full communion with its ancestral home but altered to suit its new African surroundings.[1]

But the work of the African writer in the English language would be in vain if the educational system were rebelling against English. In Asia, English is to some extent on the defensive. In Malaysia, there has been a strong desire to make all communities speak Malay, and the ambition has been pursued to make Malay not only a compulsory subject in all the schools but finally the sole official language of the country. Experiments in providing university education in Malay are certainly under way. In India, a similar tendency is observable to reduce the areas of education that are covered by English, and increase the utilization of Hindi for primary education in at least some parts of the country. It has been estimated that within forty years a third of the urban population and one-fifteenth of the rural population in India may become literate in English, but that literacy in Hindi may be equal to that in English for people in the towns and five times as great in the country. The greatest growth in literacy, so it is estimated, will be in indigenous Indian languages. In fact, literacy in languages other than both Hindi and English by the year 2000 could account for more than half the total literates in India. The concept of "Indo-Saxons" is basically more remote than the concept of "Afro-Saxons".

Certainly, on the linguistic front the African situation in education contrasts starkly with the Asian. There is less of a push in Africa to promote indigenous languages as media for literacy, though some attempts in that direction are under way in places like Tanzania. There is also less linguistic nationalism generally in Africa than has been observable in places like Malaysia, India and Bangla Desh. The African situation is characterized by an expanding utilization of English; whereas in Asia there is a declining utilization of English. African governments are introducing English at an earlier phase in the educational pyramid than the British themselves had done. As Geoffrey Moorehouse once put it:

On both sides of Africa, moreover, in Ghana and Nigeria, in Uganda and Kenya, the spread of education has led to an increased demand for English at a primary level. The remarkable thing is that English has not been rejected as a symbol of colonialism; it has rather been adopted as a politically neutral language beyond the reproaches of tribalism. It is also a more attractive proposition in Africa than in either India or Malaysia because comparatively few Africans are completely literate in the vernacular tongues and even in the languages of regional communication; Hausa

---

[1] Chinua Achebe, "English and the African Writer", *Transition* (Kampala) 4 (18) (1965), 29-30. See Appendix B of this book.

and Swahili, which are spoken by millions, are only read and written by thousands.[2]

It is these considerations favouring the growing ascendancy of the English language among black people that continue to assert the likelihood of an expanding population of Afro-Saxons.

Winston Churchill once wrote a mammoth three volume study entitled *A History of the English-Speaking Peoples.* Churchill lived at a time when the English-speaking peoples were overwhelmingly white, and he was basically right about the Anglo-Saxons. A future Churchillian historian writing a similar study might have to pause and reflect whether the English-speaking peoples did not include a population of Afro-Saxons greater in number than the population of Australia, New Zealand, and Great Britain, put together.

And when a William Wordsworth of the future asserts his people's love of freedom, he might reflect upon the increasing ambiguity of these immortal lines:

> We must be free or die, who speak the tongue
> That Shakespeare spake; the faith and morals
> hold
> Which Milton held.[3]

Those who speak the tongue that Shakespeare spake will by the end of the twentieth century include the descendants of Julius K. Nyerere, President of Tanzania and translator into Swahili of Shakespeare's *Julius Caesar* and *The Merchant of Venice.* Those holding the faith and morals which Milton held might be deemed to include the descendants of A. Milton Obote, former President of Uganda, who adopted the name Milton in admiration of the author of *Paradise Lost* and some of his moral principles. The Afro-Saxons are not only here to stay; they are probably here to multiply.

---

[2] Geoffrey Moorehouse, "Tongue Ties", *Manchester Guardian Weekly* (London and Manchester) July 16, 1964, p. 5. The estimates of likely proportions of literacy among Indian languages are also from Geoffrey Moorehouse's two articles in the *Manchester Guardian Weekly* in that year.
[3] William Wordsworth, "London, 1802".

1

THE KING, THE KING'S ENGLISH AND I

PREFACE

Not long after the death of Sir Edward Mutesa, the former Kabaka of Buganda, I received one morning in my office an anonymous note. The note was on fairly rough paper, and seemed to have been delivered surreptitiously and left on my secretary's desk.

The note requested me to deliver a public lecture about Sir Edward Mutesa. Why me? The note asserted that I was the only one left in Uganda who could in fact give a public lecture about Sir Edward Mutesa following his death. The writer could not be expected to know what I would say about Sir Edward, but assumed that I would at least try to be fair. And a fair lecture about Sir Edward in the political climate of Uganda at that time seemed sufficiently sensitive to make my correspondent prefer to remain anonymous in his communication to me, although all he was doing was to request such a lecture.

I thought very hard about the challenge which that unknown writer had put before me. I consulted one or two friends, including my secretary, and they were all firmly of the opinion that I should not give such a lecture.

And yet I had been moved and to some extent flattered by that anonymous appeal. I grappled with my conscience for a solution. A few months previously, following the assassination of Tom Mboya, I had given a lecture in the main hall at Makerere under the title of "Tom Mboya, Makerere College and I". The lecture was later published in *East Africa Journal* under the title of "Tom Mboya, Underdevelopment and I" (*E. A. Journal*, September 1969). The technique I had used in the

Mboya lecture was autobiographical in part – I had linked a discussion of Mboya to self-evaluation and self-analysis. I explored and evaluated some of the meeting points between Mboya's life and my own.

Could I use the same technique in a lecture on Sir Edward Mutesa? I had known Sir Edward far less well than I had known Tom Mboya. And the meeting points between Sir Edward's life and my own were fewer than those which had existed between Mboya's life and mine. Yet the idea of approaching the second historical figure, Sir Edward, in a personalized manner did have some attraction. The writer and his subject could be made to merge into each other. The artist and his art could be fused.

The task was ambitious, but I was nevertheless attracted towards it. My first encounter with Sir Edward had been when I was in my late teens, and he was in his late twenties. That was before he had been exiled by Sir Andrew Cohen, the Governor. There had been something about that meeting with Sir Edward which I had found humanly suggestive. His intervention to spare me embarrassment when I was not authorized to show visitors workshops at the institute where I was working revealed a considerate side to the young king which I long remembered.

I decided to discuss Sir Edward and the whole imperial tradition in relation to that singular incident at the Mombasa Institute of Muslim Education. Symbolic of the imperial tradition, and of the destinies which awaited both Sir Edward and myself, was the English language as a social and historical phenomenon.

I proceeded to write the paper – and it came to bear the title "The King, the King's English and I". But should I deliver it at Makerere University in the main hall as I had delivered the lecture on Mboya? I would probably have done so if I had not been given to understand that *Transition* was about to come to life again within a few weeks of my completing the paper.

Indeed, *Transition* had expressed an interest in my lecture on Tom Mboya at the time. But the lecture was already committed to *East Africa Journal*. I wrote to Rajat Neogy explaining this. I later sent him a fragment of my essay on Sir Edward Mutesa. Rajat Neogy decided to have it.

Given the apparent imminence of the appearance of *Transition* at that time, I decided not to steal the thunder of the magazine by anticipating its appearance with a lecture on Sir Edward in the main hall. On the contrary, I decided that it was fitting that a lecture on such a politically sensitive subject as Sir Edward Mutesa should first come into Uganda within the covers of the revived *Transition*. Nothing that I had written about Sir Edward was in any way provocative, but even discussing the man in a spirit of fairness instead of animosity could have been gravely misunderstood in the last few years of Dr. Obote's regime.

I felt that an obituary on the last Kabaka of Buganda should indeed fittingly appear in the first issue of a resurrected *Transition*. The fates of Buganda under Obote's rule and of *Transition* had indeed been linked. A precipitating factor behind the detention of the editor of *Transition* and Mr. Abu Mayanja was a letter by Abu Mayanja, suggesting that some judicial positions recommended to the President of Uganda at that time had not been confirmed because the nominees belonged to the wrong tribe – the Baganda.

When the editor and Abu Mayanja were detained, it was three days before the state of emergency in Buganda was due to be extended for six more months by an act of Parliament. On the Saturday following the detention of these two people my expression of concern at their detention was publicized in the press. Late that very day Obote started thinking about his speech for the session in Parliament on the extension of the state of emergency in Uganda. He delivered the speech two days later, on Monday evening – after sending a message to me to say that I would be interested in what he had to say. Although the speech was ostensibly on the extension of the state of emergency in Buganda, it digressed into a vigorous denunciation of me for my defence of Neogy and Mayanja, and of my very presence in Uganda as a teacher at Makerere. The state of emergency for Buganda had also become with that single speech a state of emergency for myself and my department at Makerere, and indeed a state of emergency in the relations between Makerere and the Uganda Government under Dr. Obote.

It was all these considerations of the original crisis for *Transition,* partly in relation to the predicament of Uganda following the 1966 ordeal suffered by Mutesa's kingdom, which somehow made it more fitting than ever that my highly personalized and semi-autobiographical discussion of the King's career in relation to my own should appear in a *Transition* rising from the ashes.

That would have been an *ad hoc* issue of *Transition* published probably from Paris. The editor received my essay in good time. And if the magazine had come out in time, this very non-provocative essay on Mutesa and myself – entering Uganda within the covers of a distrusted magazine – might have precipitated yet another crisis between myself and the authorities in Uganda's regime. But fortune seems to have intervened. The particular issue of the magazine in which the essay was to appear never saw the light of day. It was, as I indicated, supposed to be an *ad hoc* issue – pending a decision on whether the magazine should continue from an African capital later on. But when the decision was finally made to revive *Transition* from Accra in Ghana, the original idea of an *ad hoc* issue from Paris much earlier was dropped. The essay "The King, the King's English and I" – designed originally to enter Uganda while Obote was still in power – thus came to be held up for twenty-odd months. The subject matter is now no longer sensitive politically. The drama of having anything on Mutesa written by somebody in Uganda after 1966 is now no longer so dramatic. But in another sense the essay becomes extra personal, extra quiet – random reminiscences by a commoner concerning the career of a King in relation to his own.

On Thursday, April 1, 1971, I saw Mutesa's face for the last time. It was serene in appearance; it was dead. I was looking at his body in a glass case at Namirembe Cathedral in Kampala. I was not a Muganda, and so those symbolic filial feelings of personal bereavement which many Baganda were experiencing that day were remote from me. And yet, I remembered for one brief second that it was also on the 1st of April – way back in 1947 – that I first looked at the serene face of a corpse. It was the dead face of my father. I was a boy of fourteen. I wondered whether that was a point of contact between my feelings and those weeping Baganda as they queued past the dead body of one who was perhaps the last of their kings.

I had come to Namirembe Cathedral with some flowers. A woman attendant signalled me pointing to the floor. I bent, and placed my flowers on the floor. They were among the very first to be brought to the body lying in state at Namirembe. To the best of my memory there were only three other bouquets before me. As I straightened myself up again I took one last look at the little card I had attached to my flowers. The card said

> To Sir Edward Mutesa – In memory of
> a brief encounter in Mombasa in 1952.

THE ISSUE

How important a factor is the English language in the lives of individual Africans? The question is too vast to be attempted in a single chapter. But there are in any case a variety of ways in which it can be approached. We will examine the English language and its influence on the growth of African nationalism, the English language and its impact on African international relations, and the English language and its interaction with religion in Africa. This exercise is an attempt to look at language as a factor in the careers of two people – one a king and the other a commoner. The king was Sir Edward Mutesa who was once Kabaka of Buganda. The commoner is myself. Behind both stories is the imperial tradition in whose embrace East Africa had remained for so long. Symbolizing the imperial tradition are two Governors who touched the lives of Mutesa and myself in different ways. One Governor was Sir Philip Mitchell, a towering colonial figure who ruled both Uganda and Kenya at different times and made an impact on the history of colonial East Africa. The other Governor was Sir Andrew Cohen, the man who deported Mutesa in 1953 and caused one of the most dramatic crises colonial Uganda ever underwent.

By a curious destiny the two figures we are looking at were native speakers of languages which came to have important political consequences. Mutesa was of course a Luganda speaker, and I was born a native to the Swahili language. The two languages came to have important areas of rivalry in the life of Uganda, while at the same time serving significant cultural roles in their different areas. Swahili had been introduced in Ugandan schools quite early, and if the policy had continued, substantial cultural interpenetration would have taken place between Uganda and her neighbours. But partly because of linguistic nationalism among the Baganda, the language was eliminated from schools in Uganda. Where it did remain was in the armed forces. And this, as I shall briefly indicate, came to have important political meaning after independence.

THE IMPERIAL BACKGROUND

The importance of the Kabakaship in the national politics of Uganda was substantially due to that massive political fact, the British policy of indirect rule. Institutionally, indirect rule was a commitment to utilize native institutions in the task of governing the colonies. In the Buganda kingdom indirect rule fostered among the Baganda a pride in indigenous culture combined with a marked interest in metropolitan ways. There was respect for Kiganda culture as a moral force, combined with a keenness on the acquisition of Western education and the adoption of certain British modes of behaviour. Even the devotion to Luganda as a distinguished medium of local culture was combined with a quest for competence in the English language and an attachment to English as a symbol of intellectual modernity. The capacity of the Baganda to imbibe the new Western civilization without straining their indigenous cultural attachments has been one of the most remarkable feats of acculturation in the history of Africa. In Buganda the Kabakaship survived not only in spite of the introduction of the English sub-culture and its secular tendencies, but in some ways almost because of that introduction. There was a fusion of the old indigenous civilization with the newly imported sub-culture. Indirect rule in Buganda not only protected both the Kabakaship and the English language; it made the English language, as we shall indicate, one of the qualifications for accession to the Kabaka's throne.

Let us now look at that other personality moulded by the English language – that is, myself. By religious affiliation I was nearer to the emirs of Nigeria than to the Kabaka of Buganda. I was, in other words, a Muslim. When I left school I worked for a while in an educational institution which was built precisely because the Muslims of the coast of Kenya had been left behind educationally as a result of their distrust of Christian missionary schools. There was no "Ibo problem" on the coast of Kenya arising from the importation of educated manpower from other parts of the country. But there were nevertheless elements of backwardness within the Muslim community which needed to be rectified.

I said that by religious affiliation I was nearer to the Sardauna of Sokoto than to the Kabaka of Buganda. But in status I was distant from both. They were kingly figures, and I was a commoner. And the role of the English language in my life was different from what it must have been in theirs.

A KING CALLS

But one day the King and the commoner met for the first time. My role in the Mombasa Institute of Education was that of "Boarding Supervisor". Essentially the job was that of a domestic warden. I was the one who ordered the rice and the onions and the meat for the resident students in the Institute, and I was the one who supervised the houseboys and cooks – all much older and more experienced than I.

The Institute was one of the show-places of Mombasa. The architect had been a Captain Beaumont, a retired aristocratic English sailor with Middle Eastern experience, who had been specially chosen by Sir Philip Mitchell, the Governor of Kenya, to furnish the designs for the new technical institute for Muslims in Mombasa. The word "Muslim" gave the captain his cue. The architecture aspired to be Islamic, and it certainly succeeded in acquiring this personality. There was a quiet elegance, partly Arabian and partly reminiscent of Persia. There was, of course, no attempt to be imitative in detail. All that Captain Beaumont had aspired to do was to create an Arabian atmosphere in the architecture and arrangement of the campus of the Institute.

One day I received a phone call from my uncle, Abu Suleiman Mazrui. He said that His Highness the Kabaka of Buganda was in Mombasa and was staying with Bwana Mdogo, a wealthy and prominent member of the old Zanzibari aristocracy who had lived in Mombasa for many years. Bwana Mdogo himself also got through to me and re-affirmed that the Kabaka was interested in seeing the Mombasa Institute of Muslim Education and would be coming with his entourage sometime after four o'clock. Could I be available to show them around?

Of course I said yes. The idea of meeting one of the kings of Uganda was very attractive. But I was a little nervous about the prospect and not quite sure how to handle this royal visitor and his group. As the domestic warden of a Muslim institution I would not have dreamt of serving alcohol in my flat. But there was always tea.

Four o'clock came and the tension started. The minutes ticked away. Four thirty came and went; five came and went; five thirty came and went; six came and went. I began to give up hope. Perhaps the royal visitor was not coming after all. I paced up and down the flat uncertain whether to be angry or disappointed or simply indifferent. It was getting dark. Before long I would simply have to give up. It was all most inconsiderate I thought.

But then, the sound of a car – no, the sound of more than one car. It was not completely dark yet but they had their lights on. They were large cars. There was no doubt about it – my royal visitor had arrived with his entourage.

I hurried downstairs to greet the visitors. There must have been ten or twelve people. The centre of gravity within the group was evidently the handsome little man, elegantly dressed with easy self-confidence. I greeted them all and asked them to follow me to my humble flat. My small sitting room was a little too small for the group, but they managed to squeeze in somehow. I do not think I can remember who the other members of the group were. One or two, in retrospect, must have been big physically, unless it was the force of their personality which left this impression on my nineteen-year-old mind.

It was late already for the tea that I had originally intended. Nevertheless I asked if His Highness would like some tea. My cakes and samoosas were also available. The Kabaka thanked me graciously but said they were all right. I then indicated that I was available to show them round the Institute as soon as they were ready. We got up and started the tour.

In some ways the most important part of the Institute, to the extent that it was a technical institute, were the workshops further down the hill. But the workshops were strictly out of bounds at night, and heavily protected by "askaris". If the Kabaka had arrived at tea time with his entourage I would have been able to take them round the workshops as well. But now it was after dark and I did not have the authority to take visitors to an area of the Institute which was out of bounds at that time of day. Very timidly and apologetically, I explained to the Kabaka that I was unable to take them to the workshops. He himself took it very well, but I got an inkling of Buganda arrogance in the reaction of two members of his entourage. Their eyes flashed when I indicated that I did not have the authority to take the visitors there. One of them indicated that there should be no problem of authority where the visitor was a monarch from a neighbouring country. I was getting a little flustered and embarrassed by this challenge, when Mutesa came to the rescue. He said they should respect the rules of the place and should not expect me to break them. They would see the workshop on some future occasion if they came early enough. I was greatly relieved. But I was also impressed by the king's understanding.

Some time in the course of the tour I was asked if all the members of the staff were Muslim. I replied that almost all the teaching members, both the technical instructors and the academic tutors, were Europeans. There was only one Muslim among the teaching members, a British-educated Ismaili scientist.

The Institute was Muslim by virtue of the composition of its students but not by virtue of the composition of its staff. All those applying for entry into the Technical Institute as students had to be Muslim, though there was very little religious instruction in the syllabus. The idea was simply to provide the relatively backward Muslims of East Africa with an institution capable of providing them with technical education and advanced vocational skills.

"Do you yourself do any teaching?" asked a member of the Kabaka's entourage.

"No", I answered. I did have some responsibility for discipline within the residential sector of the Institute, but this was outside teaching hours, and mainly at night.

"You are yourself a Muslim, though?" enquired the Kabaka. I was indeed wearing a red fez, and I had mentioned my first name when introducing myself. Yet for some reason His Highness seemed to be interested in getting a confirmation. I said yes indeed I was. It was not until many years later that I discovered the reasons behind that enquiry.

I saw my visitors to their cars and said goodbye to them. The Kabaka himself was very gracious, and I looked at him as he got into his car and drove away. More than twelve years were to pass before I saw him again. And they were twelve momentous years both for him and for myself. Little more than a year after he left Mombasa he hit the headlines of the world as an exiled king. After a confrontation with Sir Andrew Cohen he was sent away into exile in England. I read avidly about the event and its sequels and all the controversies which surrounded the deportation of the African king. I remembered his considerate attitude

to me when I declared my inability to show them the workshops of the
Mombasa Institute of Muslim Education.

A CHAT WITH SIR PHILIP

In the life of the Kabaka before independence two British Governors
were cast in particularly symbolic roles. One was Sir Philip Mitchell who
was Governor of Uganda in 1939 when the Katikiro of Buganda announced: "The fire of Buganda is extinguished. Our beloved Kabaka,
His Highness Sir Daudi Chwa, released his hold on the shield at seven
o'clock this morning."

Daudi Chwa's three chief officers made their choice of the successor
from among the princes. It was not of course necessary that the successor should be the eldest son. The choice fell upon Mutesa. It was approved unanimously by the Lukiiko. Under the 1900 Agreement, the
Governor of Uganda, Sir Philip Mitchell, had in turn to approve the
choice. There was no special problem about British recognition of young
Mutesa as the new Kabaka. He was only a minor then, and the three
officers were sworn in as regents pending Mutesa's full accession.

If it fell upon Sir Philip Mitchell to be the inaugurating Governor for
the reign of Mutesa, it also fell upon Sir Philip Mitchell to be the inaugurating Governor of the Mombasa Institute of Muslim Education ten
years later. Indeed the whole idea of an institute to teach technical subjects to Muslims in East Africa was virtually a brain child of Sir Philip
Mitchell. He had heard the old Aga Khan once say that the educational
retardation of the Muslim communities of East Africa would only be
solved if a special university for Muslims was ultimately established.
Sir Philip Mitchell approached the old Aga Khan when an opportunity
arose and indicated that what the Muslims needed was not a university
as yet, but a technical college to give them important vocational skills
and help them enter the technological age. Sir Philip therefore proposed
the establishment in Mombasa of a special institute to provide courses
in electrical engineering, mechanical engineering and woodwork, and a
nautical school to take account of the Arab tradition as a maritime
people with an interest in a continuing sea trade between the Persian
Gulf and the East African coast.

The old Aga Khan was converted to Sir Philip's vision. The Aga Khan
made a donation of a hundred thousand pounds towards the project.
The old Sultan of Zanzibar, Sir Seyyid Khalifa bin Harub, made another
donation of a hundred thousand pounds. The Bohra community also
made a contribution of about fifty thousand pounds. With such an initial
payment made by the Muslims themselves, it became much easier for Sir

Philip to persuade the three East African governments each to make a grant-in-aid to the school.

So it was that the Mombasa Institute came into being to help divert Muslims to modern occupations and professions. Thus it was that the institution which provided the setting for my first encounter with Sir Edward Mutesa was established, to become a showplace of the town and command the interest of visiting dignitaries. It was Sir Philip Mitchell who had helped inaugurate the age of technical education for a selection of Muslims in East Africa.

While the Kabaka was in exile in England, I was myself plotting and scheming to get a scholarship to go to England for further studies. A number of times I troubled my boss at the Institute, Lieutenant-Colonel H. W. Newell, to write testimonials in support of my applications for scholarships. Colonel Newell, a tall Englishman with a bushy moustache and a fluent command of Urdu acquired as a result of prolonged service in imperial India, had regarded me as his protégé from the moment I agreed to work in the Institute for two months without pay so as to be assessed. I was only fifteen when I started, and that was before the actual Institute had itself been established physically. At that time the project had been accepted, and the money had been provided, but construction of the buildings had only just started. Lieutenant-Colonel Newell, presumably at the request of Sir Philip Mitchell, had become the Bursar of the project. He and the architect and the Director of Technical Studies were the first appointments made apart from the Secretary. I was probably the fourth appointment made, though I was only a very junior member, with no status, and trying my fingers on a typewriter under my own steam.

The offices were in Sir Philip Mitchell's own residence in Mombasa, Government House, overlooking the Indian Ocean in an elegant area of the town near the golf course. We had been given a small wing of Government House for our offices. I did learn a bit of typing on my own initiative. And later on Colonel Newell sent me to a shorthand school to take a course there. I passed in shorthand with distinction, and started using it briefly taking dictation from Colonel Newell. He did not really need me as he had a very efficient English woman, Mrs. Hutton, to do the work more professionally, but the Colonel did try to give me some practice following my confirmation as a junior clerk in the Institute.

It was during this period that I met Sir Philip Mitchell. I had been making a number of applications for those scholarships, some to the Kenya Government, and some to India. Colonel Newell graciously wrote these testimonials, but back came negative answers. One day he arranged that I should see Sir Philip Mitchell just to meet him. I went, a little nervous perhaps, but simply curious also to see this big ruler of colonial Kenya. Sir Philip put me at ease and chatted for a while. He then mentioned my educational ambitions and asked what I had been doing. When I mentioned India he wanted to know what I would study there if I was successful. When I said I wanted to study law, Sir Philip thought it would be a mistake to go to India. "In India every lawyer is a politician and every politician is a lawyer – there is no professional pride", Sir Philip asserted. I did not know what to say. We chatted a little while longer.

To this day I do not know whether the purpose of the exercise, whether the whole idea behind my meeting Sir Philip Mitchell, was to enable the big man to assess me and see if he should mention my name in the right quarters in Nairobi.

It is conceivable that Sir Philip's interest was aroused when he attended our *Maulidi* celebrations at the Institute. These were annual celebrations to mark the birthday of the Prophet Muhammed. The students chanted hymns and recited the Koran. The European members of staff attended quietly and listened to the religious aspects of the ceremonies. And then I, as Boarding Supervisor of the students and a Muslim member of staff, stood up to give a speech. My role as the speaker at these functions had started the previous year when the students asked me to do so. It had now become a tradition, so it seemed, for the Boarding Supervisor to give the speech in English marking the Prophet's birthday following the recitations in Arabic. This year Sir Philip Mitchell was in attendance, and the occasion therefore acquired extra significance. My speech was, as usual, prepared in advance, but I was extra nervous in the initial phases of the delivery. But then my confidence reasserted itself and I completed the presentation in style.

Sir Philip then gave a short speech himself. He did congratulate me on my speech, but I did not realize how much I had impressed him until later. In his many years as a towering British colonial officer, in different parts of the empire, Sir Philip had attended many ceremonies of different communities where speeches had been made. He told Colonel Newell that in all his years of attending such ceremonies, he had never heard a speech "better done" for such a purpose than my own little piece of oratory. When I was later invited to go and see Philip Mitchell and have a chat with him, my excitement was indeed complete.

Did he mention my name to the Director of Education in Nairobi when he got back? All I know is that the next time I applied to the Kenya Government for a scholarship, the answer was not totally negative. This time the Director of Education of Kenya wanted to talk to me himself in Nairobi. The big discrepancy between my School Certificate results, which had been third grade, and the favourable references that the Director of Education had since received in support of my application, needed somehow to be resolved by an intensive interview in Nairobi. I was therefore invited to go to Nairobi at my own expense. The Government was as yet unwilling to spend any money on me until they were quite sure that I had the makings of a graduate. I took the train and went to Nairobi. I was subjected to a thoroughly probing interview by the Director of Education himself and his second-in-command. When it was all over they would not tell me whether I had succeeded. I therefore had to return to Mombasa in suspense.

1955 was the year of the Kabaka's return from England back to Uganda. 1955 was the year of my own first visit to Uganda, simply as a tourist. But in addition the year of the Kabaka's return from England was also the year of my own departure for England. I had won the scholarship. What should be remembered is that by the time I won the scholarship, Sir Philip had already retired as Governor of Kenya.

But the nagging questions remained. Had Sir Philip Mitchell jotted down his impressions of me on a memo and communicated this to the Director of Education? Had the Director of Education later regarded this then as one extra reference, justifying a probing interview before a final decision could be made about awarding a scholarship to a third grade School Certificate candidate? Did I owe the opportunity to be interviewed to Sir Philip Mitchell himself? I might never know for certain since I never asked him to help me and he never said he would. But did the man who inaugurated Mutesa's kingly career also help to change the course of my own?

DESTINY AND LANGUAGE

If Sir Philip Mitchell had been instrumental, however indirectly, in securing an interview for me, I owed the impression I made on him to a little oratorical exercise in the English language. But now that the interview was secured, the English language had a further part to play. I had to be articulate enough in my conversations with the Director of Education in Nairobi to impress him as potential academic material. The Director of Education in fact interviewed me in company with his deputy. I still remember those two earnest Englishmen, putting me in the middle in a little office in the Department of Education in that old colonial Nairobi. Their questions were diverse, ranging from the nature of my work at the Muslim Institute to what I thought of Darwin's theory of natural selection. My ambition at that time was to study either law or journalism. Journalism would have given me an opportunity to use the English language in writing as a career and law would have given me the opportunity to use the English language on my feet in a court of law. The Education Officers at Nairobi told me quite firmly that a Kenya Government scholarship to study law was out of the question. As for studying journalism, they felt that it made better sense for me to go to the United Kingdom and take a degree in an appropriate subject rather than go to a school of journalism as such. They kept on saying that all the best journalists they knew had not been to a school of journalism and had in fact been to a university to do a Bachelor of Arts degree. Would I accept a Kenya Government scholarship if it was neither for journalism nor for law but for English and History, for example? Of course I said I would – but then went on to ask if that meant I stood a good chance. The two Education Officers were obviously readier with questions than with answers. They said I would hear from the Department of Education in due course.

I returned to Mombasa. I waited for the decisive letter which was going to determine my future one way or the other. I am not sure whether there was any undue delay but it did seem to take the Education Department ages to respond. Then one fine day I saw that suggestive envelope with the bold letters "On Her Majesty's Service". The postal frank was Nairobi. I tore it open with a sense of anxiety. Yes – the tide had turned at last. They were sending me to England. As my School Certificate results had amounted to only a Third grade, the Kenya Government wanted me to start with two more years of schooling in an educational institution in England before I could proceed to university. I was now launched on the first important stage of my career since my miserable results in the School Certificate in 1948. The English paper in the School Certificate had in fact won me my best grade in the examination as a whole. My credit was the best. But my results in the examination as a whole certainly were not. It took further linguistic and oratorical accidents in the years ahead to re-open the gates of academic advancement for me.

In Mutesa's career, too, the English language was an important factor. Born in 1924, Mutesa had more than a dozen half-brothers, though not a single full brother. Mutesa explains to us in his autobiography that the question of which of the sons of a Kabaka is to succeed is never decided until after the Kabaka's death. When a Kabaka dies the Lukiiko chooses the successor. Mutesa himself was not the eldest son, and it is not necessary that the successor should be legitimate, though Mutesa himself was. Since the 1900 Agreement of Buganda with Britain it had come to be increasingly accepted that a Kabaka had to be versed in English ways if he was to protect his people adequately in their relations with the British Government. Command of the English language had, by the time of Mutesa's accession to the throne, become virtually a distinct qualification for the great royal office of Buganda. Mutesa himself was not the only one of the old Kabaka's sons to have been initiated into English imperial ways. Mutesa's command of the English language was not decisive in securing him the choice of the Lukiko. But had he been ignorant of English ways, this fact would have been decisive in putting the throne beyond his reach. Mutesa tells us in his autobiography:

During his life a Kabaka may hint as subtly or blatantly as he wishes as to whom he personally favours, and such hints may well carry weight, but he cannot will the Kabakaship as you will a possession. I think my father did drop such hints, and it is true that I had an English tutor, as he had done, but this was by no means conclusive – my eldest brother, for example, was educated in England.[1]

When Mutesa went to Budo special arrangements were made to give him an extra exposure to British ways.

King's College Budo, is confident that it is the best school in Uganda and has been so since it was founded in 1906. . . . At first I stayed with an Irish family, Robinson by name, so that I heard English and was familiar with European ways at an early age even if I made little of them at first. . . . When I was thirteen a young Englishman, Freddie Crittenden, came to Budo as my tutor and an attractive red brick bungalow was built for us. He taught me, among other things, to enjoy P. G. Wodehouse and Thackeray . . . When my tutor left for the war in 1940 I moved into the house of Lord Hemingford, the headmaster, and formed a friendship with him and his wife that lasts to this day.[2]

With such tutoring and cultural exposure, it was not long before Mutesa experienced that curious imperial phenomenon. As he himself put it, "Oddly enough, I was more fluent in English than in Lugada."[3]

THE BAGANDA AND THE "B-A-RITISH"

The other great Governor in the life of Mutesa was Sir Andrew Cohen. Cohen was one of the most radical governors in the history of British Africa. Faced with the consequences of the 1900 Agreement of Uganda, which gave pre-eminent status to Buganda, Cohen was apprehensive about the long-term viability of Uganda as a united nation if the Agreement continued to determine relationships between the parts. Cohen was also temperamentally suspicious of authority based on royal power. He

---

[1]   Mutesa, *Desecration of My Kingdom* (London: Constable, 1967) 76.
[2]   Mutesa, *Desecration*, 77, 79, 83-84.
[3]   Mutesa, *Desecration*, 84.

was therefore interested in cutting the kabakaship down to size and transforming it into a constitutional monarchy. Cohen and Mutesa had had their ups and downs already before those few ill-chosen words by Oliver Lyttelton rocketed Uganda into a crisis of international dimensions. Oliver Lyttelton – now Lord Chandos – was then Secretary of State for the Colonies. In an after-dinner speech about Central Africa, Lyttelton had defined a vision "as time goes on of still larger measures of unification and possibly still larger measures of federation of whole Eastern African territories". A little post-prandial expansiveness became the ignition for one of Buganda's great battles with the British. Mutesa himself admits that the federal issue was indeed only an ignition device. More fundamental was the tension between the British Governor's reformist radicalism on the one hand and an African king's defence of his institutions on the other. To use Mutesa's words:

> The mention of federation in East Africa was enough to bring all Baganda anxiety frothing to the surface, and this in turn emphasised our political position. The speech (by Lyttelton) was not the real subject of the dramatic events that followed, which concerned the relationship of the British with the Baganda, but it was their immediate cause.[4]

One thing led to another. Sir Andrew wanted to use the crisis as a stage towards the evolution of his idea of a unitary state of Uganda. Buganda responded with an attempt to consolidate its privileged position in the country. Buganda wanted to be transferred from the responsibility of the Colonial Office to the responsibility of the Foreign Office, arguing that it was not colonized territory but had entered into a treaty with the British voluntarily. Demands for a date for independence for Buganda began to be heard. Few speeches made in England could ever have had more dramatic consequences within Africa than the little after-dinner chat in which Oliver Lyttelton chose to indulge himself.

Early on the morning of November 30, 1953, Mutesa was called for an interview at Government House. He found the Governor at his desk. Mutesa sat on his right. The Governor repeated an ultimatum he had issued before for greater cooperation from the Kabaka. The Kabaka had in fact given some concessions, but there were compromises he could not make without alienating the Lukiiko irreparably and doing great harm to his stature among his people. Mutesa refused. Sir Andrew Cohen drew from under his blotter the papers which withdrew recognition from the Kabaka as "native ruler". Sir Andrew rose and walked out of the room. Instantly two policemen appeared through another door. One said: "This is a deportation order, Your Highness, and I have

---

[4] Mutesa, *Desecration*, p. 118.

been instructed to carry it out." The crisis of the Kabaka's exile, which was to last for two years, was well under way.[5]

In the course of that period of exile that other Governor important in Mutesa's career, Sir Philip Mitchell, played a brief role. The British Queen was scheduled to visit Uganda in 1954. Oliver Lyttelton records in his autobiography that Sir Philip Mitchell wrote suggesting that the Queen's visit might be used as an occasion for a gracious gesture by her to allow the Kabaka's return. Lyttelton liked the idea, but Sir Andrew Cohen emphatically advised against it, arguing that the country was settling down and no such gesture was needed. In the battle between Cohen and Mutesa, Mutesa finally won when he returned triumphantly to his mother-country in October 1955. But, taking a longer historical perspective, the victory must be transferred back to Sir Andrew. His belief in a unified Uganda, and his commitment to reduce the powers of traditional institutions and democratize decision-making in the country, has at least partially been realized. A unitary Uganda, republican in constitution, came into being a decade and a half after that momentous confrontation between a British Governor and an African King.

My own encounter with Sir Andrew Cohen was much later and in different circumstances. When he was Governor, Cohen had been so far ahead of his time that when colonial rule in Africa was coming to an end his views and calibre were regarded as relevant enough by the British Government to have him entrusted with the position of Permanent Secretary in the British Ministry of Overseas Development. He was the only British Permanent Secretary who was at the same time an ex-colonial Governor.

I first saw him at a conference on development in Jesus College at Cambridge University. It was an international conference and he attended one or two sessions. I saw him but we did not actually meet. I knew about him already, of course, but I do not think he knew about me.

It was at another conference the following year that we actually met. The conference was at the University of Sussex this time, and was the inaugural conference to launch the new Institute for Development Studies at Sussex. I was among the speakers in the first session in that conference, responding to Paul Streeten's paper. I met Cohen at a later session. He was intrigued to learn that in a speech, commenting on a paper by an economist, I had used English creative literature in the texture of my reasoning.

---

[5] For Mutesa's interesting account of this scene, see *Desecration*, 120-122.

SIR ANDREW LISTENS

But it was not until October 1967 that I had any extended conversation
with Sir Andrew. We met in Nairobi at a meeting which was described
as "the second Como conference", consisting of representatives of foun-
dations and relevant ministries of donor countries, alongside representatives drawn from the different sections of the University of East
Africa. The purpose of the meeting was to investigate and exchange
ideas on where the University was going next and what role external
financial support might play. But before Sir Andrew came to Nairobi
he stopped in Uganda. We did not meet in Kampala. But he was interviewed by *The People*. The first question which the interviewers asked
him was based on something I had said some weeks earlier. This was
the question posed to Sir Andrew:

African countries have been insisting on "aid without strings" from the
donor countries. But recently a Makerere professor remarked: "Foreign
aid without strings is an insult to human dignity." Which of these two
views do you support?

Sir Andrew later told me in Nairobi that he had been a little startled
by the remark attributed to "the professor", and he did not know at the
time that it was I who had made it. In fact, I had had occasion to make
that remark at a public meeting in Kampala. My argument was that
free aid totally without strings should be avoided unless the situation
was one in which no conceivable reciprocal service was feasible between
donor and recipient. The truth was that aid was hardly ever granted
totally without strings, and if it were, it would definitely denote a lack
of equality between the donor and the recipient. A relationship of absolute charity was, I argued, a relationship of inequality. No two developed states ever gave to each other major economic gifts without an
attempt to arrive at some form of reciprocity, and the more nearly equal
the negotiating states, the tougher the bargaining about reciprocal concessions and benefits. I had indicated that there could be no major
transfers of economic advantages from, say, France to Britain without
a close calculation on what the French would get in return. Even in
relations between the United States and Britain, though less equal than
relations between Britain and France, the idea of what one party gained
from a special favour it did for the other was never absent. When a
developing country demanded, therefore, to be given aid completely
freely, with no strings attached whatsoever, it was demanding absolute
charity – and absolute charity was not a normal relationship between
real peers.

Of course the very fact that one country was receiving aid was an

admission of at least temporary inequality. The more one gave in return
for that aid, the less it was aid. Strings attached to aid helped to make
the exercise a mutual transaction; the donor was not entirely a benefactor, but also a beneficiary. The recipient of the aid was not entirely
a beneficiary but became in his own right a benefactor by extending
some reciprocal favour to the donor. The real issue between equals in
matters of aid was not whether there were strings, but what kind of
strings. And the whole business of scrutinizing strings and negotiating
about them was, I insisted, an assertion of parity of esteem.[6]

Sir Andrew did not know the full reasoning behind my assertion
when Luke Kazinja and Charles Binaisa confronted him with the question as to which of the two views he supported – the nationalists insistence on "aid without strings", on the one hand, or the professor's
remark that "foreign aid totally without strings is an insult to human
dignity", on the other.

Cohen became the supreme diplomat. He said:

Well, I support both statements because I think that African and other
countries which make use of aid don't want political strings to be attached.
In other words: "We give you aid if you give us your vote at the United
Nations" which is obviously unworkable and undesirable. But aid ought
to have strings in the sense that there ought to be an agreement between
those who give aid and those who receive it about the conditions under
which it should be given. The project should be properly worked out,
should have a high priority according to the development plan and should
be efficiently managed by the people who receive it . . . therefore saying
"We refuse to impose conditions" is an insult to dignity because a proper
agreement between two people conducting a piece of business involves
certain conditions relating to the carrying out of the business.[7]

The same radicalism which had animated Andrew Cohen in his relations with the Kabaka in the 1950's was obviously still at play in his
mind as Permanent Secretary to the Ministry of Overseas Development
in the United Kingdom. But he might in addition have acquired a capacity to be more tactful and diplomatic without sacrificing his un-
doubted sense of social conscience and commitment.

It would have been interesting to know what he had to say about my
book *Towards a Pax Africana*. Sir Andrew had accepted an invitation
from Helen Kitchen, the editor of *Africa Report* to review the book.
But Sir Andrew postponed the review for *Africa Report* a little too
long. He died suddenly about a year later. What I did get from him

---

[6] The argument also occurs in my article "The Functions of Anti-Americanism
in African Political Development", *Africa Report* 14 (1), January 1969.
[7] See *The People*, October 28, 1967.

briefly in Nairobi in October 1967 were some comments on some of the issues I had raised in the book.

But although Cohen never had a chance to review a book of mine, he did have a chance to respond to a speech of mine. Contact was here established once again with that old experience with Sir Philip Mitchell at the beginning of the 1950's in Mombasa. In the speech he had heard at the Mombasa Institute of Muslim Education, Mitchell had been intrigued by *how* I said things. And, at a certain level of education in the colonial period, how someone used the English language was a more important criterion for evaluating him than what he actually said in the English language. Bad ideas expressed in good English made a greater impact than good ideas expressed in bad English. I am not sure whether what I said in the speech at the Institute which intrigued Sir Philip Mitchell was indeed something worth saying at all. It may have been very ordinary. But the important thing was that it was expressed in a certain way.

Much later in one's career it is no longer enough to perfect a style of expression. What is said becomes as important, and sometimes even more important, than how it is said.

The situation in my dealings with the second Governor in Mutesa's life was therefore significantly different from what it was when I had had brief dealings with the first Governor, Sir Philip Mitchell. My speech to the external donors at Nairobi in October 1967 warned the donors against being so carried away in their enthusiasm for projects of practical utility in the University that they completely neglected the principle of *balanced* growth for a University. The impact of projects on the realities of societies could not easily be estimated in advance. The donors would be naive if they imagined that supporting this or that practical enterprise was a direct contribution to stability, or development, or any of the major imperatives of academic investment. One could assess, but one could never be sure. I said to the donors:

You cannot be sure that we shall become more stable, or better developed. You cannot make us happier. You can only make us more knowledgeable. I ask you therefore to be a little more daring in your selection of enterprises to support. Do not overcalculate. After all, there are occasions when wise men rush in where fools fear to tread.

Later in the conference I heard Sir Andrew comment that there were two statements he had heard at Nairobi which by themselves made his trip from London worthwhile. One was a statement by Principal Arthur Porter, Head of the University College, Nairobi. Dr. Porter had asserted: "In our policies at our University College we are guided by two basic principles – relevance and excellence in that order of priority." Sir

Andrew's orientation made him react favourably to such a scale of priorities. The philosophy I had enunciated in my speech was in many ways radically different from what was implied by Dr. Porter's assertion. I was warning my audience against too narrow a definition of "relevance". Yet somehow my speech also touched something important in the whole temperament of Sir Andrew Cohen. Both in his days as Governor and in the years which followed, Sir Andrew had often been daring in some of the decisions he had taken. He was a man of imagination and had that rare quality, genuine vision. He sometimes bungled in his daring. But there was a moment of brief immodest self-recognition on his part when I said, "After all, there are occasions when wise men rush in where fools fear to tread." Cohen had had on occasion the wisdom to risk a bungle in pursuit of daring ideals.

At the time of that conference in Nairobi, Cohen knew that Mutesa was in his second exile in London. Indeed, 1967 was the year of the Republican Constitution in Uganda. The monarchies of old were abolished that year. And the country was at last declared unitary. I wonder what went on in the mind of Sir Andrew Cohen.

A PALACE FALLS

The second exile of the Kabaka had started dramatically in 1966. In a confrontation with the central government of independent Uganda the Kabaka and the Lukiiko of Buganda had overplayed their hands. They had issued an ultimatum to the central government, virtually asserting their autonomy of central control. Events culminated in a military confrontation at the Kabaka's palace. The palace fell, and Mutesa fled, through Zaire and Burundi, and then onwards to England. With that English upbringing he had had as Kabaka, England was like a second home to him. His Cambridge days and even his exile had deepened further Mutesa's basic Anglophilia. At the end of his first exile he said he was sorry to leave England. "It can never be pleasant to be an exile. My first year was miserable, though I was living a life that must have looked easy and luxurious from a distance. As the certainty that I should return grew, however, my love for England was able to struggle with my pain at being forced away from Uganda."[8]

I went to look at the palace at Mengo not long after his second fall in 1966. There were signs of bullet marks on the outside walls of the Palace, the marks of the traffic of history. I was in a car with a colleague from University College, Nairobi, and my wife and one of our children. There being no sign warning us against approaching, we drove

[8]   Mutesa, *Desecration*, 139.

up to the closed gates. We observed the small scars of battle with an air of solemnity.

But the gates were suddenly flung open, and a soldier stood there with a gun aimed at us. He demanded that we get out. The colleague, who was driving the car and did not understand Swahili, thought that the order was for us to depart. He started reversing the car. The soldier shouted and seemed about to fire. I said to my friend, "For heaven's sake stop!" He did, and the soldier came and demanded that we come out. The alarm was raised and other soldiers came. With commendable humaneness they left my wife and child alone while we were taken into the quadrangle of the palace. I spent five hours in military custody, accused of simply trespassing. Our defence that there was no notice to say that we were not to approach, and no soldier outside the gates to indicate this prohibition, was not regarded as convincing.

But from the point of view of language a curious thing happened in that confrontation. I heard one soldier say to another that we were to have our Swahili tested. We suspected that if we failed the test the treatment given us might have been different. I suppose the Swahili test was in part to try to ascertain whether or not I was a subject of the departed Kabaka. The Baganda's disdain of Swahili had caught up with them in a traumatic way. A linguistic test had begun to be used as a way of determining the degree of humiliation to which a captured person was to be subjected. Several years later, in December 1969, a Jamaican colleague of mine was subjected to severe manhandling by soldiers following the attempted assassination of President Obote. Again one of the factors behind the severity of the treatment he got was that he failed to pass the test of Swahili.

My own fate that day in the courtyard of the palace was happier. I passed the Swahili test with flying colours, and was spared some of the physical humiliation which might have ensued upon failure. The historic battle between Luganda and Swahili against the background of the English language had assumed dimensions of political pathos.

I indicated earlier that on that day early in the 1950's when the Kabaka visited the Muslim Institute he was particularly anxious to know whether I was myself a Muslim. Much later when I was on the staff of Makerere, I was introduced to the Kabaka's uncle, Prince Badru Kakungulu. It was then that I discovered that one of the things that had impressed Mutesa was the phenomenon of a young Muslim speaking English so fluently. When I met his uncle more than ten years after the event, and it was explained to the Prince who I was, complete with my family background, his eyes brightened up. He remembered so late in the day the comments made by the Kabaka about a young Muslim in Mombasa who spoke English fluently.

As my Swahili was being tested in military custody that memorable day in 1966, I had a passing memory of my first encounter with Mutesa against the elegant Arabian architecture of the Muslim Institute in Mombasa. In that stream of consciousness I might also have thought of Sir Philip Mitchell with whom I so closely associated those early days of the Institute. I do not remember for certain. I looked at the palace and its scars once again. The voice of the soldier commanded, "Njoo hapa!" We drew near in obedience.

2

ENGLISH AND THE ORIGINS OF AFRICAN NATIONALISM

Many of the things which one can say about the significance of the
English language for the development of African ideas one can also say
about the French language. But there are certain areas of thought where
one of these languages has been more important than the other. Among
the areas where English has been particularly significant is in the development of certain notions of self-determination.

But ideas of self-determination have their roots in ideas of "freedom"
at large. The minimal sense of freedom is the condition of not being a
slave. The story of African liberation therefore takes the form of liberation from slave traders and slave owners before it takes the form of opposition to colonial rule.

What is the place of the English language in either form of liberation?

A background factor to be borne in mind is that the Anglo-Saxons *
were pre-eminent both in the acquisition of slaves and in the building of
empires. It later became a matter of direct political significance not only
that England had had the biggest single share of Africa in the "scramble"
as a whole, but also that the largest group of blacks in the New World
were English-speakers. What might also be remembered is that these
same Anglo-Saxons who took the lead in enslaving blacks were later

---

* The term "Anglo-Saxon" is here definable by combining a linguistic criterion
with a criterion of colour. In other words, "Anglo-Saxons" in this article are
white people who speak English as a first language. Please refer also to my
companion piece "The English Language and Political Consciousness in British
Colonial Africa", *Journal of Modern African Studies* 4 (3) (1966). I am indebted
to my wife for guidance on some aspects of language, with special reference to
French.

to produce from their ranks the foremost champions of abolition. In England they produced William Wilberforce. In the New World they produced John Brown and Abraham Lincoln.

But what was to be done with the blacks once they were freed from slavery? The term "colonization" came into the vocabulary of black politics. Today the word itself connotes Africa's loss of freedom on the advent of imperial rule. But in much of the Nineteenth Century the term "colonization" was more closely associated with the liberation of blacks outside Africa – and their repatriation back to Africa. Here again the English-speaking world stands out as exceptional. There were black slaves in Portuguese Brazil, in Spanish Cuba, and in the Arabian peninsula, but the most enduring "Back to Africa" projects were in the English-speaking world. Why did this happen? [1]

Two factors help to form part of the explanation. On the credit side is Anglo-Saxon liberalism. The same human impulses which demanded freedom for the black slave went a step further – and demanded that he be taken back "home" from where he had been uprooted. There was a humanitarian logic in the naiveté of taking the black man back to his ancestral soil.

But there was also a less favourable side to Anglo-Saxon impulses. To a greater extent than either the Portuguese of Brazil, the Spaniards of Cuba or the Arabs of Saudi Arabia, the Anglo-Saxons were unhappy about racial integration. No people managed to combine more effectively such a high degree of humanitarian sensitivity with such a highly developed sense of racial exclusiveness. Both the humanitarianism and the racial exclusiveness contributed to the idea of repatriating blacks back to Africa. The same Lincoln who felt so passionately about emancipating slaves subscribed to the idea of encouraging blacks to return to their ancestral land. Nnamdi Azikiwe of Nigeria reminded us of this latter side of Lincoln in a book he wrote in the early 1930's. Azikiwe recalled that on meeting a deputation of American blacks on August 14, 1862, Lincoln said:

You and we (Caucasians) are different races. We have between us a broader difference than exists between almost any other two races. . . . There is an unwillingness on the part of our people, harsh as it may be, for you free coloured people to remain with us. . . . I suppose one of the principal difficulties in the way of colonization is that the free coloured man cannot see that his comfort would be advanced by it. . . . For the sake of your race you should sacrifice something of your present comfort for the

[1] For a brief discussion of the Afro-Brazil story see Jose Honorio Rodrigues, "The Influence of Africa on Brazil and of Brazil on Africa", *Journal of African History* 3 (1), 49-67. See also James C. Brewer, "Brazil and Africa", *Africa Report* 10 (5) (May 1965).

purpose of being as grand in this respect as the white people ... General Washington himself endured greater physical hardships than if he had remained a British Subject.[2]

Sierra Leone is a part not only of the history of freedom in Africa, but also of the spread of the English language in West Africa. In his book on the origins and future of Pan-Africanism, George Padmore tells us about the role of English among the freed slaves in Sierra Leone in those early days. Padmore says:

The Creoles of the Colony rapidly became the first Westernized community in Africa. Drawn as they were from the heterogeneous elements, cut adrift from their ancestral cultures, traditions and customs, the repatriates intermarried and adopted the English way of life. The Queen's language became their normal medium of communication.[3]

But the Queen's language came to be radically Africanized in Sierra Leone. English gradually became Krio, the lingua franca between the Creoles and the indigenous tribes in and around Freetown. Blyden described Krio as a "convenient bridge" between African dialects and the English language.[4]

But the impact of Sierra Leone on West Africa as a whole was perhaps more in the spread of the English language than of Krio. There did arise people like Bishop James Johnson who championed the adoption of Krio as the national language of Sierra Leone and as the medium of instruction in schools. But the weight of opinion in Sierra Leone, among both Europeans and Creoles themselves, was against such a move. Indeed, it was almost part of the educational policy of the country to try to eradicate Krio.[5]

---

[2] Cited by Azikiwe in Nigeria in *World Politics* (London: Arthur H. Stockwell, 1934), 234-235. For the quotation from Lincoln, Zik refers to Nicolay and Hay, *Abraham Lincoln, Complete Works* (New York, 1894), Vol. 1, 222-225.

[3] *Pan-Africanism or Communism? The Coming Struggle for Africa* (London: Dennis Dobson, 1956), 38.

[4] Edward W. Blyden, *Christianity, Islam and the Negro Race* (London: W. B. Whittingham, 1888), 223. Born on a West Indian Island in 1832, Blyden went to New York at the age of fifteen seeking higher education. The Colonization Society of New York offered him a free passage to Liberia where he landed in January 1850. There he got an education in classics and languages. He later became professor and President of Liberia College, Secretary of State for the Interior and served twice as Liberian Ambassador to the Court of St. James. For Blyden's contribution to the concept of an "African Personality" see Robert W. July, "Nineteenth Century Negritude: Edward W. Blyden", *Journal of African History* 5 (1), 73-86.

[5] See Letter from the Reverend James Johnson, the African Bishop, in *Sierra Leone Weekly News*, 22 February, 1908. The letter is partially reproduced in Christopher Fyfe's *Sierra Leone Inheritance* (London: Oxford University Press,

A more concrete contribution which Sierra Leone made to the spread of English in West Africa came to be centred on Fourah Bay College, established in 1827 as virtually the first modern institution of higher learning in sub-Saharan Africa. Year after year the College sent out Africans to propagate the Gospel and to spread liberal education in the English language in different parts of Western Africa.

Partly out of the stimulus of the Gospel, and of Western liberal education, a new black ambition came into being. In discussing this ambition we might start with a remark made by a great user of the English language, George Bernard Shaw. In April 1933 Shaw said something which, in an important way, touched the deepest ambition of the nascent African nationalism at the time. Shaw said: "Civilizations grow up and disappear, to be replaced by other and stronger civilizations. For all I know, the next great civilization may come from the Negro race".[6]

It is possible that the reason why Shaw illustrated with the Negro race was because in his time that race was regarded as the least likely source of a great civilization. And perhaps precisely because of that prejudice, this socialistic Irishman wanted to make sure that the black man was credited with the same human potential as anyone else.

Such sentiments concerning black repatriation had by then already started to affect the African continent. British humanitarianism was giving birth to Sierra Leone; American philanthropy was helping the creation of Liberia. Both countries came to assume symbolic significance for African nationalism later on. And both have their place in the history of the English language on the continent.

A glance at the significance of Sierra Leone might form a useful starting point. Edward W. Blyden, the Nineteenth Century black intellectual and precursor of Negritude had this to say about Sierra Leone:

It is a very interesting fact that on the spot where Englishmen first began the work of African demoralisation, Englishmen should begin the work of African amelioration and restoration. England produced Sir John Hawkins, known to Sierra Leone by his fire and sword policy. Two hundred years later, England produced Granville Sharp, known by his policy of peace, of freedom and of religion. The land of Pharaoh was also the land of Moses. Alone, amid the darkness of those days stood Sierra Leone – the only point at which the slave trade could not be openly prosecuted – the solitary refuge of the hunted slave.[7]

1964), 221-222. See also Fyfe, *A History of Sierra Leone* (London: Oxford University Press, 1962), 468-469; and Hollis R. Lynch, "The Native Pastorate Controversy and Cultural Ethno-Centrism in Sierra Leone, 1871-1874", *Journal of African History* 5 (3) (1964), 395-413.
[6] *New York Times*, April 13, 1933.
[7] Padmore, *Pan-Africanism*, 23.

Whatever the real motives of Shaw's line of speculation, however, it was a line which evoked a response from Nnamdi Azikiwe. For a member of the most humiliated race in recent history, the vision of Africa as possibly the next great source of human regeneration was both frustrating and inspiring. It was frustrating because it was so hypothetical and long-term. It was inspiring because such an eventuality would be the ultimate vindication of black potential. It might well have been considerations such as these which made Azikiwe embrace Bernard Shaw's line of speculation. And yet at that time the only country in Azikiwe's part of Africa which was already independent was not Sierra Leone, but Liberia. To George Padmore, Sierra Leone might indeed have been "the greatest living monument to the memory of the Abolitionists",[8] but to Azikiwe the greatest symbol of the coming Africa was Liberia, the only sovereign country at the time. Azikiwe saw Liberia as "the nucleus of black hegemony. . . . the soil where the seed of an African civilization is destined to germinate."[9]

Nor was Azikiwe unusual in his romanticism about Liberia. The country retained this special place in the imagination of West African nationalists well into the 1940's. In 1945, when voices were saying that it was time that the next pan-African conference be held in Africa, the influential West African Students Union in London wrote W. E. B. Du Bois urging that "the fifth Pan-African Congress" should be held in Liberia.[10] In his autobiography Nkrumah, too, confesses to having once been inspired by Liberia as a symbol of African sovereignty. "I judged Liberia not from the heights it had reached but from the depths whence it had come."[11]

In the context of the history of the English language in Africa, Liberia, too, holds a significant position. It is essentially the only country in Africa which owes its English to the New World rather than directly to British rule on the continent. And today Liberia is the only black African country in which English is a native language – at any rate English is the first language of the country's black elite.

Historically, Blyden had seen broad linguistic and cultural implications in the very territorial contiguity between Liberia and Sierra Leone. In the 1880's Blyden had made the following observations.

For 200 years, the Portuguese language was spoken along this coast. Vil-

---

[8] See George Padmore (ed.) *History of the Pan-African Congress* (first published 1947) (London: Hammersmith Bookshop). Second edition 1963.
[9] Azikiwe, *Liberia in World Politics* (London: Arthur H. Stockwell, 1934), p. 395. The italics are original.
[10] Padmore, *History of the Pan-African Congress*.
[11] *Ghana, the Autobiography of Kwame Nkrumah* (Edinburgh: Thomas Nelson and Sons, 1957), 184.

lauit says when he landed here, at Cape Mount and at Cape Mesurado in 1666, "all the Negroes who came to trade spoke the Portuguese language." But the English language has everywhere driven it out. . . . We have a continuous English-speaking Negro State from the Sierra Leone River to the San Pedro River. . . . "

Blyden went on to philosophize about the suitability of the English language for Africa as compared with either Portuguese or French. He saw English as a mongrel language – a product of the mating of diverse cultures. It was less of a stickler for purity than its Latin neighbours tended to be. The English language was pre-eminently a language of accommodation and pragmatic synthesis. It was therefore the more suitable as a lingua franca in multi-lingual situations. In Blyden's words:

English is, undoubtedly, the most suitable of the European languages for bridging over the numerous gulfs between the tribes caused by the great diversity of language or dialects among them. It is a composite language, not the product of any one people. It is made up of contributions by Celts, Danes, Normans, Saxons, Greeks and Romans, gathering to itself elements. . . . from the Ganges to the Atlantic.[12]

This function of English as a vehicle of communication among Africans of different tribes was later to take a continental dimension. The language was to play a succession of important roles in the movement which came to be known as Pan-Africanism.

But in discussing the origins of movements for unity in Africa one ought to draw a distinction between Pan-Africanism and Pan-Negroism. Pan-Negroism is that movement, ideology or collection of attitudes which is primarily concerned with the dignity of the black people wherever they may be. The banner of Negroism therefore brought sub-Saharan Africans and Afro-Americans together. Pan-Africanism, on the other hand, gradually became an essentially continental movement within Africa itself. And from the point of view of Pan-Africanism the Arabs of North Africa are today more important than the blacks of the United States. In fact, Tom Mboya of Kenya had even suggested that the proof that Pan-Africanism was not a racial movement was the fact that the Organization of African Unity included Arab as well as black states.[13]

Historically, Pan-Africanism was born out of Pan-Negroism. But while the loyalties of Pan-Negroism were, as Azikiwe put it, "ethnocentric", those of Pan-Africanism became essentially intra-continental.[14]

[12] "Sierra Leone and Liberia", in: Blyden, *Christianity, Islam and the Negro Race*, 243-244.
[13] *Freedom and After* (London: Andre Deutsch, 1963), 231.
[14] See Azikiwe "The Future of Pan-Africanism", *Presence Africaine* 12 (40)

Among the towering founding fathers of Pan-Negroism must be included American blacks like W. E. B. Du Bois and West Indians like George Padmore and, indirectly, Marcus Garvey. But racial affinity alone could not have converted these feelings of distant fellowship between Africans and Afro-Americans into an international movement. Race alone could not have brought those black fighters together in those early pan-African conferences. After all, there has been little political intercourse between the blacks of Brazil and nationalists in English-speaking or French-speaking Africa. Given the limitations of those early years, it was indeed a matter of direct significance for African nationalism that American blacks were English-speakers.

Admittedly, Martinique has made an important contribution to African cultural revivalism, especially through the poetry of Aimé Césaire. And more lately there has been the ideological influence in Africa of the late revolutionary Frantz Fanon.[15] Even Haiti has sometimes attracted symbolic salutation as the first black republic outside the African continent.

But English-speaking blacks in the Americas by far out-numbered French-speakers. And this helps to account for the basic Anglo-American orientation of those pan-African conferences in the early part of this century. Nkrumah's first trip to continental Europe in the 1940's was in an attempt to get French-speaking Africans more actively involved in Pan-Africanism. As Secretary of the West African National Secretariat in London he went to Paris to see the African members of the French National Assembly – Sourous Apithy, Léopold Senghor, Lamine Gueye, Houphouet-Boigny and others. As a result of Nkrumah's visit, Senghor and Apithy went to London to attend the West African Conference which Nkrumah and his colleagues had been organizing. What is significant about this is not that French Africa was represented at the conference in London, but that special acts of encouragement had to be initiated by the English-speakers to get Francophone Africans involved.[16]

(First Quarter, 1962), 7-12. For a historian's view of the influence of American blacks on African thought see George Shepperson, "Notes on Negro American influences on the emergence of African nationalism", *Journal of African History* 1 (2) (1960), 299-312. See also Shepperson's article, "Abolitionism and African Political Thought", *Transition* (Kampala), 3, (12) (January-February 1964), 22-26.

[15] In the English language see especially Fanon's *The Wretched of the Earth* (trans. by Constance Farrington), (New York: Grove Press, 1963). Fanon was born in Martinique, later joined the ranks of the F.L.N. and fought for Algeria's independence, and wrote psychoanalytical studies on racism and the purifying potential of violence.

[16] Nkrumah's account of this is at once friendly and detached. See his *Autobiography*, 54-58.

This West African get-together had been preceded by a broader venture – the historic fifth Pan-African Congress held in Manchester in 1945. The towering figures of that conference too were overwhelmingly English-speakers. Two of the most famous came to be Presidents of their countries – Nkrumah himself and Jomo Kenyatta. Virtually the only representation that French-speaking Africa had was in the person of Dr. Raphael Armattoe from Togoland. Armattoe was not really committed to the cause. He was very much a detached guest among African militants. As a measure of his aloofness we might perhaps recall the story that Nkrumah, as Secretary of the Organizing Committee of the Conference, had to tell about him:

I remember one evening Makonnen came to see me behind the scenes in a state of great agitation. Could I possibly see a Dr. Raphael Armattoe, he said. Dr. Armattoe, a native of Togoland, who had been invited to speak at the conference, came in and declared that he had lost his portmanteau in which he had several things of value. He felt that since we had been responsible for his attendance at the conference, we should make good the loss he had sustained. He proceeded there and then to list the items and assess their value and presented me with the account. The Congress was already very much in debt but I decided it was better to pay the man and get over it the best way we could.[17]

But while this fifth Pan-African Congress was still more a conference of English-speaking blacks than of Africans regardless of language, it was nevertheless more Pan-African than any of its predecessors. Here again Nkrumah, as a participant, gave us a useful insight into the significance of the Congress. He argued that, like Garveyism, the preceding four "Pan-African" conferences were not born of indigenous African consciousness. "Garvey's ideology was concerned with black nationalism as opposed to African nationalism. And it was this Fifth Pan-African Congress that provided the outlet for African nationalism and brought about the awakening of African political consciousness."[18]

But why did Pan-Africanism in this intra-continental sense then gain an ascendancy over Pan-Negroism? When did the leaders of black Africa become more conscious of the African continent itself and relatively less interested in fellow black people in the New World? One possible answer is that the change took place when anti-colonialism replaced black dignity as a slogan for the African sector of the black movement as a whole. For as long as the dominant battlecry was black dignity, this encompassed both Africans and Afro-Americans. But when independence became the paramount fighting slogan of the African sec-

---

[17]   Nkrumah, *Autobiography*, 54.
[18]   Nkrumah, *Autobiography*, 53-54.

tor, the links with the non-colonized blacks of the New World were weakened. Apart from movements like that of the Black Muslims – which in any case came later – self-government was not a meaningful ambition for Afro-Americans in the United States. And this factor diluted the sense of fellowship in diversity between them and African nationalists.

But just as the English language had once helped to make Pan-Negroism possible, it now indirectly helped to weaken Pan-Negroism. It had this latter effect when it facilitated the growth of anti-colonialism in the African continent itself.

But how did it facilitate that growth?

In trying to answer that question we might usefully start with a quotation. In her first Reith Lecture in 1961, Margery Perham made a claim which is perhaps all too familiar. She said: "The ideal of democratic freedom ... (has) been learned very largely from Britain herself." [19] Her observation was itself part of the imperial tradition – the oral tradition that the ideas which were turned against the Empire were themselves imported by the Empire.

This is an exaggeration which has tended to cloud many people's thinking. And one of the factors which has led to this confusion is that the later African demands for freedom were expressed in words which were indeed "imported". And so, many an observer failed to distinguish between new ideas and a new way of expressing old ideas. In English-speaking West Africa this distinction was made more obscure to observers by the use of actual English slogans. The central slogan had to be something which expressed the desire for liberation. In East Africa the word came to be the local Swahili word, Uhuru, but in West Africa it was the actual English word "Free-Dom", partly Africanized, which was the more common platform song.

Wilfred Whiteley had been known to reflect on the "irony" that the word Uhuru – the rallying point of East African liberation movements – was a loan word from Arabic. It was borrowed from, to quote Whiteley, "those by whom so many were formerly enslaved".[20] To that extent, both the West African slogan of "Free-Dom", and its African equivalent Uhuru, were terms inherited from those who had, at least for a while, denied many an African the very thing which the words denoted. But on the evidence that the word Uhuru is derived from Arabic, it would be rash to conclude that East Africans learned about the virtues of liberty by listening to the wisdom of the Arabs. Yet many a Westerner has tended to regard the use of words like "Free-Dom" or

[19] *The Colonial Reckoning* (New York: Knopf, 1962).
[20] "Political Concepts and Connotations", *St. Anthony's Papers* 10, *African Affairs*, Number One (London: Chatto and Windus, 1961), 18.

"self-determination" by Africans as conclusive proof that it was colonialism which tutored Africans into a love for liberty.

We know that there were pockets of resistance to European intrusion
among different tribal communities from the outset. Groups like the
Ashanti and the Matabele provided adequate evidence of their opposition to being ruled by foreigners from distant lands. It would therefore
seem that the love of freedom in this sense among such people owed
nothing to European influence. On the contrary, the European intrusion
seems to have violated that love. We might then ask in what sense it
could still be true that these people learned about self-determination
from colonial tutelage. This is where the English language comes into
relevance. Resistance to foreign rule in Africa does indeed antedate the
coming of the English language, but that resistance did not become
"nationalistic" until its leaders became English-speakers. When the Ashanti, the Masai or the Kikuyu harassed intruders with spears three or
four generations ago they were "hostile natives". But when they came
to attack colonial rule in "sophisticated" language they became "nationalists". In a variety of ways the English language was an important
causal factor in the growth of African national consciousness. Indeed,
learning English was a detribalizing process. If one found an African
who had mastered the English language, that African had, almost by
definition, ceased to be a full tribesman. To an extent which was later
to be exaggerated, there was indeed a "Westernizing" process implicit
in the very act of learning English.

But why should the learning of a language have this effect? The
reason lies in the relationship between language and the culture from
which it springs. Language is the most important point of entry into
the habits of thought of a people. It embodies within itself cumulative
associations derived from the total experience of its people. The English
language as a partial embodiment of Anglo-Saxon habits of thought
must therefore carry with it seeds of intellectual acculturation for the
Africans who learn it. That is why learning English was, to a non-
Westerner, a process of Westernization. And to the extent that an English-speaking African was thus partly "Westernized" he was indeed
partly detribalized.

Yet to be detribalized was not the same thing as to have national
consciousness. Partial detribalization was a necessary condition of
nationalistic feeling but not a sufficient condition. By learning a Western
language an African might indeed move from tribalism to non-tribalism. But it would be pertinent to ask what kind of non-tribalism.
After all, the quality of being detribalized could, in one case, take the
form of neo-universalism, a sentiment of African identification with the
metropolitan power. But it could, in another case, take the form of

nationalistic self-consciousness *as an African*. On balance detribalization in English-speaking Africa took a more decisive turn into nationalism than it did in French-speaking Africa. Togoland's Dr. Armattoe
said something appertaining to this at that fifth Pan-African Congress:
"It is sometimes questioned whether French West Africans have any
feeling of national consciousness, but I can say that French West Africans would be happier if they were governing themselves." Nevertheless, Armattoe went on to add that French West Africans "sometimes
envy the British Africans their intense national feeling." [21]

That was in 1945. In September 1958 it was still possible for French-
speaking Africa to vote, in a popular referendum, for a *continuation* of
French imperial rule. What was remarkable about the De Gaulle referendum of 1958 was not that Guinea had voted in favour of independence, but that she was the only one. Had a similar referendum been
held in English-speaking Africa, the results would probably have been
very different. Both the French and English languages had indeed helped
to detribalize the leaders of Africa – but on balance it was more English
than French which produced practising nationalists.[22]

But was this because the English language lent itself more to nationalism? On the contrary, it was French more than English which commanded the militant love of those who spoke it. When this love is evoked
in the French people themselves, the result is linguistic nationalism.
For French is, after all, their own national language. But when a passionate love for French is aroused in those to whom French is only an
adopted language, the result is a kind of linguistic universalism. To put
it in another way, a Frenchman passionately in love with the French
language is a nationalist; but an African passionately in love with French
is, at best, a cultural cosmopolitan. Among French-speaking Africans
Léopold Senghor is perhaps exceptional, not in his love for French, but
in the frankness with which he expresses it. He tells us: " ... If we had
a choice we would have chosen French." He then goes on to rationalize
this affection by saying:

First, it is a language which has enjoyed a far reaching influence and
which still enjoys it in great measure. In the 18th century French was
proposed and accepted as the universal language of culture. I know that
today it comes after English, Chinese and Russian in the number of

[21] See Padmore (ed.), *History of the Pan-African Congress*, 36.
[22] Paul-Marc Henry, former head of the Division of Sub-Saharan Africa in the
French Ministry of Foreign Affairs, said in 1959 that "between 1946 and 1958
one does not find any trace of activity by any French-speaking politician in the
various stages of the Pan-African movement, as interpreted and operated by
Mr. Padmore and Dr. Nkrumah". See Philip W. Quigg (ed.) *Africa, A Foreign
Affairs Reader* (New York: Frederick A. Praeger, 1961), 162.

people who speak it, and it is a language of fewer countries than English. But if quantity is lacking there is quality.

Senghor then goes on to assure us:

I am not claiming that French is superior to these other languages, either in beauty or in richness, but I do say that it is the supreme language of communication: "a language of politeness and honesty", a language of beauty and clarity.... [23]

In part it is this militant linguistic cosmopolitanism among French-speaking African leaders which arrested the growth of real nationalism in their part of the continent. The English language, by the very fact of being emotionally more neutral than French, was less of a hindrance to the emergence of national consciousness in British Africa.

But there were other factors, too, about English to be taken into account. Among these was the simple but persistent fact once again that the United States was English-speaking. This provided an alternative country of higher education for African leaders from British Africa. Education in Britain or France was indeed quite capable of producing nationalism in its own right. But the fact that these were the imperial countries themselves could sometimes create an ambivalence in an African's attitude towards the country of his education. An African educated in England could indeed hate England but he might also make a few English friends. Even if he did not make friends, he was bound to find out that not all English people were "colonialist" in their sympathies. He might find himself marching with British radicals against this or that policy of the British government.

In addition, there was the element of anglicization which a student usually underwent if he spent more than two years in England. The student might never grow to love England, but by being anglicized a little he would have rendered his anglophobia less pure psychologically. Perhaps even "British empiricism" might rub off on him – and he could become a gradualist in his attitude to decolonization.

An African from Francophone Africa educated in France might become even more ambivalent in his attitude to French colonial rule. He might make more French friends than his Anglophone counterpart might make English friends in England. And it might be even more effectively demonstrated in France than in England that colonialism was not universally applauded by the citizens of the colonial power. On the whole there have always been more French radicals in existence than there have been English radicals.

---

[23] "Negritude and the Concept of Universal Civilization", *Présence Africaine* 18 (26) (Second Quarter, 1963), 10.

What emerges from these considerations is the fact that the imperial country itself was not conducive to single-minded nationalism in an African. There were factors which got in the way of total psychological hostility to the country concerned.

But unless he was prepared to learn a new language altogether the Francophone African did not have many alternatives to France as a source of higher education. At any rate he had before him no French-speaking equivalent of the United States – in terms of scholarships available.

What these factors added up to was this historical phenomenon. Firstly, English-speaking Africans were, on the whole, more national-istic than French-speaking Africans. Secondly, among the English-speakers, those who were educated in the United States tended to be more single-minded in their nationalism than those educated in Great Britain. It was perhaps not accidental that the leadership in Ghana passed from British-educated personalities to the American-educated Nkrumah. Nor was it entirely a coincidence that the founding father of Nigerian nationalism was Nnamdi Azikiwe.

What made American-educated Africans more militant in their na-tionalism than British-educated ones? There was indeed the tradition of anti-imperialism which many Americans continued to subscribe to even if their governments did not always do so. There was also the factor that America was, in any case, a more ideological and more rhetorical country in its politics than Britain usually was. *The Observer* of London might have been overstating the case when it described Com-munist China and the United States as "the two most ideologically in-spired States of the modern world".[24] But it is certainly true that political beliefs tend to be articulated with greater passion and more hyperbole by Americans than by the British. And exposure to such a climate could make an African educated in the United States more ideological and more rhetorical in his own stand of anti-imperialism than his fellow African in the British Isles.

A third factor which made education in the United States conducive to militancy was the racial issue. In his book on Nigeria, James S. Cole-man put the question in these terms:

The special situation of the American Negro, into whose company an African student is inevitably thrown was... an important conditioning factor. African students in America were perforce made acutely aware of colour discrimination, in itself provocative of racial consciousness.

Coleman goes on to point out that West Africans did not meet in their own countries the highly institutionalized and omnipresent discrimina-

---

[24] Editorial, *The Observer* (London), May 9, 1965.

tion characteristic of Southern states, and to a degree also of Northern states, in America. Racial discrimination in Nigeria (formally outlawed in 1948) was irritating mainly as a symbol of European imperialism, but "it did not engulf the individual and plague him at every turn". Thus, Coleman tells us, many Nigerians encountered racial discrimination on a large scale for the first time when they arrived in the United States.[25]

Coleman was on less solid ground when he went on to suggest that the same sort of racialistic cultural shock, though less pronounced, hit an African student studying in England. On the contrary, a reverse type of shock was more usual. In other words, what impressed African students in England in those early days was the apparent racial broad-mindedness of the British people in England as compared with the type they encountered at home. Many a student came to draw a sharp distinction between those two types of Britons in his experience.

And so while African students studying in the United States found themselves in a more racialistic society than they had in their colonial homes, African students studying in England found themselves less so. It is therefore not surprising that the American-educated African was the more single-minded in his nationalism.

On a broader linguistic plane this is another factor which spared Francophone Africa the passions which come with highly institutionalized racial discrimination. There was no French-speaking "Jim Crow". The United States within her own borders had contributed at least as much as British settlers in Africa to the racist image of the Anglo-Saxon peoples. Because of this general image of Anglo-American racial arrogance French-speaking Africans found it possible to congratulate themselves on having fallen under French imperial rule on the grounds that it was a lesser evil. As for those occasions when even French policy betrayed signs of intolerance, the nefarious influence could conceivably be traced to "the Anglo-Saxon example". It might be fitting here to conclude with a remark by Raphael Armattoe, once again, at that Pan-African Congress:

At one time all Africans born in the French Empire were citizens. It was only when the Anglo-Saxons brought their influence to bear on the French that the position changed and fewer Africans were regarded as citizens.[26]

In his own confused way Armattoe was making at least one valid

---

[25] *Nigeria, Background to Nationalism* (Berkeley and Los Angeles: University of California Press, 1958), 245. This point is also analysed in my paper "Borrowed Theory and Original Practice in African Politics", in: *Patterns of African Development*, ed. Herbert Spiro (Englewood Cliffs, N.J.: Prentice-Hall, 1967).
[26] Padmore, *History of Pan-African Congress*, 36.

point. He was alluding to the role of the British as pace-setters in matters of imperial conduct. Those who were ruled by the British became in turn pace-setters in the general movement against imperialism at large. Through their arrogance the British and the Americans had helped to arouse the black man's pride. Through the paradox of their leadership in humanitarian ventures they had helped to restore black dignity. And through their language they had helped to detribalize the African's mind – and to give it a nationalistic dimension in modern terms.

3

ENGLISH AND ISLAM IN EAST AND WEST AFRICA

Muslims in Africa south of the Sahara have been both among those who have been relatively suspicious of the English language as a factor in cultural transformation and among those who have shown an aptitude for speaking it well. Their suspicion of English has been partly connected with the role of missionary schools in Africa. Indeed, English itself was later to find that its strongest indigenous rivals for supremacy in Africa were the leading Islamic languages of Africa.

This chapter concerns itself with that interplay between language and religion in Africa's political experience.

RELIGION, LANGUAGE AND EDUCATION

Christian missionaries were of course a critical factor in the spread of education in Africa, especially in the early days of colonial rule. The only real alternative to the Christian mission as a major agency for building schools would have been the government, but at the beginning of this century state responsibility for education was not fully acknowledged even in Britain itself, let alone in its colonies. In the field of welfare services the general ethos of *laissez faire* still exerted considerable influence. There was a similar belief in restricting the participation of the state in education and comparable areas of social endeavour. In the colonies the educational initiative was thus firmly left to private agencies, pre-eminently the Christian missionaries.

From quite early therefore the idea of Western education in Africa came to be almost equated with Christian education.

But education in British colonies was also increasingly equated among simple folk with ability to speak English. There is no doubt that there was a strong connection between the prestige of the English language and the prestige of education at large. The command of the English language was often used as a criterion of one's level of education: "And still they gazed and still the wonder grew / That one small head could carry all the English he knew."[1]

A simplistic syllogism emerged out of this dual connection. The partial equation of education with Christianity, coupled with the partial equation of education with the English language, produced a partial equation of Christianity with the English language. In other words, given that education was Christian and the English language was the very basis of education, was it not to be inferred that the English language was itself Christian too?

Of course this was not a rigorous exercise in logical reasoning, but simply an exercise in psychological association. There was a time when an African who spoke English well was assumed, almost automatically, to be a Christian. In the trial of Jomo Kenyatta on charges connected with the founding of Mau Mau, you could almost see Judge Tucker's mind associating English with Christianity in the following brief exchange between him and a witness. The witness had expressed a preference to give his evidence in English.

Magistrate: "Very well, you can give your evidence in English. You seem to speak it very well. Are you a Christian?"
Witness Kegeena: "Yes."[2]

The equation of the English language with missionary education was a major factor in conditioning Islamic attitudes towards it. Muslims became suspicious of the English language on the basis of a presumed guilt by association. This was aggravated by the sense of cultural defensiveness which developed among Muslim communities in Africa as in other parts of the world. As I have had occasion to argue elsewhere, Islam has a deep-seated sense of insecurity in relation to Christianity. As modernization gathered momentum in the Nineteenth and Twentieth Centuries, it was clear that Christian countries were leading the rest of the globe towards new technological and intellectual achievements. Within the Christian countries themselves industrialization and modernization were sometimes recognized as dangers to Christianity itself. They

---

[1] This point, including the paraphrasing of Goldsmith, is also discussed in my paper "The English Language and African Political Consciousness", *The Journal of Modern African Studies* 4 (3) (1966).
[2] Montagu Slater, *The Trial of Jomo Kenyatta*, second edition, revised (London: Mercury Books, 1965), 40.

were in themselves secularizing agencies and were therefore corrosive factors on religion and tradition. But observers in Muslim countries in the Middle East and elsewhere were not always aware of the fears entertained by Christianity itself about the new forces let loose by the Industrial Revolution. All that Muslim observers could see was that white countries still professing Christianity were in the vanguard of modernity. And European faith in progress and the rightness of their political and economic systems created in Islamic countries a great sense of unease.[3]

In Africa south of the Sahara, perhaps even more clearly than in any of the Arab countries, these new forces of modernity came riding on Christian horses. The civilizing crusade which came with Christian missions, and the evangelizing commitment of the early mission schools, helped to emphasize the intimate association between the forces of modernity and the forces of Christianity in a newly colonized Africa. The sense of insecurity among Muslims helped to aggravate their suspicion of these new forces, and encompassed also a suspicion of the linguistic medium in British Africa, the English language itself.

RELIGION, LANGUAGE AND COLONIAL POLICY

Although the mission schools were agencies for the spread of the English language, that linguistic dissemination was not always warmly welcomed by colonial authorities. Colonial administrators were on the one hand interested in the possibility of producing literate Africans to help in some of the more menial clerical positions in government and the private sector; and on the other hand they were all too aware of the potential for agitation inherent in the Western type of education in the colonies. In Ghana the word "scholar" came into being in the middle of the Nineteenth Century to designate the products of the new schools in the country. Before long there developed a so-called "Colonial Office attitude" to educated Africans – perhaps typified by an assessment registered in Colonial Office records in 1875 that " 'educated natives' or 'scholars' . . . have always been a thorn in the side of the government of the Gold Coast. They have been at the bottom of most of the troubles on the Coast for some years past."[4]

---

[3] See my chapter, "Islam, Political Leadership and Economic Radicalism in Africa", in : Mazrui, *On Heroes and Uhuru-Worship* (London: Longmans, 1967).
[4] Minutes of 6 February, 1875 by A. W. L. Hemming (later head of the African Department of the Colonial Office), C.O./96/115. See David Kimble, *A Political History of Ghana, The Rise of Gold Coast Nationalism, 1850-1928* (Oxford: The Clarendon Press, 1963), 91.

Knowledge of the English language was critical in all this. In the words of Lugard, perhaps the greatest of the English administrators in Africa, " . . . the premature teaching of English . . . inevitably leads to utter disrespect for British and native ideals alike, and to a de-nationalized and disorganized population."[5]

And even the missionaries themselves were sometimes accused of attempting to suppress the spread of the English language. This arose mainly because of the Christian missionaries' brave attempts to develop orthographies and systems of writing for local languages. F. B. Welbourn has gone as far as to assert: "It was, indeed, in the field of language and literary education that the missionaries were to make their most important contribution outside the strictly religious field. The local languages had to be learned and reduced to writing."[6]

But way back in the 1920's the missionaries were being criticized even by British government officials for their tendency to "discourage the teaching of English by the teaching of the native language and dialects and to seek to perpetuate them as written language".[7]

And yet, in spite of some distrust by colonial administrators of the impact of the English language on "the natives", and in spite of the effect of missionary promotion of African vernacular languages, the English language assumed a vital role in education above the primary level in both East and West African British colonies. And the missionaries disseminated the metropolitan language almost in spite of themselves. They were instrumental in spreading the language because of their commitment to augmenting educational opportunities for Africans, and because of their near-monopoly of school education in British colonies for quite a while.

But if Lugard did not succeed in denying Africa the English language, he certainly did succeed in slowing down its spread in the Muslim areas he controlled. The whole doctrine of indirect rule which Lugard propagated found its finest fulfilment in the Muslim areas of Northern Nigeria. As we have seen, indirect rule was an atempt to utilize native institutions in governing the colonies. But indirect rule has also had broader cultural implications. In this latter context it constituted a re-

---

[5] F. D. Lugard, *Annual Reports, Northern Nigeria 1900-1911*, 646, cited by James S. Coleman, *Nigeria Background to Nationalism* (Berkeley and Los Angeles: University of California Press, 1958), 137.
[6] See F. Welbourn, *East African Christian* (London: Oxford University Press, 1965), 82.
[7] *Annual Report*, Department of Education, Southern Province, 1926 (Lagos, 1927), 7, cited by Coleman, *Nigeria Background*, 443. On the role of missionaries in the development of the vernacular, see also Diedrich Westermann, *The African Today and Tomorrow*, third edition (London, 1949), 117-128.

luctance to tamper too radically with the belief systems as well as the political institutions of subject peoples.

Among such peoples indirect rule worked best in those societies which had developed institutions of the kind which were either relatively familiar to the conquering power (as for example Islamic institutions observed elsewhere in the Muslim world before, and then found in Africa as well) or relatively centralized in their authority structures (as for example the institutions of Buganda in the eyes of Stanley and other European explorers at a critical stage of imperial evaluation).

The finest realization of Lugardism was, in fact, among the Emirates of Northern Nigeria. And this realization deliberately excluded Christian missions from the North. In Southern Nigeria there was a growing desire for education among the masses, arising out of a belief that "Western education, and especially a knowledge of the English language, would equip them with the technique and skills essential for the improvement of personal status in the emergent economic and social structure".[8]

But in the North applied Lugardism excluded the missionary agent of change and, with him, English as a medium of intellectual transformation, occupational and social mobility and the crystallization of national consciousness. There were long-term consequences of this. "In the first place, the absence of an English-speaking educated class in Northern Nigeria in the early period necessitated the importation of thousands of Southerners into the North as clerks and artisans."[9]

Uganda was also a major achievement of applied Lugardism; and here too, the Muslims were strikingly deficient in their possession of Western academic and linguistic skills. In 1893 the Muslims had been defeated in Buganda, and from then on remained a small, even if politically significant minority. Inevitably, they were not among the great beneficiaries of missionary education. Uganda Muslims have developed as simple traders, butchers, taxi drivers, petty shopkeepers and soldiers.

In political affiliation the Buganda Muslims were often supporters of some Protestant fight as against the Catholics. But even this had connections with the nature of missionary education. It has been suggested that the Protestants have perhaps been "more ready to admit [the Muslims] into denominational schools without proselytism" than the Catholics have been.[10]

---

[8] Coleman, *Nigeria Background*, 124-125.
[9] Coleman, *Nigeria Background*, 140. The growth of a Southern population in the North holding skilled or affluent positions later became one of the precipitating factors behind the massacre of the Ibos in Northern Nigeria and some of the other events which led to the civil war.
[10] Welbourn, *East African Christian*, 61. Consult also D. A. Low, *Religion and*

But whatever the relative affinity between the Muslims and the two Christian denominations, the reduced access to mission schools relegated the Muslims to a modest status. The contrast in Buganda was perhaps particularly striking – certainly more conspicuous than in other parts of the country where Muslims and Christians lived together. The commitment to the creation of an educated African elite was stronger among missionaries operating in this region than elsewhere. Mackay defined the general direction: "Instead of vainly struggling to perpetuate the method of feebly manned stations, each holding a precarious existence, and never able at best to exert more than a local influence, let us select a few particularly healthy sites, on which we shall raise an institution for imparting a thorough education even to only a few." [11]

As David Apter has pointed out, this was precisely the model for the later pattern for education which resulted in Mengo High School (later King's College Budo) and St. Mary's College, Kisubi. [12]

Evidently indirect rule in Buganda was not protecting the Baganda from the influence of missionary education, in the way that the Northern Nigerians had been protected under similar doctrines. As we have noted, indirect rule in Uganda managed to foster a pride in indigenous culture among the Baganda and, at the same time, an interest in metropolitan ways.

ENGLISH, ISLAM AND AFRICAN LANGUAGES

Looking at Africa as a whole, the strongest rivals to European languages are, in fact, Muslim languages. The term "Muslim" or "Islamic" language is here used either in the sense that those who speak it as a first language are overwhelmingly Muslim, or in the sense that the language itself reflects a very strong Islamic influence at both the explicit and the suggestive levels; or in both those senses simultaneously.

The three strongest rivals to European languages in Africa are Arabic itself, dominant especially in the North; the Hausa language, leading in the West; and the Swahili language, leading in the East. The Arabic language is of course the most explicitly Islamic

Society in Buganda, 1875-1900 (= *East African Research Series 8*) (Kegan Paul, 1957).

[11] See J. W. Harrison, *Mackay of Uganda* (London: Hodder & Stoughton, 1890), 470.

[12] David E. Apter, *The Political Kingdom in Uganda* (Princeton, N.J.: Princeton University Press, 1961), 74. Consult also D. A. Low and R. Cranford Pratt, *Buganda and British Overrule, 1900-1955* (London: Oxford University Press, 1960).

of them all, partly because it is the language in which Islam was revealed by the Prophet Mohammed, and also because of the continued influence of Arabic in the cultural and religious life of Muslims almost everywhere.[13] In Africa the language's area of concentration is North Africa, but Arabic also plays significant national roles not only in the Sudan, but also in countries like Chad and Somalia.

Then there is the Hausa language in West Africa. More than 40% of the population of Northern Nigeria speak Hausa as their mother tongue. But in addition, Hausa-speaking groups are scattered all over West Africa, and the Hausa language and culture have exerted significant influence on the direction of cultural change within neighbouring communities.

Then there is the Swahili language in East Africa. Only a small minority of those who speak the language speak it as a first language. The language's greatest success is perhaps in its effectiveness as a lingua franca over an area which includes not only Tanzania, Kenya and Uganda, but also Zaire, Malawi and Burundi. It has been estimated that the language is the seventh most important international language in the world.[14]

These are the three most important non-European languages in Africa as a whole. Some might argue that Wolof is the fourth most significant trans-national indigenous African language on the continent. This is more debatable. And yet if it is accepted as a proposition, Wolof too qualifies as a Muslim language in the senses mentioned above.

The relevance of these languages for African cultural nationalism is quite striking. The richness of the languages is sometimes attributed to their original indigenous subtleties, but it is also at times attributed to their association with Islamic dynasties and Islamic cultural movements in the past.

Edward Blyden, perhaps the father of modern cultural nationalism in Africa south of the Sahara, discussed the role of the Arabic language in intellectualizing indigenous African languages where Islam held sway:

Different estimates are made of the beneficial effects wrought by Islam upon the moral and industrial conditions of Western Africa . . . ; but all

---

[13]   For some background of the Islamic factor in East African education, see *Kenya Education Report* (The Ominde Commission), Part I (Government of Kenya Publication, December 12, 1964), 33-39; T. W. Gee, "A Century of Muhammedan Influence in Buganda, 1852-1951", *Uganda Journal* (Kampala) 22 (1958); J. Spencer Trimingham, *Islam in East Africa* (Oxford: Clarendon Press, 1964), esp. pp. 171-174; I. M. Lewis (ed.), *Islam in Tropical Africa*, esp. chapters IX, XIV & XV.
[14]   A useful study of the "heart" of the Swahili-speaking population is A. H. J. Prins, *The Swahili-Speaking Peoples of Zanzibar and the East African Coast* (London: International African Institute, 1961).

careful and candid observers agree that the influence of Islam in Central and West Africa has been, upon the whole, of a most salutary character . . . Large towns and cities have grown up under Mohammedan energy and industry . . . Already some of the vernaculars have been enriched by expressions from the Arabic for the embodiment of the higher processes of thought.[15]

Later on those African languages which were deeply Islamized did in turn become carriers of Islamic influence to others, partly because of the prestige they had accumulated. Coleman and others have talked about the powerful "cultural attraction" that the Hausa had exercised on the smaller tribes of the middle belt and indeed on some southern nationalists in old Nigeria. The prestige of Hausa for such nationalism stems partly from its relatively rich historical tradition, partly because of the pomp and splendour of the ruling class in the community which spoke the language, and partly because of distinctive architectural accomplishments associated with Hausa civilization.

. . . The culture provides an alternative to the white European culture which the Hausa have been taught to emulate. . . . Culturally conscious Nigerians, both Hausa and non-Hausa from the South, seek to identify themselves with this tradition. In their view it provides positive proof that the white man is mistaken when he states that Nigerians have no culture, no history, and no experience in large scale political organization. This tendency toward identification is manifest even among the educated Nigerians from the South who do not take on the externals of Hausa culture.[16]

In East Africa Swahili is by no means uniformly prestigious. In fact, in Uganda the language seems to carry proletarian associations, partly because many of those who speak it are migrant labourers away from home who have had to resort to Swahili as a lingua franca in their dealings with members of other tribes.

But in Kenya, and even more in Tanzania, Swahili is associated with a highly developed cultural tradition, and the language enjoys enough prestige to be a serious candidate as an educational medium in schools.

In fact, on this issue of national languages, it has indeed been precisely such Islamic or neo-Islamic languages which have even remotely approached the status of the metropolitan language in countries previously colonized. The case of Somalia is of course distinctive as it is almost the only nation-state of some size in Africa south of the Sahara

---

[15]   See Edward W. Blyden, *Christianity, Islam and the Negro Race (1887)* (Edinburgh: The University Press, 1967 reprint), 174, 186-187.
[16]   Coleman, *Nigeria*, 22, Consult also J. P. Mackintosh, *Nigerian Government and Politics* (London: George Allen & Unwin, 1966), and Richard L. Sklar, *Nigerian Political Parties* (Princeton: Princeton University Press, 1963).

in the classical European sense of cultural homogeneity. The country has a language of poetic power which has only just found an adequate alphabet. But in Somalia the rivalry is perhaps ultimately between two Islamic languages, Arabic and Somali itself. English and Italian are at a second level of competition.

In Nigeria debate has intermittently erupted as to whether Hausa should become the national language. When in the old Federal Parliament it was proposed that Hausa should be so adopted, strong voices were heard against the proposal. Chief Anthony Enahoro, for example, said in Parliament:

As one who comes from a minority tribe, I deplore the continuing evidence in this country that people wish to impose their customs, their languages, and even more, their way of life upon the smaller tribes.[17]

And a Nigerian Minister visiting India in 1953, in relating his country's problems with a comparable multilingual situation in India, reaffirmed that:

We are not keen on developing our own languages with a view to replacing English. We regard the English language as a unifying force.[18]

Yet, the advocates for Hausa have by no means been silenced. Of particular interest has perhaps been the campaign of Mr. Tai Solaria, a weekly contributor for quite a while to the *Daily Times*, Nigeria's leading newspaper. Mr. Solaria established himself as a campaigner for the adoption of Hausa as the national language of Nigeria both in his articles in the newspaper and in supplementary pamphleteering.

When the status of Israel was established the Israelis chose Hebrew which was least spoken by any group of Israelis ... because it is native; it is indigenous. ... We now come to Nigeria. ... I have noticed that the defenders of "English shall be our lingua franca" are invariably those of us who appear better dressed in the "English" suit than the English themselves. ... Whatever Nigerian language we choose is, psychologically, a more acceptable language than any foreign language.[19]

In the wake of the Nigerian Civil War, and the suspicions in some quarters of the potential Hausa domination of the country as a whole, it would now be rash to re-activate the campaign for Hausa.[20]

---

[17]   Cited by F. A. O. Schwarz, Jr., *Nigeria: The Tribes, The Nation and the Race* (Cambridge, Mass., M.I.T. Press, 1965), 41.

[18]   Reported in *Uganda Argus* (Kampala) November 13, 1953.

[19]   See *Daily Times*, 20th October, 1966. See also Solarin, "A Native Tongue as Lingua Franca", *Daily Times*, February 5, 1965. I am indebted to Oluwadare Aguda, *The Nigerian Approach to Politics* (= *African Studies Seminar paper 2*), Sudan Research Unit, Faculty of Arts, University of Khartoum, 14-20.

[20]   For general discussions on the Nigerian Civil War, refer to *Africa Report*, April 1968; *Current History*, February 1968; and *Transition* 36 (1968).

That other neo-Islamic language, Swahili, has fared better in the struggle to win recognition as a national language. In Tanzania especially, there has been a big push forward to give Swahili a widening role in the national life of the country. Most political activity in the country is now conducted in Swahili. There is an increasing emphasis on its use as a medium within the educational system. A brave attempt has also been made to Swahilize the vocabulary of legal discourse and judical transactions in the country. And organizations like the Poets Association have received encouragement and support from the government in their bid to "enrich the nation's language and cultural heritage".[21]

In Kenya Swahili's triumph is much less clear, though the language seems to have made significant gains in the last two decades. It is more widely understood than ever before, and its role as a national language is now debated with greater feeling than ever before. It seems likely that Swahili will ultimately conquer Kenya as effectively as it has conquered Tanzania, but this is a prediction which only the future can confirm.[22]

The chances are that the Swahili which could conquer Kenya would be somewhat less Islamic in its cumulative associations than the kind of Swahili heard in many parts of Tanzania. But the Islamic influences on the language are for the time being very much in evidence wherever Swahili is spoken correctly. Here again, then, it remains true that a major rival to a metropolitan language is an African language with Islamic associations.

LANGUAGE, THE KORAN AND THE BIBLE

At the back of the Islamic influence on such African languages as Hausa, Wolof, and Swahili, is the influence of the Koran. And this influence has been important in conditioning Muslim attitudes to European languages in Africa. Edward Blyden, who had himself knowledge of Arabic, and taught it, had occasion to quote a European Koranic scholar who wrote in 1869:

[21] Vice-President Rashidi Kawawa committed the Government more formally to support the Poets Association in a speech he gave in January 1965. These cultural and linguistic groups are by no means consistently active, but the political atmosphere in Tanzania is still very favourable to endeavours in this direction. See also *The Nationalist*'s enthusiastic response to Kawawa's speech on the future of Swahili in Tanzania. "Our National Language", editorial, *The Nationalist*, 20th January, 1965. See also renewed discussion on widening the role of Swahili, in Tanzanian newspapers in January 1967.

[22] See my paper, "The National Language Question in East Africa", *East Africa Journal*, June 1967. A version of the paper also appeared in *Africa Report*, June 1967.

The Koran suffers more than any other book we think of by a translation, however masterly. The grandeur of the Koran consists, its contents apart, in its diction. We cannot explain the peculiarly dignified, impressive, sonorous mixture of semitic sound and parlance; *sesquipedalia verba,* with their crowd of prefixes and affixes, each of them affirming its own position, while consciously bearing upon and influencing the central root, which they envelop like a garment of many folds, or as chosen coaches move around the annointed person of the king.[23]

Blyden goes on to observe that the African Muslim is no exception among the adherents of Islam in his appreciation of the sacred book. "It is studied with as much enthusiasm at Boporo, Nisadu, Medina and Kankan, as at Cairo, Alexandria, or Baghdad."[24]

It has also been suggested that the Baganda were first attracted to the Arabs by the magic of reading and writing. Joswa Kato Mugema, a leading Muganda Christian, baptized in 1885, is reported to have started the art of "reading" with the Arabs. "He was still signing his name in Arabic characters as late as 1904. But reading meant, largely, reading the Qur'an."[25]

Because of the special status of the Koran in Muslim theology, there is a linguistic dimension in Islam which has no real equivalent in Christianity. The Koran is regarded not merely as divinely inspired, but as literally the utterance of God. Every word, every syllable is supposed to be directly emanating from God. The Prophet Mohammed, when revealing the Koranic verses, was serving as no more than a channel of communication. In fact, in such moments of Koranic utterances by the Prophet, God was almost a divine ventriloquist, giving the Prophet a voice which was, in fact, God's own.

The language in which the Koran was originally revealed assumes therefore a special meaning within this belief system. The Authorized Version of the Bible in the English language may be as holy to the Protestant as any other version, but the Koran in translation loses much of its original spiritual stature. Since every Arabic syllable in it is directly from God, a substitution of syllables in the English language or in Gujerati dilutes the ultimate authenticity.

Related to this literal Godliness of the Koran is the doctrine of its inimitability. This is the assertion that the diction and structure of the

[23] The quotation is from Emmanuel Deutsch, *Quarterly Review* (London), October 1869. Consult also Alfred Quillakme, *Islam* (Harmondsworth, Middlesex: Penguin, 1962 edition), especially Ch. 3.
[24] Blyden, *Christianity, Islam and the Negro Race*, 178. See also James Kritzeck, *Anthology of Islamic Literature: From the Rise of Islam to Modern Times* (Harmondsworth, Middlesex: Penguin, 1964), especially 33-74.
[25] Welbourn, *East African Christian*, 60. See also Welbourn, *Religion and Politics in Uganda, 1952-1962*, (Nairobi: East African Publishing House, 1965).

Koran can neither be equalled nor imitated by a mortal author. And yet, curiously enough, the very prestige that the Koran has enjoyed as a work of literature has played a great role in stabilizing the evolution of the Arabic language. It seems almost certain that the Arabic language in its written form would have changed more radically over the centuries had it not been for a constant attempt of Arab writers to imitate precisely the language of the Koran. This recurrent attempt to imitate the inimitable has been one of the major stabilizing influences on written Arabic over the centuries.

In Africa south of the Sahara the classical neo-Koranic form of Arabic is important not only in written literature but also in Arabic speech where it occurs. What Edward Blyden said in the Nineteenth Century about the classical nature of African Arabic is true today as well:

Those who speak Arabic speak the Koranic or book Arabic, preserving the final vowels of the classical language – a practice which, in the hurry and exigencies of business life, has been long discontinued in countries where the language is vernacular; so that in Egypt and Syria the current speech is very defective, and clipped and corrupted.[26]

The importance which the Koran has enjoyed in Muslim thought has at times retarded the evolution of secular schools. This was certainly true in those British colonies with a sizeable Muslim population. Koranic schools, in many ways deficient as instruments of education, were often a serious rival to modern schools in Muslim areas. And the very importance of the Arabic language as something to be coveted by those who do not speak it as a first language complicated the scheme of linguistic priorities in Muslim areas in Africa. In a Hausa-speaking region, for example, should the educational system promote Arabic first as the next target for acquisition, or should it promote the English language? The answer, at least in the earlier stages of colonial penetration, was by no means easy.

In addition, there was a tendency to assume that just because the believers could look to an ultimate authentic language of their faith, so too, could the nonbelievers be associated with a language of their own. Among simple people in British Africa the English language was at times regarded as a language of nonbelief, a language of the *kafir*. Indeed, the Jesus of Christianity – unlike the Isa of orthodox Islam – was often conceptualized as a European. Where churches could be segregated, and angels described as white, it was not difficult to make Jesus wear the nationality of Europe. But a nationality, it was assumed, carried a language of its own. And in British Africa the European was

[26] Blyden, *Christianity, Islam and the Negro Race*, 185.

decidedly English-speaking. It was an easy step to move from a white Jesus to an English-speaking Jesus. And the Bible in English coming into Africa was too readily made analogous to the Koran in Arabic entering the continent. The special status of Arabic in Islam led to assumptions about a special status of English in Christianity.[27]

Gradually many of the Islamic inhibitions in regard to the English language have been weakened. Lamu, which used to be profoundly distrustful of the English language and the culture it represented, has now found a new enthusiasm for government secular schools. Zanzibar capitulated much earlier, taking a dramatic lead in East Africa in per capita graduates. Islamic distrust of the English language and the civilization it represented, in Mombasa and its vicinity, began to crack after World War II, but it still remains true that Muslims in Kenya are among the least educated of the communities. As we have seen, Sir Philip Mitchell, when he was Governor of the country, was so aware of the educational retardation sustained by Muslims in Kenya that he made a special effort to obtain the necessary funds for the establishment of the Mombasa Institute of Muslim Education referred to earlier. The Institute, designed to be mainly technical, was intended to rescue Arab and African Muslims from general educational lethargy and occupational narrowmindedness. In their defensiveness against Christianity, these Muslims had been letting modernity pass them by.

But where Muslims have finally capitulated to the pull of the English language as a medium of intellectual modernity, they have been among the better speakers of the language. As it happens, this is basically a linguistic accident. In East Africa among the best speakers of the English language in diction and pronunciation are Zanzibaris, coastal Tanzanians, and native-speakers of Swahili along the coast of Kenya. It seems quite clear that the command of the English diction which these people manage to achieve is directly due to the structure and sound range of the Swahili language with which they started. In other words, there was something in the kind of Swahili spoken in these areas which gave the native speaker a degree of adaptability in the acquisition of the sounds of the English language.

A similar phenomenon has been observed among Hausa speakers in Northern Nigeria. Where they do get round to accepting the English language, and when they do succeed in learning it well, the sound range of their native Hausa facilitates their assimilation of the sound habits of the English language. It was for good reason that Alhaji Sir Abubakar

[27] In his trial on Mau Mau charges Jomo Kenyatta was accused, among other things, of having gone so far in associating Christianity with colonialism as to actually assert that Jesus Christ was an English gentleman. See Montagu Slater, *The Trial of Jomo Kenyatta*, 153. Kenyatta denied this charge.

Tafawa Balewa, the last Prime Minister of the Nigerian Federation be- fore the first coup, acquired the admiring name of "The Golden Voice of the North" among fellow-Nigerians.

CONCLUSION

We have attempted to demonstrate two major themes in this chapter. One is that Islamic attitudes towards the English language in Africa have been conditioned by the missionary genesis of secular education in British colonies, as well as by the place of Arabic in Islamic systems of thought. The missionary factor behind the spread of education and of the English language retarded Muslim involvement in this wave of modernity. The place of Arabic and the Koran within the complex of Islamic attitudes complicated the problem of priorities and choices in African Muslim communities, and diverted energies toward Koranic schools at some expense to other forms of education. Among the more simple of the adherents of Islam there was also an easy assumption that just because Islam had a pre-eminent and divinely hallowed language of its own, Arabic, so Christianity, too, must have one of its own, readily assumed to be the pre-eminent European language of the conquering power. It took a while therefore before Muslim attitudes to the English language were freed from a neo-religious suspicion.

The second theme of this paper has concerned the simple proposition that the strongest rivals to a metropolitan language in Africa have, in fact, been languages of Muslim communities or of Islamic cultural deri- vation. Arabic, Hausa and Swahili especially have come nearest to chal- lenging the supremacy of a metropolitan language in the evolution of modern Africa. They have also succeeded more than any other in sym- bolising a trans-national cultural pride and sense of dynastic historical grandeur.

In historiography, texts in the Arabic language have been part of the evidence that modern Africa has been producing to combat the assertion that Africa is a continent with no history. And the Sudanic civilizations, and their association with African Islam, have helped to give such lan- guages as Hausa and Fulani a cultural prestige.

In East Africa Swahili's prestige is by no means uniformly acknowl- edged. There are, in fact, parts of the region where the language is more easily associated with humble proletarian origins than with glorious cul- tural ancestry. And yet there is no doubt that in Tanzania, Kenya and parts of Zaire, Swahili enjoys sufficient status to pose a challenge to the imperial languages in at least some areas of national endeavour.

Behind these two themes of the paper – the nature and origins of

Islamic attitudes to the English language, and the potential of the Islamic languages as rivals to imperial media – is the simple curiosity that among the best articulators of English sounds in African societies are precisely people who grew up speaking Swahili, Hausa and perhaps Arabic.

This last paradox is essentially, as we indicated, no more than an accident in phonemes across distinct languages. But perhaps even such accidents have a wealth of symbolism in them. After all, Nkrumah defined his concept of *consciencism* as being a diffusion in the African consciousness of the three dominant traditions in Africa's intellectual evolution. These are, *firstly*, the indigenous elements themselves, *secondly*, the impact of Islam on Africa's history, language and cultural trends, and *thirdly*, the influence of imperial Europe on Africa's entry into the modern era.

The interplay between competing religions and competing languages is simply one aspect of this tripartite structure of Africa's cultural evolution.[28]

---

[28] Consult Nkrumah, *Consciencism* (London: Heinemann, 1964).

4

THE RACIAL BOUNDARIES OF THE ENGLISH LANGUAGE

When C. G. Seligman brought out his classic but controversial book *Races of Africa*, the first problem he had to confront was the definition of a race. Who are the Bantu? What constitutes a Nilote? Who are the Hamites and Nilo-Hamites? Seligman admitted that language by itself was not an adequate guide to "race".

Yet the study of the races of Africa has been so largely determined by the interest in speech, and it is so much easier to acquire a working knowledge of a language than of any other part of man's cultural make-up, that names based upon linguistic criteria are constantly applied to large groups of mankind and, indeed, if intelligently used, often fit quite well. Hence, in describing the great racial groups of Africa, terms such as "Bantu" which strictly speaking have no more than a linguistic significance, are habitually employed ... [1]

In general, Seligman used the term "race" to mean a family of related tribes – like Bantu and Nilotes – but even the definition of tribal groups, in turn, had to be overwhelmingly reliant on linguistic criteria. The Nilotes are those who speak Nilotic languages; the Bantu are those who speak Bantu languages. In this case we mean speech in terms of the mother tongue rather than a second language.

Even with regard to tribes we can say the Baganda are those to whom Luganda is the first language. Imagine applying the same criterion to the English language. The English are those to whom English is the first

---

[1] C. G. Seligman, *Races of Africa*, third edition, (London: Oxford University Press, 1957), 1-2.

language. What would the Scots have to say about this? Imagine the response of Jamaicans and Trinidadians.

The point becomes even clearer if we move from language to community. It may be defensible to say those for whom Luganda is the first language are Baganda. It becomes much more controversial to say those for whom English is the first language are themselves English.

LANGUAGES: COMMUNALIST AND ECUMENICAL

What we have here is a distinction between communalist languages and ecumenical languages. Communalist languages are those, like Luganda and Luo, which can be used to define a race or a tribe. Communalist languages are race-bound or tribe-bound, and serve to define as communities those who speak them as mother tongues.

Ecumenical languages are extra-communalist, they transcend these boundaries of racial or ethnic definition.

Communalist languages could be highly absorptive in the sense of allowing even newcomers to the language to be categorized racially or tribally as natives, provided they have, in fact, succeeded in being linguistically assimilated. This phenomenon has been striking in Buganda itself, where new groups coming in during the last two or three generations, acquiring Luganda gradually as a first language, have in time become Baganda. They become Baganda once Luganda has become their first language.

Are communalist languages spoken only by one or two million people? The answer, of course, is no. There are communalist languages that are spoken by millions. It is indeed arguable that the language which has the most speakers in the world, Chinese, is itself a communalist language – with its expanding eight hundred million speakers. The situation is still such that we can say that the Chinese are those to whom Chinese (Cantonese or Mandarin) is the mother tongue. If they live in Japan and are gradually assimilated into the Japanese language and culture, then after a generation or two they become Japanese.

In Africa, the most important non-European languages are Arabic Hausa and Swahili. All are communalist languages in their different senses, but Swahili may be gradually ceasing to be so. At the moment the majority of those who speak Swahili speak it as a second language, but there is an increasing number of people in Tanzania and Kenya who are growing up bilingual in Swahili and their own tribal language. It will become increasingly difficult to say that whoever speaks Swahili as a first language is an Mswahili. Swahili is, therefore, less absorptive than even Hausa, but that may also be its strength. The *Waswahili*, in the original sense of "the people of the coast", were defined by reference to some degree of Arabization and Islamization. Because they are now politically unimportant, their language stands a chance of being acceptable to others.

But the same cannot be said of Hausa. In the old Federal Parliament before the first *coup* of January 1966, it was proposed that Hausa should be adopted as the national language of Nigeria. We will recall that strong voices were heard against the proposal, fearing that it would result in a Hausa domination of the smaller tribes' customs and ways of life.[2]

Since then, in the wake of the Nigerian Civil War, the fears of a potential Hausa domination of the country as a whole have increased still further. For the time being, then, Hausa is doomed to be basically a communalist language.

A more startling communalist language is Arabic, partly because of its distribution across different nations, and partly because of the great variety in colour of those who speak it. One would expect Arabic to be as extra-communalist as the English language. Just as English has native speakers who range from Australian industrialists and English Dukes, to black fishermen in St. Kitts in the West Indies, so Arabic has native speakers who range from white Lebanese millionaires to black Sudanese soldiers. And yet while English is ecumenical, Arabic has retained its communalist nature in spite of the diversification in the colour and origin of its speakers.

The Arabs as a "race" defy pigmentational classification. They also defy any attempt to place them on any one particular continent. Are the Arabs Asians, Africans, both, or neither? It is not often remembered that there are more Arabic speakers within Africa than outside. Arabic may have started in the Arabian Peninsula, spread into the Fertile Crescent, and then into Africa, but the balance of preponderance of speakers has changed. In some ways the situation is the equivalent of the change in relationship between England, as the birthplace of the English language, and the United States. The mother country, England, is now overshadowed by her former imperial extension – and there is the possibility of Britain becoming an extension of the United States rather than the other way around.

Does the analogy hold in the relationship between Arab Africa and the rest of the Arab world? It certainly holds as between the old Arabian Peninsula proper, on one side, and Africa and the Fertile Crescent combined, on the other. Countries of the Peninsula proper – especially Saudi

---

[2] F. A. O. Schwarz Jr., *Nigeria: The Tribes, The Nation And The Race* (Cambridge, Mass.: Massachusetts Institute of Technology Press, 1965), 41.

Arabia, from which the Arab invasions of the seventh century origi-
nated – are now overshadowed in inter-Arab influence even by Iraq
and Syria on their own. If we put Africa on one side and the rest of the
Arab world as a whole (Peninsula and Fertile Crescent) on the other,
the preponderance of Arabic speakers is still on the African side. As the
Egyptian scholar, Boutros-Ghali, put it in a book published in 1963:
"It must not be forgotten that sixty percent of the Arab community and
seventy-two percent of the Arab lands are in Africa."[3]

Although by crossing the Atlantic the English language became less
communalist, by crossing the Red Sea Arabic has remained as communalist as ever. Those who spoke Arabic as a first language became,
after a generation or so, Arabs. The result was a staggering mixture of
groups. As Erskine Childers once put it:

... the Arab world ... comprises very many widely varying races or
historical ethnic groups. The short list is bewildering, and distinguishing
"racial" definitions are themselves treacherous. From west to east, the list
must include Berbers, Carthaginians, Romans, Vandals, Arabians, Tur-
comans, Egyptians, Nubians, Haemites, Greeks, Armenians, Circassians,
Assyrians, Babylonians, Hittites, Sumerians, Kurds, Persians and a small
host of ancient migratory infusions whom it is safer to describe simply
as Semitic.

Childers goes on to say that anyone attempting to give a racial definition
of "What is an Arab" would founder hopelessly in the waves of several
thousand years of migration, invasion and intermarriage. " 'Arabism'
has nothing to do with 'race', but with language, cultural tradition and
heritage . . . ."[4]

But Childers here is using the word "race" as some kind of descent
by blood. Muddathir Abd Al-Rahim has also used the "blood" definition
of race, and rejected it as not meaningful when applied to the Arabs.

In fact, however, Arabism ... is not a racial bond which unites the members of a certain ethnic group. It is a cultural, linguistic and non-racial
link that binds together numerous races – black, white and brown. Had
Arabism been anything else but this, most modern Arabs, both Africans
and Asians, including the entire population of Northern Sudan, would
cease to be "Arab" at all.[5]

---

[3] Boutros Boutros-Ghali, "The Foreign Policy of Egypt", Chapter in: Black
and Thompson, *Foreign Policies in a World of Change* (New York: Harper and
Row, 1963), 328.
[4] E. Childers, *Common Sense About the Arab World* (London: Victor Golancz
Ltd., 1960), 70.
[5] Abd Al-Rahim, "Arabism, Africanism, and Self-Identification in the Sudan",
The Journal of Modern African Studies 8 (2) (July 1970), 248. And see also
Edward Atiyah, *The Arabs* (London: Pelican Book A 350, 1955).

But if one insists on regarding the Arabs as a race then the criterion applicable is linguistic. The Arabs are those who speak Arabic as a first language. Very often they are also Muslims, and have acquired other aspects of Arab culture, but the central defining characteristic remains linguistic. Arabic, in spite of the richness of pigmentation among its speakers, remains more "race-bound" than the English language.

What we have here, then, is a paradox. The English people are more racially exclusive than the Arabs. But precisely because a person did not become English merely by being English-speaking, the English language became less racially exclusive than Arabic. With the Arabs, those who spoke their language became absorbed into the race. With the English many of those who spoke their language were kept decidedly out of the "Race". Today, therefore, we identify those who speak Arabic as a native language as belonging to that particular race; but those who speak English are decidedly not necessarily English. The English language is less race-bound partly because the English people have tended to be racially exclusive.

Perhaps French comes in an intermediate position between English and Arabic. The French assimilation policy, and the tendency to accord French rights to those who absorbed French culture, was strikingly reminiscent of the history of the Arabs. Perhaps if the French Empire had lasted as long as the Arab Empire, we might, indeed, have arrived at a situation where we could say that those who spoke French as a first language were French, be they white, brown or black. But the French language did not have enough time to become like Arabic.

TOWARDS THE GLOBALIZATION OF ENGLISH

There have been occasions when the racial exclusiveness of the English people has tended to make them possessive about the English language itself. This is, in fact, one of the major paradoxes of the comparative history of the English language and the French language.

French was, on the whole, intended by France to be disseminated across the globe to become the language of high culture and high diplomacy and to recruit to its ranks more and more creative users of the medium. There was a time when French seemed to be winning that battle. Its prestige did make it the language of the aristocracy in countries as varied as Czarist Russia and Lebanon, Chile in Latin America and Egypt under Ottoman rule.

The English people, on the other hand, were less preoccupied with the imperative of spreading their language. On the contrary, they were sometimes arrogantly possessive about it, particularly in their Colonies.

Many were the Englishmen in the old Colonial days who insisted on speaking Swahili to an African in Kenya, even if neither of the two spoke Swahili while both of them spoke fluent English. It became a point of honour sometimes to maintain the linguistic distance between the Englishman and his coloured subject, as a way of maintaining the social distance between them.

On occasion, colonial administrators were, as we have seen, disturbed by what were regarded as the political consequences of teaching the English language to the natives. Lord Lugard, the greatest of the British administrators in African history, also shared some of these reservations.[6]

Yet, in spite of these influential reservations about the "reckless" spreading of the English language, the language gathered its own momentum and rapidly outstripped French, both in the number of countries that adopted it as a major national medium, and in the number of speakers. The British, who did not want their language to become a universal language, are doomed to precisely that fate, while the French are embarked on a determined attempt to stop French from receding in importance.

The major instrument for the initial spread of the English language was the British Empire itself. French expansionism was also the single most important medium for the spread of French, but the British Empire was bigger and more widespread than the French Empire. Secondly, France never succeeded in producing the equivalent of a United States – that is, a linguistic child who then became bigger than the mother, and began to contribute even more than the mother to the spread of the shared language. Certainly since the disintegration of the British Empire, the biggest carrier of the English language has been the American rather than the Englishman. By 1966, it was being estimated that there were already one-and-a-half million Americans abroad on business or in technical assistance programmes, and millions more American tourists sampling the world in all its diversity.

The United States contributes large amounts of money towards the teaching of English in a large number of countries. Partly because of the American leadership in important areas of science, English has become the primary language of science, and aviation, as well as of sports, and increasingly even of literature and the theatre. As one East African publication put it some years ago in a delightfully pungent, if journalistic style: "When a Russian pilot seeks to land at an airfield in

[6] Lugard, *Annual Reports*, 125, cited by James S. Coleman, *Nigeria: Background To Nationalism* (Berkeley and Los Angeles: University of California Press, 1958), 136-137.

Athens, Cairo or New Delhi he talks to the control tower in English."[7]

The same weekly journal reproduced from a recently established report estimates to the effect that by 1966 seventy percent of the world's mail was written in English, and an even larger percentage of cable and wireless transmissions. Sixty percent of the world's broadcasts were already in English, and more and more countries were introducing English as a compulsory second language in schools.

Yet in spite of this phenomenal spread of the language, the British at home seem to look upon it at best as an amusing phenomenon, and at worst as something which is tending to pollute and corrupt their language.

On the one hand, because English is now no longer communalist or race-bound, many foreigners to the language are scrambling to bring it into their lives. But because the English people themselves continue to be relatively insular, none of the new native speakers of the language are admitted into the fold. Indeed, some of the new varieties of the language are not always recognized as legitimate.

An example of this scramble for the possession of English was a delightful argument which broke out in the *East African Standard* (Nairobi) in 1965. A Mr. M. S. Robinson, an Englishman, complained about the degeneration of the use of English in Kenya with particular reference to the impact of broadcasting on usage. The purist response of British users of English – as contrasted with the experimentalist tendencies of American users of English – had asserted itself in Kenya in defence of the pristine originality of the texture of the language.

Back came a reply from a non-British Kenyan, Mr. S. Meghani, disputing Mr. M. S. Robinson's monopolistic approach to the English language. Mr. Meghani said that if Mr. Robinson did not like the way other people spoke English, he should also remember that others may not like the way he did. "English as spoken by an Englishman is not at all pleasant to listen to . . . let alone easy to follow."

Mr. Meghani then went on to challenge the claims of the English people to the English language.

It is not at all wisdom on the part of a tiny English population in this wide world to claim that English, as presented and pronounced by Americans, Canadians, Africans, Indians and the people of Madras State, is not English. It may not be the Queen's English, but then what? Has the Englishman the sole right to decide upon the form and style of a universal language?

Mr. Meghani then asserted that the whole trouble lay in the name which the language continued to bear. The name, suggested Mr.

---

[7]   See the section on "Education", *Reporter* (Nairobi), December 30, 1966, p. 13.

Meghani, was now a misnomer since English had by far outgrown its origins.

Strictly speaking, English cannot be called "English" at all, since it is a universal language belonging to all. It is difficult to understand why it is still known under that horrible name; it should have had another name.[8]

Within a few days back came a reply from another native speaker of the language, seemingly from the British Isles. This new correspondent confessed that he held the view that civilization was bounded on the North by the Thames — and woe to those over-tolerant individuals who would substitute the Trent — and on the West by the Tamar and the Severn and on the South by the English Channel. He then went on to support Mr. Meghani's suggestion that English as spoken by Mr. Meghani and "others of similar linguistic and cultural attainments, including the V.O.K. announcers" should bear some other name. The new writer thought that was the most sensible suggestion he had heard for a long time.

As one who holds . . . that the English language is an autochthonous product of that civilization (bounded on the North by the Thames and on the South by the English Channel), I feel that your correspondent's suggestion should be acted on immediately or, as he would probably prefer to put it, implemented forthwith. There is, however, no need to coin a new name for the "universal" language. There is a time-honoured one – "Pidgin-English".[9]

Such was the reply from a reader with a strong possessive instinct towards that variety of the English language which was bounded by the Thames and the English Channel.

We have had, then, the spread of English, capturing peoples and nations, and yet having those new "converts" rejected as linguistic equals by the originators of that language in the British Isles.

THE EMERGENCE OF AFRO-SAXONS

Let us refresh ourselves about what we said in the Introduction. Before the end of this century there will probably be more black people who speak the English language as their native tongue than there will be inhabitants of the British Isles. Black Americans alone who speak the language as a first language are already nearly the equivalent of half the population of Great Britain. And then there are a

---

[8] See Letters to the Editor, *East African Standard* (Nairobi) February 15, 1965.
[9] *East African Standard* (Nairobi), February 19, 1965.

few more million black speakers of the language scattered round the Caribbean and the northern fringes of South America. Within the African continent, the only black native speakers of the English language so far are the ruling community of Liberia, descended from black Americans. There are also a few black native speakers of the English language in places like Sierra Leone. But at least as important a phenomenon is the growing number of educated African families that are using English as the language of the home. A number of African children, especially in West Africa but also increasingly in East Africa, are growing up bi-lingual in English and their own African language because their parents are highly educated and speak English to each other.

It is these considerations which make it likely that by the end of the twentieth century the black native speakers of the English language will outnumber the British speakers. An Afro-Saxon population, linguistically influential, will have come into being. But this kind of situation has its tensions. The Anglo-Saxons, liberal in some spheres, but racially exclusive, have tended to create complexes among those they have ruled or dominated. And where English conquers the black man as effectively as he was once conquered by the Anglo-Saxon race, tensions between dignity and linguistic nationality are unavoidable.

An important illustration comes with James Baldwin, one of the most gifted black users of the English language today. Baldwin once wrote an article on how he stopped hating Shakespeare. He admitted his hatred of Shakespeare had been, in part, a turning away from "that monstrous achievement with a kind of sick envy". In Baldwin's most anti-English days, he condemned Shakespeare for his chauvinism ("This England" indeed!). But, mainly, his revulsion against Shakespeare lay in the fact that he, as a black man, was condemned to being a native user of the English language.

... I felt it so bitterly anomalous that a black man should be forced to deal with the English language at all – should be forced to assault the English language in order to be able to speak. .... I condemned (Shakespeare) as one of the authors and architects of my oppression.[10]

Some of the irritation came from the characters created by Shakespeare himself. Baldwin mentions how some Jews have at times been bitterly resentful of Shylock. Baldwin, in turn, as a black man, was bitter about Caliban and dubious about Othello ("What did he see in Desdemona anyhow?").

Baldwin's quarrel at that stage with the English language was that it

---

[10] See James Baldwin, "Why I Stopped Hating Shakespeare", *Insight* 11, published by the British High Commission (Ibadan, 1964), 14.

was a language which did not reflect any of his experience. But when one day he found himself in a non-English-speaking situation, having to think and speak in French, Baldwin began to see Shakespeare and the English language in a new light.

If the language was not my own, it might be the fault of the language; but it might also be my fault. Perhaps the language was not my own because I have never attempted to use it, had only learnt to imitate it. If this were so then it might be made to bear the burden of my experience if I could find the stamina to challenge it, and me, to such a test.

Baldwin found support for this possibility from two "mighty witnesses" — his black ancestors, who had evolved the sorrow songs, the blues and jazz, and created an entirely new idiom in an overwhelmingly hostile place; but Baldwin also found support from Shakespeare, whom he now regarded as the last bawdy writer in the English language.

Shakespeare's bawdiness became very important to me since bawdiness was one of the elements of jazz and revealed a tremendous, loving and realistic respect for the body, and that ineffable force which the body contains, which Americans have mostly lost, which I had experienced only among Negroes, and of which I had been taught to be ashamed.

The language with which Baldwin had grown up had certainly not been the King's English. It had been the English of the black man in the New World.

... an immense experience had forged this language, it had been (and remains) one of the tools of the people's survival, and it revealed expectations which no white American could easily entertain.[11]

What ought to be grasped here, in addition, is that the bawdiness of Shakespeare was intended for public performance. The man was primarily a playwright. In Shakespeare and in drama at large we, therefore, have that important link between the literature of oral utterance and the literature of the written word. The character of Falstaff was indeed written by Shakespeare, but it had to be made to live on the stage. The actual writing down of a play would be alien to indigenous East African tradition; but the performance of that play on the stage could re-establish a link with East Africa's dramatic experience. Much of the poetry of Africa was indistinguishable from song – it was intended for recitation in a collective context, rather than for the private enjoyment of one individual lover of poetry retreating to an isolated spot for solitary indulgence.

Nor were the mighty lines of Shakespeare primarily intended for

[11] Baldwin, "Shakespeare", 14-15.

solitary indulgence. They were intended for the throbbing spontaneity of Elizabethans, reminiscent in their very sense of involvement with the performance and their hearty assimilation into the mood of the moment, of audiences in Africa, black America and the West Indies.

Yet because Shakespeare wrote his plays, the question of identity was important. There were plays by Shakespeare, whereas much of African oral literature is a literature without authors. The African experience is a collective heritage, modified and augmented, sometimes diluted, as it passes from person to person, from generation to generation. But the heritage of Shakespeare, precisely because he wrote the plays and made them bear his name, has individualized the genius. It has pin-pointed the fountain of creativity. And with that focussing there has emerged a whole branch of knowledge known as Shakespearean studies, ranging from minute discussions of original editions of this or that play, to discussions connected with the biographical details of the author.

Yet, in the case of Shakespeare, there is at least one residual link with the kind of literature where authorship retains an element of uncertainty. Disputes have erupted every century as to whether Shakespeare's plays were indeed written by Shakespeare. Arguments as to whether he was the front man for dramatic exercises written by Francis Bacon or by Christopher Marlowe have periodically animated the scholarly world. There are those who, like Africans, have argued that it did not matter who had written Hamlet – the play was a collective inheritance. Shakespeare's plays might just as well have been, according to this school, plays without authors, or plays by an anonymous contributor to English civilization.

But there are others who have disputed such a neo-African dismissal of the importance of authorship. The whole tradition of individual accountability in western civilization is called into question when it is claimed that the authorship of a particular artistic or scientific achievement is irrelevant. Did Columbus discover America? How Newtonian is Newtonian physics? Does it matter what the origins of the Bible are? Does it matter who invented the steamship?

In short, the written word and, in the case of music the written notes, have so far been indispensable both in preserving the details of what was originally created and, often, in preserving knowledge about its creators. The two forms of preservation are, of course, inter-related. Just a written record that at the Globe theatre a play called *Hamlet* was performed, authored by William Shakespeare, would not be enough if the play then became transmitted from generation to generation by memory. The entire structure would change, the outlines of the characters could be transformed, the whole exercise might become radically different. A play transmitted by word of mouth from generation to generation, from the sixteenth century, would hardly survive intact by the time it was being enacted from memory at the National Theatre in Kampala. The written word, then, becomes important both in determining authorship and in preserving the original text.

And precisely because the written word is a method of conservation, it also helps to stabilize a language. Ideas which are not reduced to writing can be very perishable indeed. Where is the complete wealth of Africa's wisdom over the centuries? Africa must have had great philosophers, great mystics, even great eccentrics, trying out new ideas. But much of that old intellectual activity has simply been lost to us. Yes, Africa does indeed have oral tradition. Some of Africa's wisdom has been transmitted from generation to generation by word of mouth. But oral tradition tends overwhelmingly to be the transmission of consensus rather than heresy, of accepted ideas rather than innovative intellectual deviations. In Africa's history, many of the latter kind of ideas, which might indeed have commanded acceptance one or two generations later had they been preserved in writing, died very early because they were never so recorded. Ancient radicalism did not find the conserving blessing of the written word.

Among the things which change very fast when there is no widespread tradition of writing is, quite simply, language itself. Swahili has had a written tradition for two or three centuries, but it has not been very widespread. One consequence of this is the fact that Swahili has changed more between the eighteen-fifties and the nineteen-seventies than English has during the same period. English has changed less rapidly partly because of the conserving influence of a literate culture. It is true that literacy in the early part of the nineteenth century in England was far from universal. But the literate section of the community had become so big, and its impact on the rest of the population so great, that much of the language of the other classes of nineteenth century England has survived with little change to the nineteen-seventies.

But there are also disadvantages in the preservation of all aspects of language. The disadvantages might lie partly in consolidating and deepening even those aspects of the language which need to be changed. One of the least explored of these aspects is *metaphor*. Metaphor accumulates certain associations, some negative or perjorative. When language undergoes relatively little change, it becomes difficult to revise such metaphor and its outdated associations.

BLACK METAPHOR AND ENGLISH SEMANTICS

This is what brings us to the residual racialism in English metaphor in matters connected with white and black colours.

A few hours before I started writing this particular part of the Chapter, I received in the post an issue of the monthly magazine *Africa Report*. In the correspondence columns there was a bitter complaint from a Tanzanian critic of President Nyerere's régime – a Tanzanian living in the United States. The Tanzanian complained that articles published about his country tended to "whitewash" the régime and its failings. I have sometimes caught myself saying that one of "the blackest stains" on Nyerere's career was his decision to let his former ambassador in Washington, Othman Sherrif, be taken to Zanzibar, probably to his death.

I suppose, in such a context, one could attempt to use a different metaphor if one could stop oneself soon enough. But how much of a choice in synonyms do I have when I want to discuss blackmail? Or something sold on the blackmarket?

It is true that most of the time when we are using these words we are not connecting them with any racialist tradition which associates black with evil and white with goodness. The metaphor is so much part of the English language, so beautifully integrated, that it is ready for use unconsciously, in a spontaneous flow. In the metaphor of the English language black has repeatedly, and in a variety of contexts, strong negative connotations. White has ambivalent connotations but, more often, favourable ones. The connotations have been so stabilized that users of the language are unconscious of those wider links with racialist traditions. But does not the lack of awareness make the situation worse than ever?

It would matter less if English continued to be the language of only the English people. But precisely because it is the most eligible candidate for universality, and also because black native speakers of the language are on their way towards becoming the most numerous, the case for a gradual diversification of English metaphor in the area of colour becomes important for African writers. They need not change the word blackmail into whitemail, or blackmarket into white or brown market; but a new consciousness of the residual racialism of the English language, and new imaginative coinings of alternative metaphors, at least within African versions of the English language, would help to improve the credentials of the English language as an African medium. In accepting the English language as their own, black people should not accept passively and uncritically. There is a case for the deracialization of the English language.

As a starting point in such an endeavour, we should at least be clear of the broad negative connotations which the metaphor of blackness has assumed in the English language. There is, first, the association of blackness with evil; secondly, there is the association of blackness with void and emptiness; thirdly, there is the association of blackness with death. These three areas of negative association have, in fact, multiple sub-associations. The association with death, for example, also makes black the colour of grief. Conversely, if war is death, white becomes the colour of peace. The white dove becomes the messenger of reconciliation.

But let us take each of these three broad negative connotations in turn – black is evil, black is void, black is death.

In some ways, most deeply structured into the language is the notion that black is evil. To some extent the difficulty has its origins in the Europeanization of Christianity. As Christianity became a religion whose chief champions were white people, angels gradually became white and the devil black.

The biblical heritage of the West profoundly influenced metaphorical usages in more popular literature. With regard to the English language, the Bible and Shakespeare might well be the greatest contributors to popular metaphor.

Nothing has captured the association of black with evil more poignantly than Blake's Poem *The Little Black Boy*. The poem exclaims with a startling revelation of this whole universe of metaphor: "And I am black but O My soul is white."

John Bunyan and other religious writers also have suggestions about washing a black man, or an Ethiopian, white, as a way of conferring upon him salvation.

But John Dryden puts limitations on the degree of blackness which is admissible in heaven, as well as on the degree of whiteness which could ever deserve hell. In Dryden's *The Hind And The Panther* the agony of purgatory is the predicament of one who is "too black for heaven, and yet too white for hell".

But, as we indicated, next to the Bible it is Shakespeare who has had the greatest single impact on the metaphorical evolution of the English language. Problems therefore arise when African literary figures, and even African Heads of State, find themselves imbibing the Shakespearean idiom.

President Julius Nyerere has even had to confront the ominous task of translating the Bard into Swahili. The plays which Nyerere has translated so far are *Julius Caesar* and *The Merchant of Venice*. Both include negative metaphors of blackness. *The Merchant of Venice* is, in any case, a play partly concerned with racial or religious consciousness.

There are references in the play to black people and customs of colour. But there is also a very explicit association of the dark complexion with the devil.

Portia has had to deal with earlier suitors including a French Lord, a Baron of England, a Scottish Lord, a German Duke. But also among those who courted her was the Prince of Morocco. In Act I, Scene 2, she notes the importance of his dark complexion, even if his entire behaviour is saintly. Blake may have been satisfied that a black boy could have a white soul, but Portia has different ideas about the black-skinned Prince interested in her:

If he have the condition of a saint and the complexion of a devil, I had rather he should shrive me than wive me.[12]

Mwalimu Julius Nyerere had to grapple with this racialistic insinuation, in order to render it into Swahili. He decided to translate "complexion of a devil" more as "face of a devil" than "colour".

... kama ana hali ya malaika au sura ya Shetani ni heri anighofiri makosa kuliko kuniposa.

President Nyerere was an admirer of Shakespeare, but his friend Dr. Milton Obote, was perhaps an even greater admirer of John Milton. The Satan portrayed by Milton in *Paradise Lost* had, at least in the initial phases of the rebellion, a heroic stature. Satan had rebelled against the tradition of kneeling to pray, of flattering the Almighty with grand epithet, of singing hymns in His praise. Until he rebelled, Satan, like all angels, was of course white. At school Obote admired, not Satan as a symbol of evil, but Satan as a symbol of rebellion against total tyranny. Indeed, Obote adopted the first name of Milton in honour of the author of *Paradise Lost*.

Satan and his followers were driven out of Heaven into the great depths. They found themselves lying on the burning lake of Hell. In Book I John Milton has an epithet for Hell – it is "Black Gehenna".

From being a white angel, Satan was becoming a black devil. We might almost say that this heroic figure portrayed by Milton and admired by Obote was the first black person in eternity. And God had sentenced him to a life of perpetual hell.

Related to the whole tradition of identifying blackness with the Devil and whiteness with the angels are the metaphors of shepherds, flocks, sheep and lambs in the figurative language of Christianity. "The Lord is my shepherd". But what is the Lord to do with the black sheep of Africa?

---

[12] *The Merchant of Venice*, Act I, Scene 2, Lines 151-153.

We are back to the colour prejudices of Christianity and of the English language. The sheep and their wool are usually white. The black sheep of the family is the deviant, sometimes the wicked, exception.

From blackness and its association with evil there is an easy transition to blackness and death. Sir Patrick Renison, then Governor of Kenya, defiantly resisting pressures to release Jomo Kenyatta, bracketed these two associations of darkness and death in his very denunciation of Kenyatta. He called Kenyatta "Leader into darkness and into death".

The concentration of darkness in the middle of the night carries ominous suggestions of danger and evil. The owl, because it hoots in the night, is often an omen of bad luck. The worst luck was death, and the worst omen, impending death. Alfred Tennyson described a grave as "the gross blackness underneath".[13] The black band round the arm at funerals, the black suit that the dead man is sometimes supposed to wear, the black dress the widow is expected to use – all are cumulative associations of blackness and death. In translating *Julius Caesar*, Mwalimu Julius Nyerere had to translate the phrase by Octavius – "Our black sentence". This was the sentence of death passed by the counter-conspirators against those who might have been implicated in the assassination of Caesar in Act IV, Scene 1.

Nyerere's compatriot and fellow translator of Shakespeare, S. Mushi, had, in turn, to grapple with the dark recesses of Macbeth's mind. In Act I, Scene 3, Malcom speaks of Macbeth as "black Macbeth", referring to the foul nature of Macbeth's soul, as well as suggesting its orientation towards murder and death.

BLACK IDENTITY AND LINGUISTIC REFORM

As for the association of blackness with the void, this has given rise to a number of sub-associations, ranging from emptiness, ignorance and primitiveness, to sheer depth. The Dark Ages are dark both because we do not know very much about them and because they are presumed to be barbaric and primitive.

It is partly because of these preconceptions of emptiness and barbarity, that many African nationalists, black as they were in colour, objected to Africa being described as a "dark continent". Why were these dark people indignant that their ancestoral landmass should bear the title of "dark continent"? Precisely because their initiation into the connotations of the English language had sensitized them to the negative implications of such a description of Africa.

[13]   Alfred Tennyson, *Supposed Confessions Of A Second-rate Sensitive Mind*, Conclusion.

Darkness as emptiness and barbarity certainly influenced Professor Hugh Trevor-Roper in his dismissal of the concept of a meaningful African history. In his own infamous words:

> Perhaps, in the future, there will be some African
> history . . . but at present there is none: there is
> only the history of the Europeans in Africa.
> The rest is darkness . . . and darkness is not
> a subject of history. [14]

Darkness as a characterization of Africa's past is thus resisted by the darkest in colour of all peoples – the African nationalists south of the Sahara themselves. The connotations of the English language, with all its cumulation of negative associations in relation to blackness and darkness, are pre-eminently to blame for these anomalies.

The starting point of black aesthetics must, therefore, be not only the black power motto "Black is Beautiful", but also the insistence that black is not evil, nor is it emptiness, nor indeed is it death. The Christian symbolism of the black soul, of the black devil, of the black armband at a funeral, might need to be transformed in the pursuit of new aesthetics for the black man.

Sometimes a resort to symbolism from African traditions can help gradually to provide alternative metaphors for African English. Death certainly can be as legitimately portrayed by whiteness, if African traditions of body-painting are involved. In the third dimension of Islamic tradition, the dead body is covered in white cloth. And a completely white cloth could be ominously reminiscent of what the Waswahili call *sanda* – the white material that is the last apparel of man.

Of course, there are occasions when African customs themselves equate blackness with negative connotations. But these anomalies are present even in the English language. The simile "deathly white" is perfectly English, if one remembers that a white man, when he is dead and no longer has blood flowing in his veins, becomes indeed, at last, really white.

But, on balance, the Africanization of the English language must definitely include the deracialization of English. Black aesthetics has to rescue blackness and darkness from the stifling weight of negative metaphor.

---

[14] Opening lecture of the series on *The Rise of Christian Europe*, broadcast by Hugh Trevor-Roper, reprinted in *The Listener* (London), November 28, 1963, 871.
    For one response to these remarks see J. D. Fage, *On the Nature of African History* (Birmingham 1965).

5

ENGLISH AND THE EMERGENCE OF MODERN
AFRICAN POLITICIANS

In his contribution to the first series of St. Anthony's Papers on African
affairs, Wilfred Whiteley, the late linguist and Africanist, argued that "to
some extent the nature of political action . . . may be related to a people's
conception of what constitutes politics".[1] Formulated in this way,
Whiteley's argument seems to assume that every people has *some* conception of what constitutes politics – the only difference being in what
kind of conception. But can the assumption be taken for granted? In
1952 – to take an example at random – Nnamdi Azikiwe, the Nigerian
leader, referred in a speech at Port Harcourt to "the growth of political
consciousness" in Nigeria. What did he mean? Had the Africans of Nigeria known no political activity until then? If they had, had they not
been "conscious" that the activity was "political?" Or was it a case of
having no special name for this kind of activity as something distinct?
If none of these hypotheses applies, what then was meant by this kind
of reference to "political consciousness" as if it were something new
among Africans?[2]

A step towards an answer can be taken by examining what another
African nationalist put forward at about the same time, virtually as a

In the course of developing some of the ideas in this chapter I benefited from
the comments of a number of friends, especially Professors John Plamenatz and
Colin Leys.
[1] "Political Concepts and Connotations", in: Kenneth Kirkwood (ed.), *African
Affairs* 1, (London: Chatto and Windus, 1961).
[2] The particular speech of Zik cited here was given at a meeting of the
National Executive Committee of the National Council of Nigeria and the
Cameroons held at Port Harcourt in October 1962. See *Zik* (Cambridge University Press, 1961), 85.

definition of politics. According to Laminah Sankoh of the Sierra Leone People's Party:

The central problem of politics is . . . the management of the affairs of the country for the purpose of maintaining or augmenting the rights, duties and privileges of the citizens.[3]

Members of a tribe before the advent of colonialism had "rights, duties and privileges". They were presumably "citizens" in this basic sense. We can also safely assume that such a tribe had some system of "maintaining" if not "augmenting" such rights, duties and privileges. To that extent the tribesmen were engaged in an activity concerning what Sankoh regards as "the central problem of politics". What then made "political consciousness" such a novel phenomenon in the Nigeria which Azikiwe was talking about?

But perhaps tribesmen were not really "citizens" in more than a figurative sense. This would hold if we accepted Ronald E. Wraith's assertion that "that mysterious quality which we call citizenship was a child of city life". Wraith has maintained that "not only have the arts of civilization been born in cities, but also so has the art of politics". He cites linguistic evidence to support his claim – "in the language of Greece and Rome politics and civilization were so closely allied to city dwelling".[4]

And yet Wraith himself speaks of Nigeria as an area with a long tradition of city life. He says:

Not all West African peoples are alike in this way by any means, but it is generally true that people had lived in towns long before they were deeply influenced by European contact. . . . There is a great difference between flying over Nigeria [with its many cities] and flying over any part of East Africa.[5]

On East Africa itself Wraith observed "how far and how fast African political consciousness has travelled in twenty-five years".[6]

And when we turn to examine the region, proceed to take Mombasa as one of the oldest cities there and accept the local Arabs and Arab-ized Africans of the coast as having almost the longest urban tradition in the area, we find that it was still possible in 1956 to classify these particular East Africans as "the least politically minded" of the local communities.[7]

---

[3] *Politics for the People* (Freetown: Waitic Printing Works, 1952), 2.
[4] Wraith, *East African Citizen* (London: Oxford University Press, 1959), 51.
[5] Wraith, *East African Citizen*,
[6] Wraith, *East African Citizen*, 7.
[7] See, for example, *Race and Power*, in *Bow Group Series "Studies of Leadership in Five British Dependencies"*, (London, 1956), 58.

It therefore seems inadequate to attribute the birth of political consciousness merely to the tradition of dwelling in cities. An additional hypothesis which might now be advanced is that politics is an activity not simply of cities as centres of population but of cities as centres of something approaching what "the Greek and Roman languages" tell us about "civilization". On the basis of this new hypothesis a tribesman becomes "politically conscious" not simply by virtue of dwelling in a city, but by virtue of being part of, or exposed to a complex system of, communal relationships and social values.

If this were so, and if it were further conceded that the Muslim North of Nigeria was the part of the country which had had the longest experience of a complex way of life by 1952, it would be in the North that one would have expected to find "political consciousness" at its most developed stage at the time that Azikiwe was referring to its growth in the territory as a whole.

And yet, if the growth of political parties is a measure of the growth of political consciousness, in Nigeria that growth was almost in inverse proportion both to the history of city-dwelling and to traditions of complex indigenous political relationships in the three regions. The National Council of Nigeria and the Cameroons (later renamed National Council of Nigerian Citizens) was in effect the first on the political scene – and it emerged out of the originally dispersed and loosely organized Ibo of the Eastern Region. The Action Group was not launched until several years later by the Western Region, despite the Region's pre-eminence in indigenous urban traditions and despite the complexities of its pre-colonial systems of government. And it was the North which came out last with its Northern Peoples Congress.

But perhaps political consciousness is to be measured not according to when parties were formally launched but according to how far and how quickly each party became something approaching "a mass party". Here again the correlation between the given measure of political consciousness and the complexity of indigenous traditions would be inverse. The N.C.N.C. was the first to become a party of mass participation while the Action Group and the N.P.C. were second and third – and not very close to the first at that. The idea of "mass participation" is perhaps not even meaningful if applied to the functioning of the N.P.C.[8]

---

[8] For accounts of development of Nigerian parties see Coleman, *Nigeria, Background to Nationalism* (Los Angeles: University of California Press, 1958) 251-365. See also Azikiwe, *The Development of Political Parties in Nigeria* (London: Office of the Commissioner in the UK for the Eastern Region of Nigeria, 1957). For a brief account of West African parties generally towards the close of the colonial period see Thomas Hodgkin, "A Note on West African Political Parties",

At this stage the question arises whether experience of a complex indigenous political system is indeed the kind of experience which leads to "political consciousness". Indeed, it can even be asked whether what anthropologists sometimes call "African political systems"[9] were, in fact, systems of *politics* at all.

This is where the semantic equipment of the anthropologist diverges from that of the political scientist. It is also where the concept of "politics" links up with the detribalizing effect of the English language. Very often what a political scientist means by "a politically conscious African" is certainly not a tribesman operating within a traditional "political system". On the contrary, the least "politically conscious" Africans were usually precisely those who were most immersed in their own tribal affairs and ancestral ways. In the colonial situation there was something rather *apolitical* about being a complete tribesman. It was not a coincidence that those who came to capture political leadership in much of Africa were precisely those who had been partially detribalized.

But where does the English language fit into this phenomenon? There is, first, the role of English in the growth of national consciousness. Linked with this is the whole concept of "the intellectual" in the development of modern politics in Africa. The first point which needs to be grasped is that the idea of "an intellectual" is a relative term. To the question "What is an intellectual?" the answer must be that it depends substantially upon the society one is looking at. In a society with a high degree of literacy the criteria of what constitutes an intellectual are more complex than they are in a poorly educated society. In Africa the concept of an intellectual is closely related to the impact of the West. One can almost say that no African is regarded as an intellectual unless he is at least partly Westernized. The two concepts of a "tribesman" and an "intellectual" are almost antithetical in popular usage.

But what degree of Westernization is needed to make an African "an intellectual"? With the spread of education and the increased number of university graduates the criteria of what constitutes an intellectual have become more rigorous and demanding. But in the initial stages of the Western impact an African in British Africa was regarded as "an

in: *What are the Problems of Parliamentary Government in West Africa?* (Conference Report), (London: The Hansard Society for Parliamentary Government, 1958), 51-62. More comprehensive works on the subject are Hodgkin, *African Political Parties* (Penguin African Series No. WA 12, 1961), and Richard L. Sklar, *Nigerian Political Parties: Power in an Emergent African Nation*, (Princeton University Press 1963.)

[9] See, for example, M. Fortes and E. E. Evans-Pritchard (eds.), *African Political Systems* (London: Oxford University Press, 1955).

intellectual" if he had acquired some fluency in the English language. Nor was this a simple case of using literacy as the ultimate test of intellectuality. An African who was widely read in Swahili literature but could not speak English was likely to be considered further from being an intellectual than a poorly read African who had acquired fluency in spoken English.

This is not quite as absurd as it might first appear. Fluency in a language other than one's own is an attribute of intellectual prestige even in the West. An English person who is not widely read but has a great command of French, German or Sanskrit is in possession of a status symbol which might outshine the lustre of a more widely read but *unilingual* compatriot. Similar considerations were at play in the prestige enjoyed by Africans who developed a good command of a European language. But these considerations were made stronger by the fact that the foreign language concerned here was the language of the ruling power. In other words, it was not merely the prestige of mastering an additional language to one's own – it was the status of having acquired the master language itself. In British Africa at that time English was *the* master language of the world. As Gustav Jahoda was given to understand in the course of studying some of the less sophisticated African attitudes to the white man in pre-independent Ghana, the quality of being native to the English language was the major linguistic difference between white people and black people at large. Jahoda was told ". . . the Europeans' language is English and the Africans' language is not English".[10]

But although English did have in this way a status independently of its role as a vehicle of literacy, there is no doubt that a connection did exist between the prestige of the English language and the prestige of education at large. This is because command of the English language was often used as a criterion of one's level of education.

In Ghana the word "scholar" came into being in the middle of the Nineteenth Century to designate a special type of African. In his book on the political history of Ghana, David Kimble tells us that "the term 'scholar' . . . aroused so much awe among illiterates". As for the definition of the term, we can discern it from Kimble's account of the strong reaction the term came to arouse in colonial administrators. The

---

[10] See Gustav Jahoda, *White Man: A Study of the Attitudes of Africans to Europeans in Ghana before Independence* (London: Oxford University Press, 1961), 24. Jahoda explains: "The reason for this widespread misconception [about English being the language of 'Europeans'] is partly the fact that the British formed the major nonindigenous group; furthermore, the term used during the interviews was *biofo*, a Ga word that can be literally rendered as 'white men's language', and thus the notion also receives semantic support."

reaction against "scholars" extended "to cover all who were articulate in English, from the barely literate to the well-informed critic".[11]

In a sense, that was the beginning of the equation between African "intellectuals" and African "politicians". As we have noted, there developed a so-called "Colonial Office attitude" to educated Africans – perhaps typified by an assessment registered in Colonial Office records in 1875 that "scholars" have always been a "thorn in the side of the government" and the traditional trouble-makers of the country.[12] This in turn was the beginning of modern politics in Africa.

But how can we find in this old situation a clue as to what constitutes "politics" in Africa? Within the more usual conceptual framework an attempt to determine whether a particular person is a "politician" logically involves ascertaining whether he is engaged in "politics". But within the African experience "politics" itself became definable by first determining whether there were "politicians" around. Politics was in this case visualized as an activity at the centre of which was a *distinct* class of people called "politicians". Traditional "African political systems", were not, in this sense, systems of politics – for under this definition there could be no politics without politicians as a discernible class of people. "Politicians" in this case are not merely practitioners in the art of politics, but the very *creators* of politics. It is because of the relative novelty of this kind of phenomenon that in the growth of political vocabularies in indigenous African languages the need has often been felt to coin a word for "politician", and sometimes even for "politics", as an activity distinct from administration.[13]

Against this conceptual background, it was possible for African nationalists outside the Belgian Congo to observe that in the Congo there were "no politics in the ordinary sense of the word".[14] Seven years earlier a Western observer had put forward, almost as a reason for this, the argument that in the Congo "you will find no black politicians".[15]

In such instances the situation seemed to be bearing out Lord Lloyd's

[11] David Kimble, *A Political History of Ghana, The Rise of Gold Coast Nationalism, 1850-1928* (Oxford: The Clarendon Press, 1963), 87-93.
[12] Minutes of 6 February 1875 by A. W. L. Hemming (later head of the African Department of the Colonial Office): CO/96/115. See Kimble, *Ghana*, 91.
[13] Swahili did have a word for "politics" but no single word for "politician". And even the term for "politics" was derived from Arabic and was not completely assimilated into the African language. The term in question was *siasa*, which also meant "policy", "cunning" or "prudence". One term for "politician" which has now emerged is the term *mtetezi* which literally means "one who struggles for something or on behalf of somebody else".
[14] Padmore discusses this phenomenon in his *Pan-Africanism or Communism?* (London: Dobson, 1956), esp. 211-220.
[15] A. T. Steele, *New York Herald Tribune*, 4 October 1952.

claim in 1933 that the masses in the colonies had no genuine political aspirations and were only being inflamed by politicians dwelling on their grievances. The masses, in other words, would have known no politics but for the politicians. All that the populace was really interested in was "good administration". And "it is because we have allowed administration to be obscured by political issues that we brought such heavy troubles upon the shoulders of all concerned".[16]

Within this reasoning of Lloyd's there are implied at least three distinctions. One is the fairly common distinction between administration and the strict act of governing on the one hand and political activity on the other. As was emphatically asserted in a Kenya newspaper not long before self-government, "to suppose that government of a country resides solely in politics is rubbish".[17] Another distinction which has, in one form or another, been recurrent in colonial disputations, is the one implied by Lloyd between "genuine" popular aspirations – presumably arising out of a "spontaneous" or "natural" growth – and aspirations which are only professed following the machinations of politicians. Linked with this is yet another distinction implicit in Lloyd – the distinction between grievances and aspirations themselves. Out of the last two sets of distinctions emerges this question: "When does a popular grievance become a popular aspiration?"

The question is pertinent in this search for the essential meaning of African "political consciousness". At this stage perhaps the whole problem of trying to ascertain what "consciousness" is in the study of African nationalism touches a similar problem in the study of Marxism. In the latter, it touches, first, on whether the proletariat is conscious of itself as a class. It touches, secondly, on whether the proletariat is conscious of what it has to protest against; and thirdly, on whether the proletariat is conscious of how it can transform the situation to its own advantage. The first is simple self-awareness as a group; the second is the collective grievance; and the third is the popular revolutionary aspiration.

The same three levels of awareness are discernible in the development of African political consciousness in British Africa. In each of them the English language and the status of "intellectuals" played an important part. At the level of awareness of what there is to protest against, it was claimed by the "scholars" from quite early that only they had the necessary linguistic access and intellectual competence to have some idea of the meaning of new governmental and legislative

[16] Lloyd, *Egypt Since Cromer* (London: Macmillan & Company Ltd., 1933), Vol. 11, 358.
[17] See "Caretaker", *Sunday Post* (Nairobi), 25 February 1962.

ordinances and regulations. As J. Mensah Sarbah, the Gold Coast nationalist, put it early in this century:

For all practical purposes, definite public opinion about the acts of the Government and legislature emanates from the educated classes, and whenever the untaught masses study and examine political questions which directly affect them, such as the Lands Bill of 1897 and the Town Councils Ordinance, they gain a great deal of their knowledge and ideas from what their privileged educated brethren tell them.[18]

Not all "intellectuals" were, in fact, sufficiently educated to understand what government documents were saying. But even a limited knowledge of the English language enabled a person to acquire, at least in the villages, the *reputation* of being quite knowledgeable about "modern affairs". David Kimble draws our attention to the testimony of a missionary in the Gold Coast who, in Kimble's words, "saw the educated African for what he was worth in his own humble environment". The missionary was D. Kemp, and he tells us about his experiences and observations in the course of his nine years at the Gold Coast:

At Abassa I had the pleasure of meeting a catechist. . . . My good friend was "passing rich on £20 a year". I suppose he was the only "scholar" in that town, but he wielded a mighty influence upon all with whom he came into contact. He was the friend and counsellor of kings and chiefs, and was held in the highest esteem among all men in the villages for many miles around. To such as he, representatives of all ranks of society came to have their domestic, social, and political grievances adjusted.[19]

It was partly this kind of status enjoyed by those who were literate in English which tended to make a "politician" out of almost every "scholar". After all, to be a "politician", even more than to be, say, a teacher, was to be some kind of a "leader". Politicians in Africa gradually came to be classified as an "African elite". To be successful in politics postulated having *followers* – and so the new activity gradually became the most important entrance to leadership in colonial Africa. What was the primary task of such political leaders at that time? The first task was precisely the task of trying to create a common consciousness of what there was to protest against in the colonial situation. On February 25, 1947 – to take an incident at random – the *Daily Express* of Nigeria reported that Ivor Cummings of the Colonial Office Welfare Department was refused accommodation by the white-owned Bristol Hotel in Lagos on the grounds that he was coloured. It was not long before the Editor of *Pan-Africa*, a nationalist publication

18 J. Mensah Sarbah, *Fanti National Constitution* (London, 1906), 239.
19 D. Kemp, *Nine Years at the Gold Coast* (London, 1898), 74-75. Cited by Kimble, *Ghana*.

published in London at the time, took up this incident and started to speculate on its broader significance for nationalism in Africa. Why had the African *employees* of the hotel failed to register their protest at this exclusion of a coloured patron? The Editor of *Pan-Africa* was convinced that in this, as in many other instances of apparent apathy or conformity by the masses of Africans, what was lacking was the ability to realize "the implications of such incidents". He therefore warned his fellow African intellectuals: "If we cannot arouse their consciousness we shall have lost a great battle."[20]

One might therefore say that African political consciousness started with a consciousness of such common grievances. That political consciousness became African *national* consciousness when the grievances were identified as "common" not only in the form they took ("We are all denied admission to the Bristol Hotel!") but "common" also in the reasons behind them ("We are all denied admission to the Bristol Hotel because we are all black.")

This kind of national consciousness became a goal-oriented African nationalism when alternatives to the *status quo* began to be conceived and to be regarded as feasible. This started with a consciousness of political status as a relevant factor towards explaining some of the grievances ("We are all denied admission to the Bristol not merely because we are all black but also because we do not possess direct political power to force the Bristol to accept black patrons.") An alternative situation to the *status quo* became a matter of calculated possible modifications to the political status of Africans. It began with an awareness of piecemeal alternatives to individual grievances. It then passed from this reformist stage to a revolutionary one ("The Bristol Hotel's insult against us stems from our whole dependent status; it is that status which must be changed completely.") By this time the politics of grievances had been transformed into a more positive force. Politics were now concerned with definable national aspirations.

But both in arousing a consciousness of grievances and in rallying support for positive aspirations, what was needed was a sense of shared group identity. A knowledge of the English language had, as we have shown, given "scholars" and "intellectuals" the *reputation* of being qualified to detect the seriousness of grievances and to devise a programme of changes which needed to be fought for. What we might now look at more closely is the contribution made by the English language to the growth of common identity in individual African colonies.

We have already mentioned how English helped to detribalize some

---

[20]   T. R. Makonnen, "The Greek Word for Colour Bar", *Pan-Africa* 1 (6) (June 1947).

African minds. But these were the minds of those who had themselves acquired a knowledge of the language. The question which now arises is how English managed to contribute to a sense of national consciousness among the rest of the population.

Part of the answer follows from the previous factor itself. We might say that English helped to make the intellectuals nationalistic, and the intellectuals in turn helped to lead the thinking of the masses in the same direction. But there were other ways, too, in which English contributed to the development of a sense of national identity in a colony. In discussing those ways we should perhaps categorize the different audiences which, directly or indirectly, were addressed by African politicians. We can then evaluate the role of English in each case. The first audience to which an aspiring "intellectual" had to get through were those people he sought to lead. But the leadership itself had to rest on an ability to communicate to the local colonial authorities the general grievances of the populace. Thus these authorities constituted the second type of audience. The third type of audience came to be government and public opinion in the metropolitan country itself. The fourth audience was the international community at large. And the fifth audience was in some ways among the earliest – it was the community of fellow politically conscious black people at home and abroad.

The English language, quite early, helped to create the fifth audience, a community of militant Africans, West Indians and black Americans brought together at pan-African conferences. As for the fourth audience, of the international community at large, this could also be reached through the English language more effectively than through any African language. Nor did the lines of communication with these outsiders flow in one direction. The nationalist movement in India and some of the ideas of Gandhi came to exert an influence on African nationalistic thought. This influence was facilitated by the fact that India and British Africa were under the same colonial power and therefore shared the same international language. Writings and utterances of Indian leaders were often accessible to Africans in British Africa in the original imperial language in which they were expressed.

Communication with government and public opinion in Britain itself was, of course, also greatly facilitated when African leaders could give their own speeches in Britain and mix with British members of Parliament without needing a special person trained in translating an African language to be an interpreter. The role of English-language newspapers published in the colonies in influencing the opinions of radicals in Britain might also be mentioned. In February 1941, in a speech to the Legislative Council in the Gold Coast, Sir Arnold Hodson, the Governor, first expressed his conviction that "ninety-nine per cent of the inhabitants of the Gold Coast" were "perfectly satisfied with the Government in its present form". He then went on to lament on how difficult it was to get this fact across to public opinion in Britain:

The views of the one per cent who want a change are being continually aired in the Press and elsewhere; whereas the ninety-nine per cent contented people do not air their views. The result is that people in England who read our newspapers are apt to get a wrong impression. . . . [21]

These external audiences that the nationalists had acquired were formative influences in the consolidation of political consciousness in the colonies. Both the radicals abroad who supported African nationalists and the conservative elements who loudly condemned "the pretensions of the upstarts" helped to strengthen nationalistic sentiments in Africa. And the English language was the medium of this ideological and verbal exchange.

Finally, we come to the two basic audiences on the local scene in each colony. There was the general populace, whom the nationalists tried to awaken and rally; and there were the colonial authorities on the scene, to whom the politicians recited their grievances. But here we ought to distinguish between African countries which had no lingua franca apart from the language of the colonial power (like Ghana and Nigeria) and those which did have an indigenous lingua franca (like Tanganyika, Zanzibar and Kenya). In both kinds of countries the political leaders who came to be classified as "nationalists", and to hold power afterwards, spoke English in addition to their own language. The ability to speak English was virtually a prerequisite – recurrent but unproclaimed – for leadership in the fight against British colonialism. But the importance of English as a vehicle of nationalism varied between the two types of territories.

If Ghana and Nigeria constitute the continental birthplace of anti-colonialism in Africa, we can say that African political consciousness in our sense was born in those territories which had no lingua franca apart from the language of the imperial power. The politicians did indeed use English in addressing the colonial administrators – but they also used English in addressing their own people at big rallies. At such rallies there were sometimes translations into other languages, but the leader himself often had to invoke the English language. In fostering national consciousness the English language in West Africa had a role

[21] Legislative Council Debates (27 February, 1941), i, 116-117. See G. E. Metcalf (ed.), *Great Britain and Ghana: Documents of Ghana History, 1807-1957* (London: Thomas Nelson and Sons Ltd. on behalf of the University of Ghana, 1964), 665.

to play which was not quite as necessary in East African nationalism outside Uganda.

The kind of role involved here is connected, but not identical, with the creation of national consciousness. It is connected, but not identical, with the creation of sensitivity to grievances. This new role of the English language has been implicit in what we have discussed before but now needs to be analysed a little more fully. By helping to produce agitating "scholars" the English language, directly or indirectly, helped to make a tribesman dissatisfied with his colonial status. We might also note how English helped to make it possible for, say, a Lobi-speaking tribesman to think of the Nzima-speaking Nkrumah as a fellow "Gold Coaster". We ought not to overlook how English could enable the tribesman to think of Nkrumah as a leader of more than the Nzima-speaking peoples. To accept Nkrumah as a fellow "Gold Coaster" was one thing: to accept him as a *leader* of all "Gold Coasters" was quite another. It would have been so much more difficult for Nkrumah to be accepted as leader outside his own linguistic group if all the political speeches he had to make were, in fact, made in the language of his own group. A Nkrumah who could communicate with others only in his native Nzima would have found it more difficult to create the image of being "above" the linguistic and tribal divisions of the Gold Coast. The role of the English language in this case was to facilitate the sheer feasibility of trans-tribal leadership.

But although the acceptance of Nkrumah as a common leader was something distinct from the acceptance of the Gold Coast as a common country, the two factors were nevertheless intimately related Capacity to follow a single leader is sometimes what converts a collection of groups into something approaching "a single people". This considera-tion has on occasion raised the question whether the apparent cohesion of a particular underdeveloped country would survive the death of its top leader. It used to be argued that a common capacity to follow the leadership of Pandit Nehru was crucial in giving the Indian multitudes a semblance of being "*a people*". It might still be true that, had Nehru died much earlier than he did, Indian unity would have cracked more seriously after his death.

Applying the hypothesis to Africa it might be argued that what made the Nigerians fall short of being "a people" was their inability to accept any single leader or unified collection of leaders. A more modest way of framing the hypothesis is to say that a capacity to be joint followers of the same leadership is evidence of some degree of integration, as well as a contributory factor towards the consolidation of that integra-tion. The Gold Coast proved that it had achieved some degree of political integration when it found it possible to be a collective follower of Kwame Nkrumah. But the experience of sharing Nkrumah as leader in turn further deepened that integration. Collective obedience to a leader, like collective obedience to the same government, has a slow but definite tendency towards unification. As a study on "Nationalism" by the Royal Institute of International Affairs put it in 1939 in a different but related context:

> Every government which has ever been set up has done something to increase the amount of homogeneity between its subjects, although it may at the same time have taken other steps which increased the differences of opinion among them and stimulated opposition to itself ... the downfall of governments may (with many exceptions) be attributed to the failure to produce cohesion among their subjects. ... The fact remains that any collection of men which has ever been subjected for any length of time to the same government will continue indefinitely to bear the marks of that subjection, and will possess a common factor making for unity among subsequent generations.[22]

To the extent that English in a country like Ghana facilitated a common acceptance of the same leadership, it gave subsequent generations of Ghanaians "a common factor making for unity".

There is one area within independent Commonwealth Africa which managed to produce a major national figure who had little knowledge of the English language. The area is Zanzibar and the figure is the late Abeid Karume, who was the First Vice-President of Tanzania. But no colony in British Africa (apart perhaps from Somaliland) was linguistically more homogenous than Zanzibar. Zanzibar did not need the English language either for trans-tribal or for inter-racial communication. Swahili was a better medium from that point of view.

Nevertheless, the lack of English was a handicap to Abeid Karume – and may have helped to keep him out of effective power in Zanzibar until after the revolution.

Neither did Tanganyika and Kenya need English to quite the same extent as British West Africa. But the national leaders who emerged were those who added a knowledge of English to their competence in Swahili. In any case the English language was important in creating a sense of East Africanism which could include non-Swahili-speaking Ugandans. And in a general area of white settler dominance – concentrated in Kenya but with an influence which was felt beyond its borders – an African politician who was competent in English had part of the necessary credentials for the kind of leadership expected by the masses. He was qualified in an important way to face up to the imperial "enemy".

---

[22] Royal Institute of International Affairs, *Nationalism* (London: Oxford University Press, 1939), 5-6.

Finally, there is the impact of the English language on the vocabulary of politics in *indigenous* languages. Talking about the impact of English and other Western languages on Asia the Indian historian, K. M. Panikkar, has argued in these terms:

Philosophy and religious thinking, however much they may influence the people in general, are the special interests of the intellectuals. . . . It is the change in the language that is in many ways the most far-reaching transformation in Asia, for it is not merely the reflection of the changed mind but is itself the instrument of continuing changes, for the new languages of Asia represent a new semantics, a new world of ideas and thought which is reaching a larger and larger circle every day.[23]

A similar phenonmenon has been unfolding even in the field of basic political thinking in Africa. As political activity became more complex the need for a new language to cope with it became more pressing. Basic notions like "vote", "local government", "responsible government" and "constitution" sometimes needed to be rendered into African languages. It should be pointed out here that although the temptation to borrow the available English terminology must often have been considerable, there were occasions when this was resisted and a word was coined from another language. The word for constitution in Swahili is *katiba*. It is a relatively new word in Swahili, starting with the nationalistic pressures for new colonial constitutions. But it was not to English that Swahili turned; it was to Arabic. With Arabic Swahili had had, in any case, a longer etymological connection than it had with English. Nevertheless, it still remains true that the impact which had forced Swahili to seek a new word from Arabic was the impact of a new idea which had come with the English language.

But how does this influence of English relate to the other criteria cited at the beginning of this chapter as to the essential character and causes of politics at large? George Bennett, the late Commonwealth historian at Oxford, starts his book on Kenya's history with a reassertion that politics, as the Greek root of the word indicated, was an activity essentially of cities. From this he draws the conclusion that the birth of modern politics in Kenya must therefore be traced to the urbanization which followed the coming of the European.[24]

Bennett's premise is very similar to that advanced by Wraith in the passage cited earlier. Is this hypothesis invalidated if the beginnings of

[23] K. M. Panikkar, *Asia and Western Dominance, A Survey of the Vasco Da Gama Epoch on Asian History, 1498-1945* (London: George Allen and Unwin [first published in 1953], Fifth Impression 1961), 329.
[24] *Kenya: A Short Political History, The Colonial Period* (London: Oxford University Press, 1963). 1.

politics in Africa are now attributed to the consequences of a linguistic revolution?

The empirical association between politics and city dwelling was not, in fact, quite broken by the advent of the English language as a politicizing factor in colonial Africa. But one distinction which ought to be borne in mind is the simple one between a *capital* city and other towns. As we have noted, it was not the oldest city in Kenya, Mombasa, which became the hub of political activity in the country. On the contrary, Mombasa retreated into a semi-boycott of politics after the capital moved to Nairobi. It was the latter city which became the centre of grievance-articulation. Among the factors which made it so was its nearness to the most sensitive area of land problems in the country – the White Highlands and the Kikuyu reserves. But modern politics – as distinct from petitions from chiefs – came when an articulate class of "politicians" in our sense began to be discernible. The Masai as well as the Kikuyu were among the tribes most exposed to the geographical nearness of the white settlers. The Kikuyu responded to that nearness by letting themselves acquire some of the "skills" which they thought they needed in dealing with the white man. Among the basics was "the skill of language". The Masai retained their old tribal ways. It was therefore from the Kikuyu rather than the Masai that the first modern "politicians" in the area emerged. And when Jomo Kenyatta came back from England to raise political consciousness in Kenya to the level of *national* consciousness, there was little doubt about his credentials for leadership in this kind of activity. He had even written a book in the English language. Capacity to write well in the language of the ruler augured well in a struggle for political power. As G. Balandier put it in discussing the status of literacy in black Africa, "The idea of power – from the example of the 'orders' or regulations emanating from the administration – tends to associate itself with the use of writing."[25]

The association of city dwelling with politics was, in a limited way, maintained when the new Kenya African Union established its headquarters in Nairobi. But a more basic link among politics, city-life and the English language lies in the fact that the educated and semi-educated Africans sought to make their homes in towns.

It is this phenomenon which made many a Colonial administrator draw a distinction between "the well-intentioned natives of the interior" and "the semi-literate malcontents in the towns".[26] But the "well-inten-

[25] G. Balandier, "Social Changes and Social Problems in Negro Africa", in: C. W. Stillman (ed.), *Africa in the Modern World* (Chicago: University of Chicago Press, 1955), 66.
[26] Kimble shows how this type of distinction started to occur in Colonial Office

tioned" acceptance of the *status quo* of the rural people did not last long. Even the countryside came to be partly politicized. As Philip Mason put it in his Burrough Memorial Lecture at Leeds University some years ago, "What a handful of intellectuals think today, the peasant will vote for tomorrow."[27]

But it was not merely with city dwelling that Wraith had etymologically associated "politics". It was also with "civilization". This latter connection between politics and "civilization" is even more effectively reconciled with the theory of a linguistic revolution than the equation between politics and city life. The major reservation which one must make is that Wraith uses the term "civilization" almost in a monopolistic sense – such that any way of life which is unconnected with his models of "Greece and Rome" somehow falls short of being a "civilization". Further, it is not at all certain that the kind of "politics" implied by what Wraith calls "the language of Greece and Rome" were present in, say, the Egyptian civilization of the early Pharaohs.[28] As we might have implied in discussing the relationship between politics and detribalization, there is a degree of *secularism* which is indispensable if a society is to become political in our modern sense. Greece and Rome were, in relative terms, secular civilizations. Ancient Egypt was not. Ancient Egypt was therefore a somewhat *apolitical* civilization. What Wraith was in danger of implying was that such a phenomenon was a contradiction in terms.

Similarly, Nigeria had indigenous African civilizations of its own before the advent of British imperial rule. But the British impact came to reduce the mysticism of ancestral ways within at least some of these civilizations. Here again the new language, as an embodiment of new ways of looking at things, helped the process. The English language, by opening up new directions of thought, had a secularizing effect. It facilitated the erosion of ancestral beliefs.

But how complete the erosion was had to depend, in part, upon how much there was to be eroded away. Partly arising out of its relative individualism, the Ibo society was already nearer to secularism than the Yoruba. This estimate is based on the assumption that the more centralized a *traditional* society is, the greater the body of legitimizing

---

memoranda from quite early in the political history of the Gold Coast. See Kimble, *Ghana*, 89.

[27] See *Christianity and Race* (London: Lutterworth Press, 1956), 121.

[28] The "political" differences among these civilizations were partly derived from a more basic difference in intellectual temper. See Henri and H. A. Frankfort, John A. Wilson, Thornkild Jacobsen, *Before Philosophy, The Intellectual Adventure of Ancient Man* (first published in 1946) (Baltimore: Penguin Books, 1963, reprint).

mores needed to maintain its cohesion. And the Yoruba were more centralized than the Ibo. As for the Hausa and Fulani of the North, these were shielded from the secularizing effects of the new English civilization. And in any case there was perhaps a longer stride to take towards secularism than was necessary with the Ibo.[29]

It is considerations such as these which help to explain the chronology of politicization in Nigeria. And it is at this point of *secularism* that politics, civilization, and English as a revolutionary language converge in the history of former British Africa.

But, as discussions of specific African ideas have recurrently demonstrated, the language of politics in Africa is still tied to the idiom of anti-colonialism and the quest for self-government, almost as if the latter had yet to be achieved. Again this comes out in the new political vocabulary of some indigenous languages. In Swahili a political party was for a while definable as *chama cha kutetea uhuru*, or "a brotherhood or society of the fight for freedom". In Nyakyusa a "politician", to the extent that such a person first emerged as a fighter against the colonial regime, came to be literally rendered as "a man who works against the government". In referring to this, Wilfred Whiteley aptly pointed out that some of these African translations from English political concepts were "clearly going to prove difficult to reconcile with political activity once self-government has been achieved".[30]

Yet if some of the translations do survive, they will at least serve as historical evidence of the gallant efforts made by local African languages to cope with the broad new world of political ideas which came with the invasion of a foreign language. To that extent the local African languages themselves will, for a long time to come, bear traces of the revolutionary impact of the English language on the intellectual and governmental experience of the African peoples in different parts of the continent.

---

[29]   See Coleman, *Nigeria*.
[30]   "Political Concepts and Connotations", *St. Anthony's Papers*, 8, 12-13, 15. See also Whiteley, "Language and Politics in East Africa", *Tanganyika Notes and Records* 47 and 48 (June and September 1957). For a more comprehensive discussion of linguistic problems in Africa see John Spencer (ed.), *Language in Africa*, Papers of the Leverhulme Conference at Ibadan on Universities and the Language Problems of Tropical Africa (London: Cambridge University Press, 1963).

6

ON POETS AND POLITICIANS: OBOTE'S MILTON
AND NYERERE'S SHAKESPEARE

The most rationalistic of all the Greeks, Plato, once levelled the "gravest charge against poetry" – namely that "poetry had a terrible power to corrupt even the best characters". Plato himself was in favour of submitting poetry to a censorship "designed to expunge everything unsuitable to its educational purposes".[1]

Plato was convinced that the poet was a manipulator of people's emotions. And the manipulation of emotions could, indeed, be a matter of long-term political consequences.

Perhaps the two greatest poets in the English language are William Shakespeare and John Milton. The two most historically significant socialists in East Africa so far have been Julius K. Nyerere and A. Milton Obote. Nyerere's socialism has deep, intimate links with his cultural nationalism. Obote's socialism had a profound area of inter-action with his partiality for republicanism and distrust of aristocratic privilege. This chapter proposes to discern the points of contact among all these factors: the two English poets, the two East African socialists, the relationship between Nyerere's socialism and his cultural national-ism, and the relationship between Obote's socialism and his republican orientation.

We may define an intellectual as a person who has the capacity to be fascinated by ideas and has acquired the skill to handle some of them effectively. We may define a *literary intellectual* as a person who is engaged in a serious way in literary activity, and who is fascinated

[1] See the Penguin Classics Edition of *The Republic*, Book X: "The Effects of Poetry and Drama" (London, 1963), 383. See also Michael B. Foster, *Masters of Political Thought*, vol. 1 (London: George G. Harrap, 1961 reprint), 62.

by literary ideas. Obote and Nyerere are literary intellectuals because they have themselves been writers and because they have been profoundly stimulated by great literature. This chapter will pay special attention to the latter factor in their intellectualism.[2]

JOHN MILTON AND MILTON OBOTE

We started by citing Plato's views about the power of poetry in the manipulation of emotions. An important poetic influence on the emotions of A. Milton Obote in his younger days was the English poet John Milton. It started at secondary school. When Obote was a pupil at Busoga College, Mwiri, he found two writers particularly awe-inspiring – one was, in fact, Plato himself, and the other was Milton.

John Milton bequeathed his very name to young Obote. Obote's Christian name, until he went to school, was Apolo. The name Milton was accorded to him, and embraced by him, in his secondary school days "because of his special liking for that poet".[3]

The story about Obote's fascination with Plato in his schooldays was reported in June 1964 in *The People,* then the newspaper of the ruling party of Uganda, in an article entitled "The Formative Years of Dr. Milton Obote". Acording to the article, Obote's headmaster at the College in Mwiri "made it a practice to read *The Republic* of Plato with the top form every Tuesday". The article then asked: "Had this reading of Plato anything to do with the moulding of Obote's thoughts?" The question at the time was left tantalizingly in the air.

John Milton, the poet, was indeed influenced by Plato. In a book entitled *Plato and Milton* a scholar claimed, not so long ago: "Milton himself did not hesitate to assert a momentous debt to Plato, and besides the Bible, he pays to no other writings an equally high compli-

[2] Dr. Obote, like Dr. Nyerere, was of course, also a political intellectual in the sense that, as President of Uganda, he was engaged in the profession of politics, and the ideas which were of most immediate interest to him were inevitably those which concerned the polity, the behaviour of man as a political animal, and the intellectual basis of political and administrative organization. These different categories of intellectuals were originally defined in the debate between myself and Mr. Akena Adoko, the then Chief General Service Officer of the Uganda Government, on "The Role of Intellectuals in the African Revolution" held in Kampala in February 1969. This debate is discussed more fully in the text of this chapter, *infra.*

[3] This anecdote is related by Akena Adoko. See Akena Adoko, "A Comparative Study of the Soviet Union and the State of Uganda", *The People,* April 25, 1970. I have since discussed the anecdote and the origins of that second name, Milton, with Dr. Obote himself and obtained confirmation thereof.

ment." The book itself, by Irene Samuel, dates back to 1947, but the discussion on Milton's debt to Plato goes further back still. It was Samuel Taylor Coleridge who, in a letter to W. Sotheby dated September 10, 1802, had occasion to say: "How little the commentators of Milton have availed themselves of the writings of Plato, Milton's darling!"[4]

It was the *political* ideas of these two thinkers which fascinated Apolo Obote most. The political meeting-point between Plato and Milton occurs on the issue of entitlement to power and of credentials for exercising rule over others. *The Republic* of Plato is clear in its insistence on intellectual merit as the ultimate criterion of the right to exercise power. The whole concept of the philosopher-king is, in some ways, profoundly republican. A philosopher-king in Plato's terms is a philosopher first, and a king only by virtue of his philosophical competence. The structure of society as a whole, in Plato's Republic, has to be derived from notions of natural aptitude. The stratification is to be based on gradations of aptitude. At the top of the social structure must be the guardians: those entrusted with the destiny and welfare of society. The guardians are to be groomed and trained on the basis of their intellectual capabilities, and to be entrusted with the power to rule on the basis of a strict leadership code.

Then there is the class of auxiliaries: those bearing the heavy burden of defence and security. Lastly, there is the economic sector of society, entrusted with the productive forces and the economic well-being of society.

The neatness of the division of labour in Plato may have fascinated Apolo Obote, as it has fascinated many another mind. What is more likely to have been an important factor behind Plato's impact on Obote lies in his concept of rule based on merit rather than on heredity; kingship derived from philosophical competence rather than hereditary descent. But also significant was the leadership code, implicit in the austerity imposed on the guardians of Plato's Republic. Positions of power were not to be positions of personal privilege. Furthermore, the sharing of power imposed the responsibility of collectivism, a doctrine of sharing things. The life-style of the guardians as decreed by Plato envisaged a renunciation of private property. And since women could sometimes be a form of property, Plato went to the extent of urging a renunciation of private entitlement to a particular woman. Plato's communism went further than anything Karl Marx entertained. Of course, it also went further than some of the deepest moral principles

---

[4] Cited by Irene Samuel, *Plato and Milton* (Ithaca, N.Y.: Cornell University Press, 1965 edition), ii.

of Obote. But the whole notion of renouncing private property, of committing oneself to a shared austerity, of being subject to the discipline of a leadership code, afforded intellectual excitement to those young political minds at Busoga College, Mwiri.

Meanwhile what, in Milton's poetry, had Obote found inspiring? What had so fascinated this young man in the heavy but grand lines of Milton that he permitted his very identity to be affected by it? What made him go through life with the name of Milton in response to the inspiration of the author of *Paradise Lost*?

TOWARDS A DIALOGUE WITH A PRESIDENT

A series of events early in 1969 conspired to afford me an opportunity of finding answers to these questions. It started with the debate in the Town Hall between Akena Adoko and myself on the role of intellectuals in the African revolution. It was in that debate that I distinguished four types of intellectuals – political intellectuals, literary intellectuals, academic intellectuals and general intellectuals. As a participant in that debate I was all too aware that much of the future potential for dialogue between intellectuals in government and intellectuals at Makerere University depended on the spirit of that public confrontation between Akena Adoko and myself. I regarded it as important that the spirit of the enterprise should be one which demonstrated Makerere's readiness to engage in discourse with leaders of thought outside the University, and also Makerere's capacity to concede that it did not have a monopoly of knowledge and wisdom, or the exclusive title of intellectualism.

The public debate was substantially vindicated by the goodwill which emanated from it. It emerged quite soon that there were others in government who were also eager to engage in debates and dialogue of that kind. Among the first to reveal such an interest was Mr. Frank Kalimuzo, then Secretary to the Cabinet of the Uganda Government. Mr. Kalimuzo indicated to one colleague at Makerere that it would be a good idea if this colleague could arrange a private opportunity, possibly after dinner, for an intellectual confrontation between Kalimuzo and myself.[5]

The colleague was reminded by Kalimuzo of this proposal at an informal gathering at Makerere, following an address by President Obote. The colleague was Yash Tandon, then a senior staff member of the Department of Political Science at Makerere.

---

[5] Mr. Kalimuzo became the Vice-Chancellor of Makerere University on July 1, 1970. He disappeared in September 1972.

"Yes, Mazrui is agreeable to such a confrontation in my house after dinner one of these nights", Tandon was saying to Kalimuzo. Akena Adoko was apparently within hearing, and expressed an interest to participate in such a confrontation. Rumour has it that President Obote soon heard what was going on – and quipped "Why leave me out?"

By this time the whole concept of the meeting was changing from that of a polarized confrontation to that of a general dialogue between intellectuals in government and intellectuals at Makerere. The idea was subsequently thrashed out further, and the President extended the hospitality of his Lodge in Kampala for such a dialogue. The groups grew in size. On Makerere's side the Department of Political Science still had disproportionate representation at the meeting; but, in addition, almost all newly appointed Ugandan Professors were invited to the meeting, as were several other important members of Makerere staff. The Principal of Makerere, Mr. Y. K. Lule, was also among those present.

The group from government included Mr. Akena Adoko, Mr. Basil Bataringaya, Minister of Internal Affairs, Mr. Felix Onama, Minister of Defence and Mr. Frank Kalimuzo.

The informal dialogue went on from about five o'clock to some time after 9 p.m. Snacks were served in-between. At about 10 o'clock the intellectual activity came to an end, and a cultural feast unfolded itself. There was dancing first by Acholi dancers, and then by performers from Lango – "My constituents", said Obote. The cultural extravaganza continued to the small hours of the morning.

But it was the prior meeting of the minds from tea-time to about 9 o'clock at night which afforded some opportunities for the study of Obote's intellectual styles. The whole idea of a collection of such people, meeting in the President's Lodge with no fixed agenda but to engage purely in an informal conversation, was itself in the spirit of general intellectual engagement. The subjects discussed ranged widely, and included issues connected with Makerere and its role in society. But of more purely intellectual interest were the discussions concerning religious values and secular ideologies.

It started with an argument on whether Jesus Christ was a socialist. It was an issue which Akena Adoko had raised in a speech elsewhere, leaning in his answer towards an affirmative reply. A counter-argument made in the discussion was that Jesus was on the side of the poor, but was not a socialist. The idea of giving unto Caesar that which was Caesar's and to God that which was God's and the ethic of turning the other cheek, were counter-revolutionary values. Was Jesus simply in favour of charity for the poor? Or did he go to the socialistic extent of urging power for the poor?

In many ways the discussion could not have been more purely esoteric, engaged in exclusively for the mental stimulation it afforded the discussants. The move from Jesus and religion to John Milton was relatively easy. After all, John Milton was the author both of *Paradise Lost*, involving the sin of Adam and the conspiracy of Satan, and *Paradise Regained* involving Jesus' ultimate sacrifice for humanity.

It transpired in the course of the discussion that what Milton Obote found particularly fascinating about *Paradise Lost* was not the fall of man, but the rebellion of Satan. Was Satan's disobedience of God a case of civil disobedience? Was it the first instance of political rebellion in the history of thinking beings?

It appeared in the course of that brief interchange at the President's Lodge that Obote, like many other readers of Milton's *Paradise Lost*, had found a heroic dimension to the personality of Milton's Satan, at least before God's curse. John Milton might not have intended his Satan to be a hero, but the power of his poetry as it unfolds the personality of Satan, in the earlier parts of the narration, infuses into that personality a towering quality of heroic defiance. For that young Lango student at Busoga College, Mwiri, for the young student Obote at Makerere, and later even for an Obote prominent in the affairs of the nation, the most important single line in Milton's *Paradise Lost* was:

> Better to reign in Hell than serve in Heaven.[6]

It is a contention of this essay that it was John Milton's *antimonarchical orientation* which made him define Satan in heroic terms in spite of Milton's own theological position on the side of God. It was perhaps also this orientation which aroused Obote's interest.

DIVINE KINGSHIP AND ROYAL DEITY

During his lifetime, John Milton, as part of the Cromwellian rebellion against the monarchy in England, had ranged himself in opposition to the divine right of kings. But Satan in *Paradise Lost* quite clearly has ranged himself against the kingly rights of God. It is his second-in-command in the rebellion, Beelzebub, who adresses him thus:

> O Prince, O Chief of many throned Powers,
> That led the embattled Seraphim to war
> Under thy conduct, and, in dreadful deeds
> Fearless, endangered Heaven's perpetual King . . .[7]

---

[6] Douglas Bush (ed.), *The Portable Milton* (Viking Press, New York, 1949). *Paradise Lost*, Book I, 1: 263.
[7] Milton, *Paradise Lost*, Book I, 11: 128-131.

There is both in Beelzebub and in Satan a sense of pride in having attempted to break "the tyranny of Heaven".

Milton's own revelation of his conception of God in Book Three tends to vindicate Satan's reservations about living under his rule. God is sitting on His throne, surrounded by adoring creatures He has Himself brought into being, and accompanied on His side by His adoring Son. God Himself asks how His own wrath against the fall of man might ultimately be appeased. Satan is on his way towards tempting Adam to his downfall. Who shall redeem the sin of Adam's disobedience? The Son of God, sitting by His father, offers Himself. And Milton makes Jesus formulate his appeal to His father in terms which seem to be directed at some massive Divine vanity.

> O Father, gracious was that word which closed
> Thy sovran sentence, that man should find grace;
> For which both Heaven and Earth shall high extol
> Thy praises, with the innumerable sound
> Of hymns and sacred songs, wherewith thy throne
> Encompassed shall resound thee ever blest.[8]

And then Jesus, step by step, knowing precisely how best to flatter His Father and arouse in Him an image of supremacy vindicated, offers Himself to die for man, so that the wrath decreed on man by God might at last be negated. Jesus discusses the vision of His own encounter with death, allowing for a momentary victory on the side of death as the body of Jesus lets go of its life on the cross. But then –

> Thou wilt not leave me in the loathsome grave
> His prey, nor suffer my unspotted soul
> For ever with corruption there to dwell;
> But I shall rise victorious, and subdue
> My vanquisher....
> ....Thou, at the sight
> Pleased, out of Heaven shalt look down and smile,
> While by Thee raised I ruin all my foes,
> Death last, and with his carcass glut the grave:
> Then with the multitude of my redeemed
> Shall enter Heaven long absent, and return,
> Father, to see thy face, wherein no cloud
> Of anger shall remain, ...[9]

It is quite clear here that Jesus is playing up to His Father's pride in His Son, to filial vanity and divine grandeur. The technique works, and God is so pleased with His Son, that He turns to the rest of His

[8] Milton, *Paradise Lost*, Book III, 11: 144-149.
[9] Milton, *Paradise Lost*, Book III, 11: 247-251; 256-263.

heavenly community and commands them all to adore Jesus as they adore Him. Then Milton, against his will perhaps, reveals the tedious adoration of that life in heaven as God's command is obeyed.

> No sooner had the Almighty ceased, but all
> The multitude of angels with a shout
> Loud as from numbers without number, sweet
> As from blest voices, uttering joy, Heaven rung
> With jubilee, and loud hosannas filled
> The eternal regions. Lowly reverent
> Towards either throne they bow, and to the ground
> With solemn adoration down they cast
> Their crowns inwove with amarant and gold, ...[10]

We have in this vision of heaven, and of God as King sitting on His throne, a concept of kingly omnipotence capable of arousing understandable distaste. John Milton, the politician, rebelled against such a monarchical conception.

And surely no Christian prince, not drunk with high mind and *prouder than those pagan Caesars that deified themselves,* would arrogate so unreasonably above human condition, or derogate so basely from a whole nation of men, his brethren, as if for him only subsisting and to serve his glory, valuing them in comparison of his own brute will and pleasure no more than so many beasts. . . . It follows . . . that since the King or Magistrate holds his authority of the people both originally and naturally for their good, in the first place, and not his own, then may the people, as oft as they shall judge it for the best, either choose him or reject him, retain him or depose him, though no tyrant, merely by the liberty and right of free-born men to be governed as seems to them best.[11]

John Milton expressed such views in defence of the action which had been taken to depose Charles the First, and inaugurate a republican system of government in England. Milton was on the whole the most influential theoretician of the republican doctrine in England in his time. In the words of Francis Coker:

In the combat between Puritans and Royalists in England in the middle of the seventeenth century, the protagonists of republican ideas founded their doctrines upon general principles of political justice, not upon English law and precedent. . . . The English republican theory was set forth most eloquently and logically in the polemical writings of Milton. Milton's political essays constitute the major part of his literary output

---

[10]   Milton, *Paradise Lost*, Book III, 11: 344-352.
[11]   John Milton, "The Origin of Government and the Source and Limits of its Authority", in: *The Tenure of Kings and Magistrates* (Morley), 358-362. The emphasis is mine and is related to the discussion of Nyerere and Shakespeare below.

between 1640 and 1660. The graceful style and philosophic tone of these essays gave great currency and influence to his views.[12]

The same Milton who was so opposed to royal pomp and glittering civilian servility came to pour all his own grand imaginations into a concept of God which was truly imperial. In *Paradise Lost*, Book III, he shows us a Kingdom of Heaven filled with prostated bowing subjects gushing out divine flattery.

> Thee, Father, first they sung Omnipotent,
> Immutable, Immortal, Infinite,
> Eternal King; the Author of all being,
> Fountain of light, thyself invisible
> Amidst the glorious brightness where thou sitt'st
> Throned inaccessible, ...[13]

Is it any wonder that the Satan who rebelled against this style of life appeared in Book One as a heroic rebel against monarchical decadence, and succeeded in capturing the imagination of young Apolo Milton Obote?

We find Satan in Book One lying with his comrades on the burning lake, momentarily subdued after their defeat in the face of God's thunder and other heavenly weaponry. Then Satan awakens all his legions, and seeks to comfort them in their shared defeat. They were no longer in heaven; they were now on this uncomfortably hot lake. Then come the famous lines that moved Obote more deeply than anything else:

> . . . . Farewell, happy fields,
> Where joy forever dwells! . . . .
> The mind is its own place, and in itself
> Can make a Heaven of Hell, a Hell of Heaven.
> What matter where, if I be still the same,
> And what I should be, all but less than he
> Whom thunder hath made greater? Here at least
> We shall be free; the Almighty hath not built
> Here for his envy, will not drive us hence:
> Here we may reign secure, and in my choice
> To reign is worth ambition, though in Hell:
> Better to reign in Hell than serve in Heaven.[14]

---

[12] Francis William Coker, *Readings in Political Philosophy* (1938 revised edition) (New York: MacMillan, 1957 reprint), 423.

[13] Milton, *Paradise Lost*, Book III, 11: 372-377.

[14] Milton, *Paradise Lost*, Book I, 11: 249-250, 254-263. In Book Two we do find monarchical tendencies in Satan himself, as he sits on a throne conducting consultation with his comrades. And yet to sit on a throne on the basis of merit was

WILLIAM SHAKESPEARE AND JULIUS NYERERE

If the most important English literary figure in Obote's personal history was John Milton, the most important English literary figure in Nyerere's life has been Shakespeare.

Nyerere's style of leadership, though initially characterized by moderation and gradualism, later came to bear the stamp of the simple revolutionary imperative – "It is now or never!" Much of his ideology in later years has been animated by a sense of urgency, a feeling that Tanzania ought to take a particular course of action immediately or risk losing the opportunity for ever.

In the days when Nyerere was basically a moderate, some of the first indications of his later revolutionary style lay in the Shakespearean rhetoric he invoked. And the play from which he quoted came to haunt him in later life, urging him to use his skill in translating it.

In some ways Shakespearean rhetoric was at least as meaningful for Nyerere as Tennyson had been for Nkrumah. In 1934, Nkrumah applied to the Dean of Lincoln University in the United States for admission as a student. In his application, he quoted from Tennyson's *In Memoriam*:

> So many worlds, so much to do,
> So little done, such things to be.

In his autobiography, Nkrumah said this verse "was to me then, as it still is today, an inspiration and a spur. It fired within me a determination to equip myself for the service of my country."[15]

But for Julius Nyerere the mighty lines which gave poetic expression to the inner impatience of his revolutionary potential were Shakespearean. Among Nyerere's earliest publications was a small pamphlet entitled *Barriers to Democracy*, published in the 1950's. This was in the days when he was still organizing Tanganyikans to press for greater democracy within the colonial system, but on the road to independence. Nyerere's clarion call in the pamphlet is in lines drawn from a play which has had important cultural significance in his life.

> There is a tide in the affairs of men
> Which, taken at the floods, leads on to fortune;

---

to Milton different from Kingship by hereditary privilege. And so, in Milton's words,

> Satan exalted sat, by merit raised
> To that bad eminence ...

The meritocratic prejudice implicit in this line might well have also been congenial to Obote's own frame of reasoning.

15   *Ghana: The Autobiography of Kwame Nkrumah* (1957) (London, Nelson, paperback edition, 1960), p. v.

Omitted, all the voyage of their life
Is bound in shallows and in miseries.
On such a full sea are we now afloat,
And we must take the current when it serves
Or lose our ventures.[16]

The style of "taking the current when it serves", of doing it now or never, was more convincingly demonstrated by Nyerere in the later revolutionary days of the mid-1960's than in the studied moderation and gradualism of the previous decade. And yet the earlier period of moderation might have been a period of waiting to see at what point the tide would indeed be "at the floods".

But again, intimations of the Nyerere of the future lay in his Shakespearean rhetoric. For the Nyerere of the future had the optimism of all true revolutionaries – that man can fundamentally affect the course of his own history. It is true that Marx, in his writings, sometimes relegated man to the status of an object manipulated by the forces of history, floating on a wave of economic inevitability; but that was Marx the philosopher. There was another Marx – the Marx who said to philosophers: "Philosophers so far have only interpreted the world; the point however is to change it."

The Marx of economic determinism is the philosopher, but the second Marx is the revolutionary. "The point however is to change it" – there lay the optimism that human destiny was, to some extent, subject to human control.

The Nyerere of the 1950's did not exhibit such revolutionary fervour. But there were intimations of revolutionary immortality once again in his Shakespearean rhetoric. He concluded that significant little pamphlet, *Barriers to Democracy*, with yet another quotation from that haunting play – "Men at some time are masters of their fates."

Obote adopted a name from an English poet and became Milton Obote. But Julius Nyerere was already "Julius" when he fell under the spell of Shakespeare's *Julius Caesar*. Nyerere had been exposed to the play before, but he studied it more fully in his first year at Edinburgh University. It is one measure of the impact of that education that when Nyerere had risen to the highest office of his country the play still had a sufficient hold on him to compel him to translate it. It is almost as if the ghost of Shakespeare had accompanied this gifted African politician on his journey to the heights of eminence – and then demanded homage in African words.[17]

---

16 William Shakespeare, *Julius Caesar*, Act IV, Scene 3, 11: 217-224.
17 Nyerere's translation of *Julius Caesar* into Swahili is discussed more fully, but from a different perspective, in Mazrui, *The Anglo-African Commonwealth: Political Friction and Cultural Fusion* (Oxford: Pergamon Press, 1967), 121-133.

Curiously enough, the theme of republicanism versus monarchical tendencies is even more literal in Shakespeare's *Julius Caesar* than in Milton's *Paradise Lost*. Just as Obote's republican sympathies responded well to some of the words of rebellion in Book One of *Paradise Lost*, Nyerere's austere style of leadership also responded to the debate about leadership within *Julius Caesar*.

The discussion starts early in the play, setting the stage for the tragedy to unfold. At the centre is the discussion of whether the top leader in a society should be elevated to a monarchical, or even a divine, level.

A personality cult was gathering momentum around the prestige and reputation of Julius Caesar, the leader. Brutus had noticed it, and was about to draw Cassius into a conspiracy by pointing out to him that Rome was exposed to the risk of reverting to monarchical ways. They were standing there, when there was a flourish and shout.

Brutus	What means this shouting? I do fear, the people
	Choose Caesar for their king.
Cassius	Ay, do you fear it?
	Then must I think that you would not have it so.
Brutus	I would not, Cassius; yet I love him well.
	But wherefore do you hold me here so long?
	What is it that you would impart to me?...
Cassius	Well, honour is the subject of my story...
	I was born free as Caesar, so were you;
	We both have fed as well, and we can both
	Endure the winter's cold as well as he;...
	...And this man
	Is now become a god, and Cassius is
	A wretched creature, and must bend his body
	If Caesar carelessly but nod on him.[18]

And while they were talking more shouts and cheers were heard. Some important matters connected with issues of leadership and freedom were going on behind that boisterous acclamation.

Brutus later found a chance to ask Casca what had occasioned all that uproar.

Casca	Why, there was a crown offer'd him; and
	being offer'd him, he put it by with the
	back of his hand, thus; and then the
	people fell a-shouting.
Brutus	What was the second noise for?
Casca	Why, for that too.
Cassius	They shouted thrice; what was the last cry for?

[18]   Shakespeare, *Julius Caesar*, Act I, Scene 2, 11: 78-84, 92-99, 115-118.

Casca	Why, for that too.
Brutus	Was the crown offer'd him thrice?
Casca	Ay, marry, was't, and he put it by thrice,
	every time gentler than other; and at every
	putting-by mine honest neighbours shouted.
Cassius	Who offer'd him the crown?
Casca	Why, Antony.
Brutus	Tell us the manner of it, gentle Casca.
Casca	I can as well be hang'd as tell the manner of it.
	It was mere foolery; I did not mark it. I saw
	Mark Antony offer him a crown – yet 'twas not a
	crown neither, 'twas one of these coronets – and,
	as I told you, he put it by once; but, for all
	that, to my thinking, he would fain have had it.
	Then he offer'd it to him again; then he put it
	by again, but, to my thinking, he was very loathe
	to lay his fingers off it. And then he offered
	it the third time; he put it the third time by;
	and still as he refus'd it, the rabblement hooted
	and clapp'd their chapp'd hands and threw up their
	sweaty night-caps and uttered such a deal of
	stinking breath because Caesar refus'd the crown,
	that it had almost choked Caesar, for he swounded
	and fell down at it; and for mine own part, I durst
	not laugh, for fear of opening my lips and receiving
	the bad air.[19]

The crowds had been impressed by Caesar's modesty. But it was also symptomatic that the crowds wanted Caesar to become King. The idea of a personality cult developing into monarchical dimensions did not escape Julius Nyerere.

DIVINE KINGSHIP AND ROYAL PRESIDENTS

Nyerere came to translate *Julius Caesar*. The earlier part of the play was definitely concerned with the issue of attempts to royalize a Roman republic. Nyerere later came to discern monarchical tendencies in some of his nationalistic colleagues in Africa. Shakespeare's Caesar had been offered a crown three times, and to the applause of the masses, he had declined it. Kwame Nkrumah of Ghana was offered the Presidency of Ghana for life – and, to the acclaim of his people, he declined it. Rather than enjoy a life Presidency, Nkrumah preferred to stand for periodic election. In reality, he later changed his mind.

[19] Shakespeare, Act I, Scene 2, 11: 220-252.

From quite early Nyerere decided not to play up the personality factor in his leadership. Later on, as he grew in stature, many respected him, in spite of his deliberate reluctance to build himself up. Indeed, there were many who admired him precisely for the low key of his performance on the stage of leadership, as well as for his obvious intellectual gifts. In the words of one expatriate observer of African leaders, written on the eve of Tanganyika's independence:

Nyerere is not as flamboyant as many of the African leaders who are his contemporaries, but his astute leadership and logical and subtle mind have brought him respect and influence that goes far beyond the borders of Tanganyika.[20]

If Obote became obsessed with the idea of abolishing kings in the traditions of Uganda, Nyerere was more concerned with preventing the emergence of a new king in the wake of Tanzania's independence. When, on the eve of the Presidential election in Tanzania in 1965, Zanzibari newspapers were saying, "Let us elect President Nyerere as our President for life", Nyerere warned the people of Zanzibar about the dangers of excessive surrender to a leader. He said:

I might stay on until I am too old to do my job properly and then tell my son to act for me. When I die he might claim a right to the Presidency and call himself Sultan Nyerere the First; and there might be a second and a third.[21]

On the eve of the election in 1970 the idea of a life presidency was again in the air in Tanzania, but there was no question of its being entertained by Nyerere. Indeed, Nyerere tried to discourage even such minimal ways of personal adulation as having streets named after him, or having too many photographs of himself distributed to the public.

Later he grappled with the job of translating Cassius' response to the news that the senators of Rome intended, the next day, to establish Caesar as king. The people of Rome were themselves going meekly to the slaughterhouse of tyranny.

Cassius   And why should Caesar be a tyrant then?
        Poor man! I know he would not be a wolf,
        But that he sees the Romans are but sheep,
        He were no lion, were not Romans hinds.
        Those that with haste will make a mighty fire
        Begin it with weak straws: . . .[22]

[20]   Rolf Italiaander, *The New Leaders of Africa*, translated from German by James McGovern (Englewood Cliffs, N.J.: Prentice Hall, 1961), 81.
[21]   See *East Africa and Rhodesia* (London), Vol. 42, No. 2138, September 30, 1965, 72.
[22]   Shakespeare, *Julius Caesar*, Act I, Scene 3, 11: 103-108.

For Cassius, the people had to be protected from their own adulation of a particular leader; but he thought the solution lay in removing that leader. For Nyerere, too, the people had a right to protection but the leader must take the initiative in preventing excessive adulation. And just as Obote was engaged in establishing republicanism in Uganda, so Nyerere was absorbed in preventing monarchism in Tanzania.

A variant Caesarian formula was nearly established in Uganda in the 1970's. President Obote was not offered a crown, as Julius Caesar had been; he was not even offered a life presidency, as Nkrumah and Nyerere had been. But the National Council of the Uganda People's Congress did want to spare him the necessity of facing an electorate ever again. Obote himself had proposed an electoral formula which would have permitted the population of Uganda to vote either for him or against him as a presidential candidate, and should he lose, a new election would be necessary. But the National Council of his political party sought to protect him from a national campaign of this kind, and devised a formula whereby the President of the Uganda's People's Congress was automatically the President of the country. Since Obote had recently been elected by a delegates' conference for seven years of office, there was, thus, no need for him to face the electorate of the country as a whole – so these admirers of the President asserted. The adulation, though framed with different arguments and in a different language, did echo those offers extended to Nyerere, to Nkrumah before him, and long ago, to Julius Caesar, a symbolic historical figure in a play by Shakespeare.

But Obote fought this decision in an eloquent memorandum. He called a meeting of the annual delegates' conference of the UPC. Yet the position taken by the National Council won the day at the Mbale Conference in September 1970.

It was not until another conference, called by the President in December 1970, that Obote's resistance to this idea of protecting him from the electorate ultimately prevailed. A formula did emerge allowing for at least the theoretical possibility of a rival candidate in an election, if enough constituency conferences in Uganda were to give their backing to such a candidate. The danger of a monarchical President of Uganda, holding office by party acclamation without having to campaign to a national electorate, was averted for the time being. Like his colleague Nyerere, Obote had a reserved side to his personality. He was not given to flamboyance in his style of leadership; and even in his mode of dress he was perhaps more conservative than many of his colleagues. A personality cult did not seem on the verge of being inaugurated in the politics of Uganda, though an attempt to whip up enthusiasm behind *The Common Man's Charter* was inevitable in a situation where support for socialism could not be taken for granted.

When an attempt had been made on the President's life on 19th December 1969, and Obote was recuperating from his injuries, Julius Nyerere paid him a visit. He came equipped with a gift from Tanzania – yet another exercise in translation from English into Swahili. But in this case it was not Shakespeare; it was Milton Obote's English version of *The Common Man's Charter* rendered into the idiom of Nyerere's national language.

Way back in 1958 Nyerere had quoted approvingly Abraham Lincoln's statement that "God must love the common people because he made so many of them."[23]

Now early in 1970 Nyerere and Obote sat there in Kampala, showing once again a concern for the common man. Behind it all was that old principle of a leadership code which Obote had found in Plato's *Republic* and Nyerere had manifested in his resistance to a personality cult and in his response to *Julius Caesar*.

In 1967 Nyerere had, in fact, already converted this philosophy of leadership into a wider concrete policy. This was in the leadership resolutions of the Arusha Declaration, forbidding, among other things, anyone holding a public office (a Platonic "guardian") from having more than one source of income.

But even in this matter, Nyerere's translation of Shakespeare caught up with him. In January 1971, the British Broadcasting Corporation in London was at a loss how to pay Nyerere the £25 owed to him for the broadcast on the B.B.C. Swahili Service of one of his translations of Shakespeare. Would the fee as an additional income violate the leadership code of the Arusha Declaration? The B.B.C. was driven to consider the solution of giving the money to charity.[24]

By then Nyerere had himself become a philosopher-President, reflecting aloud, advising and teaching. And his people responded by affectionately calling him "Mwalimu", the Mentor. The translator of Shakespeare had learnt to play a platonic role on the political stage of his country.

ON VALUES AND WORDS

Two types of translation have, in fact, been important in the ideological evolution of Julius Nyerere. There is the translation of *words*, an attempt

---

[23] Nyerere, "The Entrenchment of Privilege", *Africa South* 2 (2) (January/March 1958) 86-89.
[24] Reported in the *Sunday Nation* (Nairobi), January 16, 1971.

to transfer verbal equivalents from one language to another; and then there is the translation of *values*, an attempt to transfer ethical equivalents from one culture or ideology to another.

The translation of values became very important for Nyerere on the eve of independence, as he tried to demonstrate that many of the liberal values of the West were strikingly discernible in the traditional cultures of Africa. Many of the doubts over Africa's capacity for self-government were based on fears that liberal competitive systems would not flourish and liberal democratic values not be upheld. The emphasis, in much of the debating conducted by Nyerere in the last few years of colonial rule, lay in his attempt to demonstrate that the liberal democratic values of the West had their analogues in Africa's traditional experience.

He regarded the three central elements of liberal democracy as being *discussion* as a mode of decision making, *equality*, and *freedom*. In a statement written not long before Tanganyika's independence Nyerere argued that:

Those who doubt the African's ability to establish a democratic society cannot be doubting the African's ability to "discuss". That is the one thing which is as African as the tropical sun. Neither can they be doubting the African's sense of equality, for aristocracy is something foreign to Africa. Even where there is a fairly distinct African aristocracy by birth, it can be traced historically to sources outside the continent. . . . Recently I was reading a delightful little book on Nyasaland by Mr. Clutton-Brock; in one passage he describes the life of traditional Nyasa, and when he comes to the Elders he uses a very significant phrase: "They talk till they agree". . . . That gives you the very essence of traditional African democracy. . . . If democracy, then, is a form of government freely established by the people themselves; and if its essentials are free discussion and equality, there is nothing in traditional African society which unfits the African for it. On the contrary, there is everything in his tradition which fits the African to be just what he claims he is, a natural democrat.[25]

By an eloquent translation of values from one cultural tradition to another, Nyerere sought to demonstrate that the African soil was inherently fertile for the seeds of liberal principles.

As Tanganyika entered the independence era the debate on the Africans' capacity for democratic forms continued, but it was now also joined by a debate on the issue of whether Africa was fertile also for the seeds of socialism. Again Nyerere's skills were utilized to give East Africa a place in this great debate. We distinguished earlier between the translation of words from one language to another, and the trans-

[25] Julius Nyerere, "The African and Democracy", in: James Duffy and Robert A. Manners (eds.), *Africa Speaks* (Princeton, N.J.: Van Nostrand, 1961), 29-30.

lation of values from one culture to another. We might call the latter technique *transvaluation*, and the former linguistic exercise *transverbalization*. In the debate on the degree to which socialism is indigenous to Africa the two processes converged, to some extent. If socialism was native to Africa, what name did it bear in African traditional languages?

The late Tom Mboya answered that question by arguing persuasively that a phenomenon could exist in a society even if there was no distinct word for it. Answering a critic's letter in an East African publication, Mboya accused his critic of "confusing the word socialism with its reality, its practice". Mboya asserted:

I have not suggested that we have to go delving into the past seeking socialism. It is a continuing tradition among our people. Does the writer of the letter think that socialism had to be given a name before it became a reality? It is an attitude towards people practised in our societies and did not need to be codified into a scientific theory in order to find existence.[26]

But Nyerere had already taken the issue further. He argued that the Swahili word *ujamaa*, denoting the fellowship of kinship ties and mutual tribal obligations, was, in its essence, a collective basis for socialism. Traditional African life, Nyerere argued, had been predicated on the principle of reciprocal relationships and the ethos of sharing. There was a loyalty to the larger society, and the subordination of individual prejudices to collective well-being. Hospitality was a persistent approach to one's fellow beings, and the caring of the aged and the sick was taken for granted. The acquisitive instinct was tamed, while parasitism or the tendency to live on others was severely frowned upon. A whole universe of ethical principles was compressed within that single Swahili word *ujamaa*. Nyerere's skills in transvaluation and transverbalization had merged to produce the beginnings of a language of socialism for East Africa.

Ujamaa was the key to this romantic interpretation of life in traditional Africa. Nyerere asserted:

We, in Africa, have no more need of being "converted" to socialism than we have of being "taught" democracy. Both are rooted in our past – in the traditional society which produced us.[27]

[26] See *Transition* (Kampala) 3 (11) (November 1963), 6. Mboya's critic was also an East African – C. N. Omondi by name. The critic's letter first appeared in *Kenya Weekly News*, August 2, 1963. The issue is discussed in a related context in Ali A. Mazrui, *Towards a Pax Africana* (London: Weidenfeld and Nicolson, 1967), 100-102.
[27] Nyerere, *Ujamaa: The Basis of African Socialism* (Dar es Salaam, 1962), reprinted in Nyerere, *Freedom and Unity* (Dar es Salaam: Oxford University Press, 1966).

We have in this transvaluative tendency that aspect of Nyerere's ideology which is concerned with *cultural self-reliance*. But, like the more purely ideological concept of self-reliance which came with the Arusha Declaration, Nyerere's cultural self-reliance is not to be confused with cultural autarky. There is no desire to withdraw from the mainstream of cultural interaction in the world. In some of its aspects, the situation is not fundamentally different from some of the assumptions of Léopold Senghor's philosophy of négritude. Négritude is also a romanticization of traditional Africa and an assertion of cultural self-reliance. But the Senghorian version of négritude is not an assertion of cultural autarky either. This is where Senghor's obsession with the utilization of the French language for négritude comes in. Senghor believes in the concept of "a civilization of the universal", consisting of contributions from various cultural heritages.

In the twentieth century the French language has been carrying Africa's contribution into that stream of the civilization of the universal. Indeed, in Senghorian terms, that civilization could not be fully universal until that African contribution was made.

Nyerere's use of Shakespeare is the other side of the coin of this exercise. Nyerere took a play which was already part of the civilization of the universal, and made it even more universal by translating it into an African language. Full African integration into world culture has to be a two-way process. It involves taking cultural Africa to the rest of the world, as Senghor attempts to do in rendering négritude values into French, as well as bringing the rest of the world into Africa, as Nyerere has done by translating Shakespeare into Swahili. Nyerere deliberately confronted the Swahili language with the formidable genius of William Shakespeare. He was, in part, trying to demonstrate that Swahili could indeed carry Shakespeare. His translation of *Julius Caesar* was a successful demonstration. His later translation of *The Merchant of Venice* was less impressive.

The question which arises is whether the first translation, that of *Julius Caesar*, was animated purely by Nyerere the literary intellectual and Nyerere the cultural nationalist; while the second attempt, the translation of *The Merchant of Venice*, had the additional element of Nyerere the socialist intruding into the venture. Was Nyerere's ideological bias hovering in the background as he grappled with issues of pounds of flesh demanded by money-lenders? There is evidence of disagreement between Nyerere and the Swahili advisers of Oxford University Press, his publishers, on the correct rendering of the very title *The Merchant of Venice*. Nyerere's rendering, *Mabepari wa Venisi* strongly suggests "The Capitalists of Venice", rather than "The Merchant". Nyerere even pluralized it, perhaps to imply that Venetian society as a whole was, in some important sense, "capitalistic" in its tendencies.

A more defensible translation of the title into Swahili would have been *Mfanyaji Biashara wa Venisi*, a "Trader or Merchant of Venice".

Nyerere insisted on his own "capitalistic" rendering. Perhaps in this case transvaluation and transverbalization were not in harmony, but in direct conflict.

But that itself is further evidence of how much a part of Nyerere's ideological evolution his interest in translating Shakespeare has been. Intellectual literary leanings, African cultural assertiveness, a partiality for the language of the grass-roots and the common man in relation to a piece of sophisticated culture, and a persistent impulse to see analogues in values and in words across cultural differences; all these have found a meeting point in those two little pamphlets that you sometimes see on the shelves of a bookshop in Dar es Salaam or Mombasa – *Juliasi Kaizari* and *Mabepari wa Venisi*, translated from the English by Julius K. Nyerere.

CONCLUSION

We have attempted to demonstrate in this paper an important area of interaction between literary education and ideological evolution. We have chosen for our case studies the two most historically significant socialists in East Africa, and discerned in their intellectual and ideological evolution the influence of the two greatest English poets.

In the case of Milton Obote, the acknowledged literary impact was that of John Milton, reinforced at Mwiri by an exposure to Plato. From Plato, Milton Obote derived some of his interest in meritocracy as a system of choosing leaders on the basis of merit, and his interest in a leadership code involving renunciation and austerity. In the Uganda situation, Obote was never absolutely sure how far a leadership code could be implemented without some important social and political costs to the system. His Communication from the Chair, in Parliament in April 1970, was a groping for such a code, at least in relation to the public service; but Obote remained divided about how much Platonic austerity he could impose on his ideologically mixed guardians of the Ugandan nation. His failure to deal with some of the excesses of his colleagues in government may have contributed to the enthusiasm with which Obote's ouster by the army on January 25, 1971, was received.

From the study of Milton's *Paradise Lost* came further strengthening of some of these austere views. John Milton had himself been a republican, and had been engaged in the movement which overthrew Charles the First and established, for a while, a republican Commonwealth in England. Milton's reservations about the pomp of power and the glittering disguise of royal despotism on earth helped to condition his characterization of Satan in the earlier phases of *Paradise Lost*. Milton disliked on earth divine kingship; but created in heaven kingly divinity. The Satan who rebelled against Milton's God, with all His unquestioned despotism and delight in hymns of praise, was a Satan who could not but emerge in heroic dimensions. It is that Satan to whom young Obote, with astute literary sensibility, responded positively. The future prophet of Uganda's republicanism was responding to a critical formative influence in that direction.

A close colleague, relative, and admirer of Obote, later came to use, like John Milton before him, blank verse to discuss issues concerning the struggle between republicanism and monarchism. This was Akena Adoko in his *Uganda Crisis*:

> The Divine right of Kabakas
> Mutesa's sole belief.
> Commoners like Obote,
> Were not fit to be rulers. . . .
> We have learnt one great lesson;
> All hereditary rules
> Are indeed rule by Corpses.
> No dead man has any right
> To rule over the living
> Directly through his own ghost
> Or indirectly through heirs. . . .
> Leadership must ever be
> Dependent on quality
> On strong personality
> But not on one's own parents.[28]

Obote's confrontation with Mutesa in 1966 finally resulted in the fall of the palace at Mengo, the flight of the Kabaka to England where he later died in exile, and the final consolidation of a republican system of government in Uganda.

When Obote came to issue *The Common Man's Charter*, much of the rhetoric was addressed to the remnants of "feudalism" in Uganda. There was a persistent warning in the Charter against the emergence of neo-feudalism. And by "feudalism" Obote sometimes meant no more than the monarchical systems in Uganda which he had helped to overthrow.

---

[28] N. Akena Adoko, *Uganda Crisis* (Kampala: African Publishers Limited, 1970), 11-13.

Anti-monarchism and anti-feudalism were indeed important elements in Obote's own evolution into a socialist. And yet what is not always remembered is that a capitalist need not be in favour of feudalism either. To some extent that was what the American Revolution was all about. It was at once the great initiation of a capitalistic civilization and a strong rebellion against British feudalistic tendencies. The American political culture has included a persistent theme of opposition to a hereditary aristocracy. The idea of social mobility as an imperative is well and truly within the complex of values of the American civilization. That civilization is pre-eminently capitalistic, solely derived from concepts of rugged individualism and private enterprise. But, at the same time, that civilization remains, at least in relation to its own domestic preference, opposed to feudalism and hereditary titles.[29]

But anti-feudalism can also result in a socialistic orientation. This was what happened in the case of Obote's ideological growth. There was a profound connection between his anti-monarchism, his anti-colonialism, and his socialism. He took a risk for Uganda when he led an anti-colonial movement; he took a risk for himself and the nation when he precipitated a confrontation between himself and the Kabaka in 1966; and he took a risk for the economy of Uganda on May 1, 1970, when he proclaimed drastic nationalization measures. But all these, in turn, might indeed have had some link with one immortal line in *Paradise Lost*, over which Milton Obote remained profoundly ecstatic: "Better to reign in Hell than serve in Heaven."[30]

By recognizing John Milton as a fountain of wisdom, Obote was almost reciprocating an old debt to the poet. In his views on race, Milton was not a liberal in the normal sense. He did share some of the misconceptions of his own age. Not that Milton refers very often in his works to a man of colour – Moor, Ethiopian or any other black African. But to the poet *black* was the colour of wisdom. This comes out most explicitly in that shorter but still great poem of Milton, *Il Penseroso*. In line 15 he does describe black as "staid Wisdom's hue". He continues the symbolism of blackness:

> Black, but such as in esteem
> Prince Memnon's sister might beseem,
> Or that starred Ethiop queen that strove

---

[29]   This issue is discussed in a related context in "The Different Concepts of Revolution in East Africa", lecture delivered at the University of Dar es Salaam, Tanzania, on November 23, 1970. A revised version of the lecture forms a chapter in Mazrui, *Cultural Engineering and Nation-building in East Africa* (Evanston, Ill.: Northwestern University Press, 1972).

[30]   Milton, *Paradise Lost*.

> To set her beauty's praise above
> The sea nymphs, and their powers offended. . . .[31]

Both King Memnon of the Ethiopians, as discussed by Homer in the eleventh book of *The Odyssey*, and Queen Cassiopeia, bore great attributes of beauty. But more important than this Miltonic version of the new slogan "Black is Beautiful" is the Miltonic belief that blackness was the colour of depth; depth was profundity; profundity was wisdom.

When young Apolo Milton Obote bowed in return to John Milton's own wisdom, an old African principle of reciprocity was implemented.

In discussing the symbolism of blackness from an African point of view we re-enter the whole field of négritude and cultural nationalism. Here we re-establish contact with Julius Nyerere. There is, after all, a place for Nyerere in the English equivalent of the philosophy of négritude – and he gained this place not only by writing a political pamphlet and a philosophical treatise but also by challenging the Swahili language to bear the heavy genius of William Shakespeare.

We discussed the interesting contrast between Nyerere and Senghor in this regard. Senghor had said:

It is a fact that French has made it possible for us to communicate . . . to the world the unheard of message which only we could write. It has allowed us to bring to *universal civilization* a contribution without which the civilization of the twentieth century could not have been universal.[32]

But by translating Shakespeare into Swahili, Nyerere took what was already a piece of universal civilization, and made it still more universal in an African idiom. For Senghor, négritude was served when African literature was expressed in a foreign language. For Nyerere, négritude was equally served when foreign literature was effectively re-expressed in an African language. This was not only a vindication of the African language as a literature medium, it was also an assertion both of cultural self-reliance and of persistent contact with universal trends.

What ought also to be further noted is that the translation of Shakespeare into Swahili was part of the broader ideological style of Nyerere, entailing a commitment both to transvaluation across cultures and transverbalization across languages. In this regard it is doubly symbolic that he should have chosen *Shakespeare* as a subject of translation and *Swahili* as the language thereof, if for nothing else than the fact that the two cultures, the Shakespearean and the Swahili, started by being contemporaneous, several centuries ago. It is Basil Davidson who draws our attention to this cultural parallelism in his observation:

---

[31] Milton, *Il Penseroso*, 11: 15-20.
[32] Senghor, "Negritude and the Concept of Universal Civilization", *Présence Africaine* 18 (18; 46) (Second Quarter, 1963), 10.

The earliest writing of Swahili epic poetry – and Swahili, language of the East Coast, is an authentically African language for all its Arabic infusions and inflexions – was contemporary with the epic poetry of Shakespeare's England. . . .[33]

If, then, there was a contemporaneous and parallel eruption of epic creativity between Shakespeare's England and the land of the Swahili language, Nyerere's translation of Shakespeare into Swahili four hundred years later assumes the massive symbolism of a historical destiny. What had seemed to be parallel lines of literary activity in two lands, which were oceans apart, had at last met in infinity.

Between the first production of Shakespeare's *Julius Caesar*, probably in 1599, and the first publication of Nyerere's translation of it, in 1963, a lot of history had unfolded. That history included the earlier days both of Apolo Milton Obote and Julius K. Nyerere. It included their shared educational institution, Makerere University. And it included that first production of a Shakespearean play at this African college of higher learning. The play was *Julius Caesar*, destined, as we indicated, to be translated into Swahili by one of Makerere's own sons, Julius Nyerere. The main character in that production was another literary intellectual: Julius Caesar's part was taken by Apolo Milton Obote.

Obote did not know then that he too would one day be the subject of intrigue among would-be assassins; that two decades after his portrayal of Julius Caesar on a Makerere stage, complete with the collapse after an assassin's blow, he would himself nearly die of an assassin's bullet.

But Obote rose from the nearly-dead, and said to his countrymen calmly, "I was shot at." Did the incident take him back to his feigned portrayal of Caesar falling? And did he derive courage and a new determination from Caesar's words before his death?

> Cowards die many times before their deaths;
> The valiant never taste of death but once.
> Of all the wonders that I yet have heard,
> It seems to me most strange that men should fear
> Seeing that death, a necessary end,
> Will come when it will come.[34]

---

[33] Davidson, "Black Men's Land: The Fact and the Fable", in: James Duffy and Robert A. Manners (eds.), *Africa Speaks*, 6.

[34] Shakespeare, *Julius Caesar*, Act II, Scene 2, 11. 32-37. When Milton Obote was ousted by the army coup of 25 January 1971, President Julius Nyerere attacked the new Ugandan regime in strong terms. A congratulatory message to Major General Idi Amin Dada from Binaisa and Co. had the following comment to make on Nyerere: "What you and your officers and men of the Armed Forces

With all this mention of death and human destiny, we are back to *Paradise Lost*. Two Miltons and two Juliuses merge into a literary experience in that Senghorian stream of universal civilization.

---

did was not because you loved 'Obote less but because you loved Uganda more'. A good student of Shakespeare such as Mwalimu Nyerere should be the first person to realise the full import of my quotation because he translated 'Julius Caesar' into Swahili." See *The People* (Kampala), February 4, 1971.

LANGUAGE IN MILITARY HISTORY:
COMMAND AND COMMUNICATION IN EAST AFRICA

In a world broadcast delivered on the radio on February 9, 1941, Winston Churchill, then wartime leader of Britain, had occasion to say: "In wartime there is a lot to be said for the motto: 'Deeds not words'."

And yet in that very exercise of broadcasting to the world in wartime Winston Churchill was belying his own words. Indeed, in that very broadcast, Churchill cited lines from Longfellow towards the conclusion of his speech. The verse from Longfellow had been written out by President Roosevelt in his own handwriting in a note addressed to Churchill, and the lines were intended to be a tribute to England in the throes of war with Hitler's Germany.

> ... Sail on, O Ship of State!
> Sail on, O Union strong and great!
> Humanity with all its fears,
> With all the hopes of future years,
> Is hanging breathless on thy fate!

Churchill was using Roosevelt's tribute brilliantly, as he continued to seek greater American support in the war. In that same speech in which he approved of the motto "Deeds, not words", Churchill uttered some of his most famous words. He asked the American people to give the British people their faith and their blessing. What Churchill meant was that he wanted the American people to give the British people more equipment with which to wage the war. And he assured the American people in this concluding paragraph to his broadcast:

We shall not fail or falter; we shall not weaken or tire. Neither the sudden shock of battle, nor the long-drawn trials of vigilance and exertion will wear us down. Give us the tools, and we will finish the job.[1]

General Eisenhower was later to complement Winston Churchill for having "mobilized the English language to the battlefield". At a time when the danger of low morale was ever present among his people, and the strength of Germany and its victories dominated the scene, Churchill's oratory sought to reassure his countrymen, as well as a demoralised Europe.

MILITARIZED LANGUAGE: INSPIRATIONAL AND ORGANIZATIONAL

What we have here then is the *inspirational* function of language in wartime. Language is utilized to capture certain ideals and manipulate the emotions in the direction of psychological stamina.

But at a time when Churchill was using the English language for inspirational purposes in England, the British colonial authorities were promoting the Swahili language in East Africa for *organizational* purposes. In other words, the broad functions of language in war can indeed be divided into two categories – the category of inspiration with morale as its objective; and the category of organization, with efficiency as its purpose. The King's African Rifles in East Africa had sought to recruit not only across tribal boundaries but also across territorial boundaries within the region. On a global scale the number of troops to be recruited from East Africa was indeed quite modest, but the recruitment covered a diversity of linguistic backgrounds. The King's African Rifles had already had to face the issue of the language of command even before the war. The issue was not absent even in the First World War, when East Africa was the scene of battle between Britain and Germany over the possession of German East Africa, Tanganyika. But with the imminence of the Second World War, and the possibility of wider recruitment once again, the problem of a suitable language of command, effective enough for a multi-linguistic unit of the armed forces, assumed a new persistence.

In the ultimate analysis there were three possibilities – first, a policy based on utilizing a number of vernaculars, secondly a policy based on utilizing the English language, and thirdly a policy based on utilizing Swahili. The multi-vernacular solution had a number of disadvantages. Unlike those who spoke West African languages, such as

[1] Sir Winston Churchill, "Give us the tools and we will finish the job", a World Broadcast, February 9, 1941, *Great War Speeches* (London: Transworld Publishers, 1959 edition), 84-93.

Hausa and Yoruba, the native speakers of indigenous languages in East Africa were more modest in population. Even the larger tribes like the Kikuyu and the Baganda were at the time little more than a million each, whereas Yoruba speakers in West Africa – let alone Hausa speakers – were to be counted in several millions.

There was the related argument that military command based on vernaculars would bedevil the issue of promotions within each linguistic group. The officers commanding Baganda soldiers might need themselves to be Baganda; the officers commanding Acholi soldiers might need themselves to be Acholi. If they were not drawn from the same linguistic community, the officers would need to be versed in the appropriate language.

The adoption of English would help this problem of communication across tribal lines, but would inevitably reduce drastically the sector of the population from which the soldiers could be recruited. In the 1930s and 1940s only a small proportion of the population of the East African countries spoke even rudimentary English, and those who spoke it well would look towards recruitment as officer cadets from the beginning. The King's African Rifles knew they had to recruit from a wide section of the population of East Africa and could not at the time afford to have this area circumscribed by an insistence on some knowledge of the metropolitan language.

The third possibility centred on adopting Swahili as the language of the armed forces. This would eliminate the problem of each linguistic community producing its own officers and non-commissioned officers. An Acholi could command an army consisting of Akamba, Baganda, and Wadigo. Both boundaries between tribes and boundaries between colonies within the same region would no longer need to be constraining factors in recruitment. It is true that knowledge of Swahili was not uniformly distributed throughout the region. Some tribal communities spoke it better than others. Some colonial territories preferred a more sophisticated version of Swahili than others. But a basic lingua franca, somewhat rudimentary, was already evolving. The armed forces could take advantage of the availability of such a lingua franca and could, in turn, strengthen its functions by providing, if need be, further courses in Swahili in the barracks.

This policy was adopted. Swahili became the language of the security forces in East Africa. The original reasons were organizational, rather than inspirational. The decision came to have important consequences for the future of Swahili, especially in Uganda.

While Winston Churchill was giving the English language a new area of achievement in a world of global broadcasts and unmanned flying missiles, Winston Churchill's colonial representatives in East Africa were helping to define more sharply a new role for the Swahili language in the affairs of the region.

It might be said that three wars were particularly important in the history of Swahili in East Africa. One war was the Maji Maji Rebellion in German Tanganyika which broke out in 1905. The second important war for the evolution of Swahili was World War I, and the third, as we have already indicated, was World War II.

MAJI MAJI: THE IDIOM OF A REBELLION

The Maji Maji Rebellion against German rule in Tanganyika was, in a sense, the first trans-tribal mass movement in the modern history of Tanganyika. It was a movement both because of its scale and because of the ideological content behind its assertiveness. Both the scale and the ideological content afforded a fundamental role for Swahili in its slow process of conquering Tanganyika.

As regards the scale and ideological content, John Illife has captured the significance of this particular episode in the history of the region.

Maji Maji was quite different from the early resistance which the Germans had faced when occupying Tanganyika, for that had been local and pro-fessional – soldiers against soldiers – whereas Maji Maji affected almost everyone in the colony. . . . In the long term, the movement may have provided an experience of united mass action to which later political leaders could appeal. . . . Maji Maji became a mass movement because it acquired an ideological content which persuaded people to join and fight.[2]

Illife discusses the use of religious symbols in the movement. He mentions the thrust of the "integration of diverse peoples". He also mentions the rapidity with which the revolt spread.

Within a fortnight, nearly all the peoples surrounding the Rufiji valley, from Kilosa to Liwale, were in revolt. . . . [In another two months] most of the peoples south of a line from Dar es Salaam to Kilosa and thence to the northern tip of Lake Malawi were in revolt.[3]

The Maji Maji Rebellion was important for the future of Swahili both because Swahili featured as a trans-tribal medium of communi-cation among the rebels, and because German policy concerning polit-ical penetration included a linguistic policy which favoured Swahili even more after the Rebellion than it had done before.

[2] John Illife, *Tanganyika Under German Rule, 1905-1912* (East African Pub-lishing House in association with Cambridge University Press, 1969) 6, 25.
[3] Illife, *Tanganyika*, 19-20.

Among the nationalist rebels in the Maji Maji Rebellion, Swahili was mainly organizational rather than inspirational. It made it possible for different people to communicate with each other. And yet to the extent that the Maji Maji Rebellion was a religious movement, inspired by a belief in invulnerability, Swahili did serve some inspirational functions, though the status of the language was still somewhat rudimentary in most parts of Tanganyika at that time.

A student of the history of Swahili, M. H. Abdulaziz, has drawn attention to the significance of Maji Maji in the genesis of trans-tribal and egalitarian movements in Tanzania. And he has placed Swahili at the heart of this process. In Abdulaziz's words:

Swahili has played a very significant role in the development of political values and attitudes in Tanzania. Its integrative qualities have influenced the style of Tanzania politics, especially its non-tribal and egalitarian characteristics. All movements of national focus have used Swahili as an instrument for achieving inter-tribal unity and integration. The Maji Maji war of 1905–07 against German colonial rule drew its support from different mother-tongue speakers who already possessed a rallying force in Swahili.[4]

In a statement to the United Nations Fourth Committee in 1956, Julius K. Nyerere described the Maji Maji Rebellion as the final act of violent resistance by his people, which had begun in 1885.

For fifteen years, between 1885 and 1900, my people, with bows and arrows, with spears and clubs, with knives or rusty muskets, fought desperately to keep the Germans out. But the odds were against them. In 1905 in the famous Maji Maji Rebellion, they tried again for the last time to drive the Germans out. Once again the odds were against them. The Germans, with characteristic ruthlessness, crushed the Rebellion, slaughtering an estimated number of 120,000 people.[5]

In its anti-German rhetoric, Nyerere's statement belonged almost to the same oratorical genre as Winston Churchill's wartime speeches. But what matters from our point of view here is Nyerere's conception of the Maji Maji Rebellion as the final attempt to deal with German occupa-

---

[4] M. H. Abdulaziz, "Tanzania's National Language Policy and the Rise of Swahili Political Culture", in: *Language Use and Social Change: Problems of Multilingualism with Special Reference to Eastern Africa*, edited by W. H. Whiteley and Daryll Forde (London: published for the International African Institute by Oxford University Press, 1971), 164.

[5] Statement by Julius Nyerere to the 579th Meeting of the Fourth Committee, United Nations, December 20, 1956. See Nyerere, *Freedom and Unity: A Selection of Writings and Speeches, 1952-1965* (Dar es Salaam, Oxford University Press, 1966), 40-41.

tion by violent rebellion: his assumption that the primary resistance of 1885 belonged to the same category of social phenomena as the final trans-tribal mass movement of 1905. In fact, the Maji Maji Rebellion was not the last of the movements of primary resistance starting from 1885, but rather the first of the really nationalist mass movements of Tanganyika. Illife's emphasis on the distinctiveness of scale in the Maji Maji Rebellion, and the trans-tribal ideology which seemed to animate it in spite of other religious differences, is indeed well taken. And because the Maji Maji Rebellion was the first nationalist mass movement of modern Tanganyika, it also offered the first nationalist role to the Swahili language in that country.

But the immediate shock of Maji Maji was on the Germans themselves. A reconsideration took place. Whatever complacency there might have been in German colonial policy was now shattered. The Germans decided minimal control of the hinterland of Tanganyika was no longer a sensible strategy. " . . . Maji Maji compelled a greatly increased German involvement in terms of political energy. The minimal aims of early colonial rule gave way to purposive colonial policy."[6]

The decision to embark on a more comprehensive programme of political penetration inevitably reinforced those aspects of German policy which were already strengthening the role and functions of the Swahili language in Tanganyika. The Germans had decided before the Maji Maji Rebellion that Swahili was going to be the language of administration, and efforts were already underway to document the language. Settlers and missionaries had also entered the great endeavour to make Swahili an effective lingua franca. The endeavour was partly a recognition of the role which Swahili had already assumed in this regard, and partly a commitment to make this role more efficient and more extensive. The first newspapers in Swahili came barely three or four years after the full establishment of German rule. *Msimulizi* came into being in 1888, and *Habari za Mwezi* probably came into being in 1894. Later on *Pwani na Bara* came into being, the first issue of which consisted of four pages, with an article on the Kaiser's birthday and a note on the Nyamwezi chief, Mirambo. The newspaper also contained statistics on the number of lions and leopards killed.

All this was part of the earlier colonial commitment to the promotion of Swahili. This commitment received an added impetus following the Maji Maji Rebellion and the German realization that administration in the rest of the country had to be much tighter and more responsive than it had been before the Rebellion.

---

[6] Illife, *Tanganyika*, 28.

By 1914 the Administration was able to conduct much of its correspondence with village headmen in Swahili; indeed, letters not written to the Administration in either Swahili or German were liable to be ignored. This was one feature of German Administration which proved of great value to their successors, the British, and evoked a good deal of approval in later years. The Report on the Territory for 1921, for example, stated "... the late German system has made it possible to communicate in writing with every Akida leader and village headman, and in turn to receive from him reports written in Swahili".[7]

What had happened was again a rather ruthless determination by the German administration not only to "pacify" the natives but also to centralize the system of administration in their colony. And centralization included ease of linguistic communication. The fortunes of the Swahili language in Tanganyika were greatly facilitated by the Maji Maji Rebellion both as a pioneer in mass organization and in its impact on German colonial policy in Tanganyika for the subsequent decade.

WORLD WAR I AND AFTER

World War I and its aftermath were also of importance for the fortunes of the Swahili language in East Africa. During the war itself the language helped to emphasize fratricidal aspects in the violence between local peoples themselves. The East African Coast especially was torn by the simple fact that the Germans, occupying the southern part of the Coast, were fighting the British occupying the northern part of the the Coast, and Swahili was the language of cultural and economic intercourse down the seaboard as a whole. Both the Germans and the British recruited into their armed forces local people who would not otherwise have been at war with each other, and who, in the case of the Coast, were a people culturally and linguistically related to each other. Along the coast Swahili was indeed used for inspirational purposes during that war, but its major function in the East African region as a whole was still basically functional and organizational.

More important than the actual war itself for the future of Swahili was the *outcome* of World War I. The defeat of Germany, and the assumption of administrative authority in Tanganyika by Great Britain, had long term repercussions not only for Tanganyika but for East Africa as a whole. From a linguistic point of view, the triumph of the

---

[7] See Wilfred Whiteley, *Swahili: The Rise of a National Language* (London: Methuen, 1969), 60-61. The quotation from the 1921 Report was cited by R. L. Buell, *The Native Problem in Africa* (London: Macmillan, 1928), Vol. I, 478.

British over the Germans was a mixed blessing for Swahili. The British as a colonial power were, in their attitude to language, different both from the French and the Germans. The French were tied to a missionary vision to disseminate their culture and spread their language. Because of that vision the French were among the least tolerant of colonial powers in their attitude to local cultures. The Germans, on the other hand, were not particularly keen on fostering the German language among their subjects. They sometimes even regarded it as presumptuous that a lower breed of people should seek to express themselves in German. The French tried to create a mystique of France by popularizing the French language; the Germans were tempted to create a mystique of Germany by isolating their language from the squalor of popular comprehension and making it mysteriously and powerfully distant. The French wanted to be admired for their culture. The Germans preferred to be admired for their power. Hence, the French policy of assimilation came into being, whilst the Germans emphasized mysteries of social distance. It was, therefore, basically presumptuous for an African to aspire to Germanhood in culture.

In addition, as we have indicated, German administration regarded it as inefficient to have to deal in too many different languages all over the colonial territory. There was, therefore, a case for singling out one medium or a few major media to be used for administrative purposes, and letting some of the others decay or die by administrative disuse.

The British were in an intermediate position between the Germans and the French. They believed in the ideology of indirect rule and its cultural appendages. They conceded a certain right of survival to indigenous cultural ways and indigenous languages. They even set up committees to coordinate the growth of key languages in their colonial territories. The East African inter-territorial language committee was a case in point during British colonial rule. But the British also believed, with some ambivalence, in bestowing the gift of the English language on at least the élites of the colonial territories.

As a generalization, we might then say that the British favoured a native acquisition of English a little more than the Germans had once favoured a native acquisition of German; and the British were more tolerant of smaller African languages, and more prepared to put up with linguistic plurality than either the Germans or the French.[8]

The fortunes of Swahili within Tanganyika suffered a little, though by no means fatally, when the country shifted from German control to

---

[8] This point concerning the comparative linguistic policies of colonial powers is discussed in a wider context in Mazrui, "Africa's Experience in Nation-Building: Is it Relevant to Papua and New Guinea?", *East Africa Journal* 7 (11) (November 1970), 15-23.

British control. The British toleration of smaller languages, to the extent that it was greater than the German, slowed down the spread of Swahili as a lingua franca. The British leaning towards promoting the English language, to the extent that it was greater than the German leaning towards promoting the German language, again affected adversely the fortunes of Swahili within Tanganyika. Indeed, the spread of the English language under British rule had the effect of relegating Swahili to the status of a second-class language even among Africans themselves. In the words of Wilfred Whiteley:

Whereas in German times the acquisition of Swahili represented a first stage towards participating in Government through membership of the junior Civil Service, no further stage in this participation could be achieved through the language. The next stage involved the acquisition of English, and for this reason, Swahili was seen increasingly by Tanganyikans as a "second-class" language.[9]

Educational policy was framed under the British on the basis of a declining utilization of Swahili. The language was used as a medium of primary school education, but became only one subject among several at secondary school, and disappeared completely even as a subject in Higher Education.

As time went on the difference in the quality and quantity of secondary-school materials and teachers was clear evidence to pupils, if to no one else, of the inferior status of the language. Institutions designed primarily for East Africans made no provision for the study of Swahili while their use of English simply confirmed East Africans in their belief that it was on this language that they should concentrate their sights. While the language of the lower courts was Swahili, the language of the higher courts was English. While Swahili newspapers were plentiful, the glossy magazines were in English.[10]

Of course if Tanganyika had been entrusted, as a League of Nations' mandate, to the administration of France, the fortunes of Swahili would have suffered even more drastically. French culture would have made of Swahili an even more second class language than it became under British rule. What is apt to be overlooked is that within Tanganyika the language would probably have fared better, and developed faster, as a national language enforced by the colonial power, had the Germans remained in control.

But while the fortunes of Swahili as a language of Tanganyika might thus have suffered when the country fell under British rule, the fortunes of Swahili as a language of East Africa probably improved. With the

[9]   Whiteley, *Swahili*, 61-62.
[10] Whiteley, *Swahili*, 62.

outcome of World War I being what it was, it was then conceivable for Kenya, Uganda, Zanzibar and Tanganyika to develop on the basis of increasing regional integration. Among the most unifying of factors in modern Africa has been the factor of being ruled by the same colonial power. Tanganyikans are much closer today to Kenyans and Ugandans than they would have been had Tanganyikans been German-speaking, while Kenyans and Ugandans were English-speaking. Regional organizations like the East African High Commission and its successors right up to the East African Community would not have been conceivable if there had continued to be a German East Africa in that part of the continent. The very concept of an East African Federation, hotly debated as it has been for decades, would not have featured realistically if Tanganyika had been the colony of a European power different from the colonisers of Kenya and Uganda.

Not least significant of the consequences of World War I was the fact that Zanzibar and Tanganyika now shared the same imperial power, Great Britain. Zanzibar, as the heartland of what later became standard Swahili, maintained its ease of communication with Dar es Salaam as the capital of Tanganyika. The dissemination of the Swahili language through East Africa as a whole received an additional boosting by the very fact that the Sultanate, then still relatively powerful, shared the same metropolitan "protecting" power as what later became mainland Tanzania. Indeed, the very union between Tanganyika and Zanzibar in 1964 might well have been inconceivable if the island and the mainland had reached the 1960's under the impact of two entirely different colonial powers.

The outcome of World War I was also an important factor behind the emergence of the very concept of *standard Swahili*. Because the British then controlled Kenya, Uganda, Zanzibar and Tanganyika, the idea of standardizing the Swahili language became viable. Rivalries between the colonial powers themselves over which dialect to choose for such an enterprise ceased to be relevant after the ouster of the Germans. In 1925 an education conference was convened by the Governor of Tanganyika and held in Dar es Salaam. This became an important landmark in the development of the idea of standard Swahili orthography. In 1926 a number of proposals were made concerning spelling and word division in Swahili. Meanwhile the 1925 conference had led to the establishment of a Central Publishing Committee. This body now demanded to be fully informed about projected text books for schools in an endeavour to avoid unnecessary duplication.

Kenya was also groping for some kind of standard orthography. It was in January 1928 that an inter-territorial conference held in Mombasa confirmed the decision to adopt the dialect of Zanzibar as the basis of standard Swahili. The Universities Mission to Central Africa had recommended the Zanzibar dialect in competition with the Church Missionary Society who were advocating the dialect of Mombasa. Again the whole enterprise of choosing a dialect from British controlled East Africa as the basis of standard Swahili became viable partly because Tanganyika was not controlled by another power. The range of dialects to choose from would not have been reduced to that of Mombasa and Zanzibar alone if a divided imperial presence had been an additional factor in the linguistic situation in East Africa.

On January 1, 1930, the Inter-Territorial Language Committee came into being at last. This Committee became a paramount mechanism in the process of standardizing Swahili throughout the region, as well as promoting regionally usable literature in the language.

In Uganda, Swahili was still relatively underdeveloped as compared with Tanganyika and Kenya. But even in Uganda the fortunes of Swahili began, perhaps haltingly, to take a turn for the better following the defeat of Germany in Tanganyika. In the 1920's Swahili in Uganda had at first seemed to be receding completely into the background. In 1925 A. W. Smith had observed that in Uganda "probably no person would favour the teaching of Swahili; Luganda is making headway in the provinces at the expense of the vernaculars".[11]

In 1926, special committees on language policy recommended that three languages be promoted in schools in the country. In the north Acholi should be used as the medium of instruction, in parts of the eastern province Teso should be the medium, and in the rest of Uganda Luganda should continue to dominate. Swahili did not feature very prominently in this planning. The full significance of Tanganyika's new status as a Mandated Territory under Britain had taken longer to reveal its implications for Uganda than it might have done. It was nearly seven years after World War I before Governor William Gowers of Uganda made the first major bid to pull Uganda into the mainstream of Swahili.

Gowers argued that since Tanganyika had become a British mandated territory and communication in East Africa had improved Uganda could not afford to isolate herself by ignoring Swahili which was understood in Kenya, Tanganyika and as far as the Congo . . . The possibility of federation [in East Africa] must have made the Swahili issue a matter of urgency for Gowers. But he confined his arguments to a more general discussion of

---

[11]   A. W. Smith, *Memo on the proposed International Bureau of African Languages and Literature* (Edinburgh House, May 1925), 7. The missionaries, who dominated the educational system in Uganda at the time, were hostile to Swahili because of its strong early cultural links with Islam.

the need for Uganda to integrate herself with general developments in East Africa, and to the educational advantages of Swahili.[12]

Swahili joined Luganda as one of the official languages of Uganda in 1927. But it was not for long. Missionary distrust of Swahili as an "Islamic language", Ganda suspicion of it as a rival to Luganda, and a sincere worry among educationalists that the introduction of Swahili into Uganda schools would be a retrograde step, all conspired to force the language out of the mainstream of life in Uganda.

But there was one area of national life where Swahili retained an official role. That was in the security forces. Swahili remained a language of command in the police and in the King's African Rifles. Both the fortunes of Swahili, and the spirit of regionalism in East Africa, became part of the history of the armed forces. It is to this factor that we must now turn.

WORLD WAR II AND AFTER

The man who was one day to become the first military ruler of independent Uganda entered military service soon after World War II. Some of his colleagues had fought in World War II in Burma, Malaya and Ethiopia.

One of Idi Amin's earliest exposures to the wider world had come precisely because of his military service. It might even be said that military services contributed to the rise of political awareness in Africa as a whole because of two important factors – the very factor of expanding horizons of experience in areas far away from home; and the factor of learning new skills of a technical kind in the armed forces. Both factors contributed to the frustrations of ex-servicemen in West Africa. The expanding horizons obtained as a result of seeing other parts of the world, and of knowing the white man as a fellow soldier in combat, and of seeing his weaknesses as well as his strengths at close quarters, began the process of humanizing the white man and of discovering that he was indeed fallible.

The factor of learning new skills, on the other hand, contributed to a sense of frustration after demobilization. The skills newly acquired were not always easy to utilize profitably outside the armed forces in the Africa of those days.

It is partly because of these factors that in the history of nationalism

[12] See Fay Gadsden, "Language Politics in Uganda: The Search for a Lingua Franca 1912-1944", USSC Conference, Makerere University, December 14-17, 1971.

in Africa as a whole ex-servicemen have often been among the first agitators for African dignity and greater opportunities. It has been said, for example, that the hundred and fifty thousand ex-servicemen throughout West Africa after World War II contributed to the general feeling of unrest which remained unassuaged, if it was not stimulated, by the mild constitutional reforms of the mid-1940s in West Africa. In a country like Nigeria it was not "surprising to find ex-servicemen among the more militant leaders of the nationalist movement during the post-war period".[13]

In Kenya's history too, a whole chapter stands out with the title "The Role of the Ex-soldier in Kenya's Political History". On one side we have the role of *European* ex-servicemen in the conversion of Kenya into a country with white settlers – with all the political repercussions which that entailed. As far back as World War I the War Council of Kenya concerned itself not only with the war and problems of conscription ("in which East Africa led the way in the Empire"), but it sought to strengthen the European position in particular by devising a Soldier Settlement Scheme for the post-war period.[14]

And at the end of the Second World War the Kenya Government and the British Government announced an agricultural settlement scheme for soldiers released from the armed forces – "men and women of pure European descent, who were thus eligible to farm in the area reserved for Europeans, and whose war services a grateful country wished to recognize".[15] What emerges from this is the importance of what Blundell called "soldier settlers" as a factor in the land question of Kenya's history.

As for the role of the African ex-servicemen in East Africa's history, one Kenya settler who served with Africans abroad has suggested that the first signs of nationalism in East Africa were discernible in the African *askari*. The *askari* was at last prompted to ask why only Europeans were officers in the East African army and why the food scales were different between white and black soldiers. As in West Africa, though less dramatically,

[13] See Dennis Austin, *West Africa and the Commonwealth* (London: Penguin African Series, 1957), 14. See also James S. Coleman, *Nigeria: Background to Nationalism* (Berkeley and Los Angeles: University of California Press, 1958), 254.
[14] See George Bennett, *Kenya: A Political History: The Colonial Period* (New York: Oxford University Press, 1963), 38. This earlier soldier scheme was ill-conceived and badly organized, but not without significance for future developments.
[15] Sir Michael Blundell, *So Rough a Wind* (London: Weidenfeld and Nicolson, 1964), 63.

the first real seeds of African nationalism were sown in the later years of the war, when the African just began to question the traditional differences between himself and the white man.[16]

From Uganda, according to his own account, young Idi Amin knew military service in Burma. And young Edward Mutesa, while studying at Cambridge, toyed with the idea of serving with the forces in Malaya. But it was not merely national awareness which was fostered by military experience. In the case of East Africa there was also the emergence of regional consciousness, complete with the promotion of Swahili among all members of the security forces of Uganda, Kenya and Tanganyika. This sense of pan-regional consciousness was facilitated partly by the method of recruitment into the King's African Rifles. Recruitment was conducted all over East Africa, but it did not follow that Ugandan soldiers would serve only in Uganda, Tanganyikans in Tanganyika and Kenyans in Kenya. On the contrary, an important aspect of policy was its trans-territorial dimension. In the police and the army, perhaps even more than in any other services, two factors were combined – an attempt to maintain a balance in the number of people recruited from each territory and an attempt to minimize the significance of the territorial origins of a new recruit in determining where he was to serve. Again, it is worth remembering that Idi Amin experienced military service in Kenya during the colonial period. And, even after the Ugandan coup of January 1971 there was still in the security forces of Uganda, personnel from the other two countries.

In June 1971, I went from Uganda to give a lecture at Bungoma Secondary School, just across the border in Kenya. At the border, a Kenya policeman asked me for a lift. We gave him a lift in the car and started a conversation. The policeman complimented me on my Swahili, and asked how it was that I spoke it so well. I explained that I hailed originally from the Coast. Then I asked the policeman where he was from, for his Swahili too was very good, though not coastal. He was a Ugandan it turned out. His uniform was that of the Kenya police. I asked him how long he had been in the Kenya police and he said eighteen years. He still regarded himself as a Ugandan, his children were at school in Uganda, and one daughter was expected to go to Makerere before long. By a curious coincidence, my lecture at Bungoma Secondary School was going to be precisely on issues of East African integration, at the request of the school itself. And there was this policeman in the car with us, a living embodiment of the historic connections between the security forces and East African integration.

[16] Blundell, *So Rough*, 58, 60. See also Donald S. Rothchild, *The Effects of Mobilization in British Africa* (= *Reprint Series Number 2, Duquesne University Institute of African Affairs*) (Pittsburgh: Duquesne University Press, 1961).

Nor should we forget the saga of "Field Marshall" John Okello, the man who spearheaded the Zanzibar revolution. Okello had served once in the Zanzibar police during the days of the Sultanate. Here was a Ugandan, from Lango, who had migrated to the islands as part of the general flow of population in East Africa. He still regarded himself as a Ugandan, and yet there he was spearheading a momentous revolution on an island state far from home. What was even more remarkable was that he had a following on that island, and that for at least a couple of weeks or so the limelight of the world was on him as the initiator of that revolution. "Field Marshall" John Okello was a living embodiment of East African integration in relation to the general mobility of the people.

What is the place of language in this whole phenomenon? Precisely because recruitment into the King's African Rifles was region-wide, a trans-tribal language of command was necessary. Before long Swahili asserted its credentials as the most trans-tribal as well as the most inter-territorial of all the indigenous languages of East Africa. Swahili became the language of both the army and the police, and this role in the security forces was its last remaining official function in Uganda after independence. Swahili had after all been squeezed out of Ugandan schools way back in the colonial period, partly in response to the negative lobbying of Luganda speakers. By the time of independence Swahili did not even have five minutes on Radio Uganda, or one single book in Uganda's educational system, but it retained an official role within the police and the army.

In 1967, Milton Obote and his Minister of Information assured me in a private conversation that Swahili would be introduced on Radio Uganda before long. At that time Radio Uganda already broadcast in fourteen languages on its two channels, but not in Swahili, in spite of the fact that Swahili was more widely understood in Uganda than the majority of those fourteen languages.

Obote was a genuine believer in the value of Swahili. He intended to introduce it as one of the compulsory languages to be learnt in his proposed National Service, and announced at Makerere University in October 1970 his intention to promote its teaching in the schools of Uganda. But he never got around to fulfilling these promises of a new language policy in the educational system of Uganda. He never even fulfilled the promise to introduce Swahili on Radio Uganda, which he had considered doing for many years.

And then on January 25, 1971, the military coup took place in Uganda. Within less than three weeks of the coup Swahili was on Radio Uganda and on Uganda Television. Indeed, on Radio Uganda Swahili has acquired almost the status of a national language. It is the only news bulletin in an African language to be read simultaneously on both channels of Radio Uganda. The old attachment to Swahili which the armed forces had shown, and which was a residual symbol of the connection between military service and East African integration, had found yet another manifestation. On taking over power in Uganda, the soldiers decided that one of their first policies was indeed to introduce Swahili in the mass media of the country.

Again it was fitting for a soldier-President like Amin to be so influenced by a realization of the importance of language. Shortly after taking over control, General Amin announced a pet project of his own – a dream of his to see established in Uganda a University especially committed to the study of languages. I had occasion to discuss with the General this idea of his. I asked the General what it was that had made him narrow the focus of his idea of a second university purely to the study of languages? He indicated that his idea did not preclude the study of other subjects, but the focus on language was dictated by the geographical situation of Uganda itself. The three most widespread languages in Africa as a whole are, in fact, English, French and Arabic. Uganda shares a border with one predominantly Arabic-speaking country, the Sudan; with two predominantly French-speaking countries, Zaïre and Rwanda; and with two predominantly English-speaking countries, Kenya and Tanzania. Among indigenous languages in Africa, Swahili may well be the most widely spread in terms of crossing national boundaries and serving central functions in a variety of countries. In four of the five countries that Uganda shares a border with – Kenya, Tanzania, Rwanda and Zaïre – Swahili is spoken. This special situation of Uganda in regard to the four languages of English, French, Arabic and Swahili imposes upon Uganda the necessity of being particularly conscious of the connection between language and regional integration.

Although I have used different words from those used by the General in our discussion, it was quite clear that he had worked out the idea of a university of languages in these terms. It may be that we should call such an institution an Academy of Languages or even a School of Languages, instead of calling it a University. But whatever name we give it, such an institution, if it came into being, would represent Uganda's awareness of her strategic situation in relation to four major languages of the African continent.

CONCLUSION

We may again remind ourselves here that there are two broad categories of language usage from the point of view of military performance. One category concerns the inspirational usage, and the other the organizational.

In modern history a particularly impressive example of the inspirational utilization of the English language was to be found in Winston Churchill's style of leadership in World War II. On May 10, 1940, Neville Chamberlain resigned as Prime Minister of Great Britain, and Winston Churchill succeeded him. From his very first speech to the House of Commons, on May 13, 1940, a new fighting rhetoric moved to the centre of British politics. It was in that very first speech that the first of Churchill's memorable wartime sentences came descending into the mainstream of history. "I have nothing to offer but blood, toil, tears and sweat."

The country did seem vulnerable; the enemy almost invincible. Britain stood alone, in splendid isolation, resting on fragility. The nation needed not only arms but also courage, not only a system of defence but also a source of determination. Winston Churchill rose to the occasion, and made his countrymen feel that the whole survival of civilization depended on the survival of the British Isles.

Hitler knows that he will have to break us in this island or lose the war. ... Upon this battle depends the survival of Christian civilization.... If we can stand up to him, all Europe may be free and the life of the world may move forward into broad, sunlit uplands. But if we fail, then the whole world, including the United States, including all that we have known and cared for, will sink into the abyss of a new dark age made more sinister, and perhaps more protracted, by the lights of perverted science. Let us therefore brace ourselves to our duties, and so bear ourselves that, if the British Empire and its Commonwealth last for a thousand years, men will still say, "This was their finest hour".[17]

The fighting words kept on ringing, as the nation struggled to give itself a defence system. The English language – a language which had by then become relatively prosiac, shy of flowery extravagance, distrustful of rhetoric – was nevertheless mobilized by Winston Churchill as an additional military resource.

We shall fight on the beaches, we shall fight on the landing grounds, we shall fight in the fields and in the streets, we shall fight in the hills.... Be the ordeal sharp or long, or both, we shall seek no terms, we shall tolerate no parley; we may show mercy – we shall ask for none.

But, as we have indicated in this analysis, concurrently with Winston Churchill's utilization of English for inspirational purposes was the initiation of a new phase for Swahili in East Africa for organiza-

17   Churchill, *Great War Speeches*, 33.

tional purposes in the armed forces. Swahili acquired influential friends in the barracks – friends whose power for future policy making was at the time not fully apprehended, but who later came to assume positions of critical significance in their countries. These were the soldiers of East Africa, mere instruments of high policy at the time they were being encouraged to learn Swahili so that they could more efficiently obey commands, but destined to become sources of power and initiative, especially in Uganda.

And yet, at that time, in Uganda the utility of Swahili was still basically organizational rather than inspirational. Along the coast in the 19th Century poets had used Swahili as a source of military morale. But in the hinterland of East Africa it was still true to say, as Wilfred Whiteley once put it, "Gone are the stirring phrases with which Muyaka sought to stiffen Mazrui resistance against the invaders from Zanzibar."[18]

Language for organizational purposes may be relatively simple, and yet still effective; language for inspirational purposes needs greater depths of meaning. Swahili in Uganda has not as yet acquired the sophistication necessary for effective inspirational utilization. The missing factor concerns the educational system.

As we indicated, Swahili disappeared from school syllabuses in Uganda following the controversies of language in the inter-war years. At his installation as Chancellor of Makerere University in October 1970, Dr. Milton Obote, then President of Uganda, intimated at long last that his Government intended to re-introduce Swahili into the country's educational system. Obote had also recommended Swahili as one of the languages which would be taught in his national service. When he was overthrown in January 1971 many of his ideas fell with him. But the partiality of his successors for Swahili, and indeed for language education generally, does give reason to expect moves towards resurrecting Swahili at least as a school subject in Uganda in the years ahead.[19]

It is only when Swahili acquires sophistication and depth as a result of its resurrection in the schools in Uganda that the language will at

[18] Whiteley, *Swahili*, 58.
[19] For a comprehensive study of the language situation in Uganda, consult Ladefoged, Glick, and Criper, *Language in Uganda* (Nairobi: Oxford University Press, 1971). Table 1.2 gives percentages of Ugandans able to hold a conversation in Swahili, Luganda, and English. The following are the percentages given in the book on page 25.

	Swahili	Luganda	English
Men	52	51	28
Women	18	28	13
Total	35	39	21

last find inspirational functions, in addition to organizational ones. In Kenya, Mzee Kenyatta, with his impressive mastery of the language, has gone a long way towards giving it an inspirational role even in *political* mobilization. His very concept of *Harambee*, though impure in pronunciation, has remained a throbbing slogan in the political vocabulary of Kenya. Self-help schemes ranging from water supplies to community schools have invoked the slogan of *Harambee* as a clarion call for national endeavour.

But it is plainly in Tanzania that Swahili has attained its most elaborate forms of inspirational usage. The language has been called upon to fight the battles of cultural nationalism, and demonstrate Swahili's capacity to bear the weight of social phenomena ranging from the Law to the plays of William Shakespeare. Swahili has been called upon to bear the burdens of national integration, and give Tanzanians a sense of belonging to one national entity in spite of varieties of tribal and linguistic origin. Finally, Swahili in Tanzania has been called upon to serve the inspirational aims of socialism itself, ranging from the very word *Ujamaa*, denoting kinship solidarity and fellowship on a national scale, to the slogan of *Kujitegemea*, the spirit of self-reliance. The ghost of the Maji Maji Rebellion smiles in satisfied vindication at the turn of linguistic history in Tanzania. To quote M. H. Abdulaziz once again:

The Maji Maji war of 1905–07 against German colonial rule drew its support from different mother tongue speakers who already possessed a rallying force in Swahili. . . . All movements of national focus [in Tanzania] have used Swahili as an instrument for achieving inter-tribal unity and integration.

With the use of language for socialistic inspiration in Tanzania, the concept of *war*[20] itself has become demilitarized, and both inspiration and organization as served by language are now directed towards new targets of national effort.

[20]   In his Presidential inaugural address on December 10, 1962, President Nyerere had occasion to say: "I know there are still a few people who think we are joking when they hear us use the word 'war'. Let me assure them that we are not. . . . Even if one were to take for example, the Maji Maji Rebellion and the Slave Wars, one would find no parallel to the slaughter of our people which has stemmed from poverty, ignorance and disease. . . . These, then, are not mock-enemies; they are the true enemies of our people. And anybody who refuses to take part in this war or who hinders the efforts of these labours, is guilty of helping a far more deadly foe than is he who helps an armed invader. . . . I look to every citizen of our country to join in the fight. And anyone who interferes with our efforts, I, for my part, shall look upon as a traitor and as an enemy of our country." For extracts from the English version of this speech see Nyerere, *Freedom and Unity: Uhuru na Umoja: A Selection from Writings and Speeches, 1952-1965* (Dar es Salaam, Oxford University Press, 1966), 176-177.

8

SOME SOCIO-POLITICAL FUNCTIONS
OF ENGLISH LITERATURE IN AFRICA

Within the broad discipline of sociolinguistics, or intimately associated with it, is a sub-discipline which we might call *socioliterature*. A wide range of phenomena go towards making socioliterature. In Africa one relevant aspect is the sociology of creative writing in modern forms. The social context of the literature of protest in South Africa, or the colonial background of négritude as an intellectual movement, or the cultural implications of having to use a European language as a medium of African self-expression, are all fit subjects for a student of socioliterature. So is the study of the social context of songs, burial hymns and versified invocation at circumcision ceremonies. In short the study of socioliterature is an investigation into the broad sociological meaning of literary behaviour in all its varied manifestations.

This chapter is an exercise in socioliterature. It seeks to explore some aspects of literary acculturation in English-speaking Africa and its relationship to the politics of the area.

A useful place to begin is simply to note that poetry has important points of contact with politics. In fact, several factors go towards linking poetry to politics. One factor is the phenomenon of cultural nationalism itself. Connected with this is the use of proverbs in traditional discourse. Yet another factor in the African experience is the impact of the Bible as a work of literature. And behind it all is

This paper was presented at a conference on Language Problems in Developing Countries held near Washington, D.C., in November 1966 under the auspices of the Social Science Research Council of the United States. It is printed here with the permission of the Committee on Sociolinguistics of the Council.

the phenomenon of *emotion* as a basic element both in poetry and in certain forms of political appeal.

Among the peoples of Eastern Africa perhaps none has a body of indigenous poetry which is more closely linked to nationalism than the Somali. In his book about the Somali, John Drysdale mentions how Somali nationalism is fostered with "the emotional appeal of Somali poetry".[1] And Colin Legum has examined how recent poems, in their longing for Somali reunification, have come to be "strongly tinged with ideas of 'the amputation' and 'the dismemberment' of the Somali nation".[2]

But Somalia is almost the only country in sub-Saharan Africa that is a "nation" in the neo-Western sense of linguistic homogeneity.[3] We have often mentioned Tanzania as having Swahili for a lingua franca. But having an indigenous lingua franca, though perhaps the next best thing, is not as preferable as having only one indigenous language. In effect Tanzania has a multi-lingual tribal base with one intertribal language. But Somalia has, to all intents and purposes, only one indigenous language.

But even Tanzania is considerably more homogeneous linguistically than almost all other sub-Saharan African states. The rule in Africa is, as many have noted, of a polyglottal tribal diversity. And the tradition of songs and poetry in such countries is therefore oriented towards individual tribes. The emotional appeal of such verse operates within a universe of tribal sensibilities and associations. Under the initial impact of the English language and its detribalizing effect African nationalism therefore turned *away* from tribal songs.

In English-speaking Africa we can, in fact, say that in the early days cultural nationalism was an attempt to demonstrate that the African was capable of mastering the imperial culture. As Julius Nyerere once put it, "At one time it was a compliment rather than an insult to call a man who imitated the Europeans a 'Black European'."[4]

In this first imitative phase of African cultural nationalism the English language became for an African more than merely a status symbol. The phenomenon as a whole was not of the kind normally associated with nationalistic sentiments. Frederick Hartz has seen the relationship between nationalism and language in the following terms:

[1]   *The Somali Dispute* (New York: Frederick A. Praeger, 1964), 15.
[2]   "Somali Liberation Songs", *The Journal of Modern African Studies* 1 (4) (December 1963), 505.
[3]   "Mankind instinctively takes language as the badge of nationality", one Westerner once claimed. See Edward A. Freeman, "Race and Language", *Historical Essays*, third series (London: Macmillan and Co., 1879), 203.
[4]   President's Address to the Tanganyika National Assembly, December 10, 1962, special publication, p. 21.

National consciousness sees in the national language the principal traditional bond of the community, the means for educating the people to solidarity, and a symbol of national personality. Nationalism, moreover, regards the absolute domination of the national language in its country as a matter of prestige. . . .[5]

But nationalism in much of Africa was not in a position to live up to these characteristics. The leaders had before them two possible methods of "educating the people to solidarity". The two were intimately related and were usually two sides of the same effort. One method was to stress what the people of different tribes in an African colony had in common. Another was to stress what *little* they together had in common with the imperial race that had colonized them. At the level of language the nearest thing to a lingua franca in a polyglottal African situation was sometimes the English language. It was a common language between at least the new class of educated and semieducated members of each tribe. To revel in the English language was indeed to stress what the political "intellectuals" had in common with one another regardless of tribal affiliation – but it was also to emphasize what they had in common with the imperial power from whom they had borrowed that language. The same language which was helping the growth of solidarity among "natives" was reducing the foreignness of the foreign power.

But it was open to nationalists to treat the English language as a necessary evil or a temporary expedient, as nationalists in India had sometimes done. The African nationalists at that time did not think of English in those terms. For a while they took pride in their command of the English language for reasons which were paradoxically, nationalistic. But would not this put these English-speaking militants in the same category as Léopold Senghor with his affectionate attachment to the French language? And yet we have to describe Senghor's pride in the French language as at best a linguistic cosmopolitanism. What made it possible for those early English-speaking Africans to be "nationalists" in spite of revelling in the English language?

In fact, Senghor's attitude to French is different in an important way from the attitude of early English-speaking African "intellectuals" towards English. The distinction is between taking pride in a language and taking pride in one's own command of a language. Senghor has said: "If we had a choice we would choose French. . . . It is the supreme language of communication." In this eulogy to French Senghor is taking pride in the French language as a language. But the attitude

---

[5] *Nationality in History and Politics* (London: Routledge and Kegan Paul [first edition 1944], 1951), 87.

of early Nigerian and Gold Coast nationalists was a matter of revelling in their own command of English, rather than in the "beauty" or any other inherent characteristic of the language itself. An individual can take pride in his own knowledge of a language without eulogizing the language itself. Indeed, many was a British administrator or missionary in Africa who must have felt an inner satisfaction in having mastered the language of a small tribe in Africa – without necessarily investing that tribal tongue with pre-eminence among languages at large.

This kind of pride is personal. What made the attitude of early Kenyan or Nigerian nationalists towards English *nationalistic?* Two factors converge to form part of the explanation. One was the way in which English was associated with intellectual competence. The other was the way in which blacks were regarded as incapable of attaining the heights of intellectuality. A competence in the English language was therefore a step towards contradicting the racialistic myth of the black man's "retarded mentality". Mastering another „civilization" might not prove that Africa was capable of creating one of her own, but it should at least prove that Africans had the mental capacity to absorb and command a "high civilization" should they decide to adopt one. The desire to prove that the African was educable in Western terms was therefore an element in the assertiveness of early African nationalism. And, in David Kimble's words, "education to many people came to mean simply the ability to speak and write English".[6]

But education was not merely a matter of asserting racial equality; it was also a matter of establishing class differentiation. And so a knowledge of English became a factor in social stratification as well.

Out of all these factors resulted the phenomenon of extravagant linguistic exhibitionism in the early days. The extravagance was "in the misuse or overuse of long words, in the use of pompous oratory, in the ostentatious display of educational attainments".[7]

An "expert" is sometimes definable as one who knows the least-known aspects of his subject. By extension an "expert" in the English language came to be defined as one who was familiar with the least familiar words of the language. Popular Nigerian literature in the English language still betrays this assumption. Donatus Nwoga of the English Department of the University at Nsukka refers us to certain characters in Nigerian literature.

In *Veronica, My Daughter,* Chief Jombo, feeling that Veronica, his daughter and Pauline his wife, were trying to browbeat him with their superior

[6]   *A Political History of Ghana* (Oxford: Clarendon Press, 1963), 510.
[7]   See James S. Coleman, *Nigeria, Background to Nationalism* (Berkeley and Los Angeles: University of California Press, 1958), 146.

knowledge of the English language, sent for Bomber Billy, reputed for the bomb words he could throw. . . . This concatenation of bombasts would be greatly effective on stage in Nigeria where big words do make an impact.[8]

Nwoga goes on to refer us to more established works in Nigerian literature. Achebe, Nigeria's leading novelist, points at his countrymen's love for big words in a speech he allocates to the President of the Omuofia Progressive Union in the novel *No Longer at Ease*. In a play by Wole Soyinka, Nigeria's leading playwright, a teacher assails the custom of paying bride price with a series of long English words – "and only stopped because he had only the Shorter Companion Dictionary – the longer edition which he had ordered hadn't arrived".[9]

Linked to this affection for bombast is an affection for quotations from major figures in English literature. One of the first warnings which Nnamdi Azikiwe sounded on his return to Nigeria from the United States in 1934 was a warning against what he called "the by-products of an imitative complex". He urged his countrymen to go "beyond the veneer of knowledge". And he emphasized that "ability to quote Shakespeare or Byron or Chaucer does not indicate original scholarship".[10]

Azikiwe's warning might have been pertinent if what the quotations sought to demonstrate was, indeed, "original scholarship". But what the quotations in fact sought to display was "scholarship" rather than "originality" a wealth of learning rather than a brilliant turn of mind. The desire to assert Africa's intellectual capacity was indeed often present either in the speaker himself or in the audience which craved and extolled such displays. But the intellectual capacity which was being asserted at this time was capacity to *absorb* the imperial culture at its most refined. Originality of mind as a form of intellectual non-conformity might have militated against this initial ambition of *assimilating* the imperial culture.

And yet that very love of long words and abundant utilization of literary quotations was itself a form of originality in English usage. It is a prejudice of the "founders" of the English language that short "Anglo-Saxon" words are to be preferred over long Latinized ones. It is also a prejudice of those "founders" that great literary figures who are revered precisely for the "universality" of their human sensitivities should nevertheless be cited only very rarely as authorities on some point of human interest. By ignoring both these conditions imposed by

[8]   Nwoga, "Onitsha Market Literature", *Transition* 4 (19) (1965), 28-29.
[9]   Nwoga, "Onitsha", 29. Soyinka's play in question is *The Lion and the Jewel*.
[10]   A speech given in November 1934 in Lagos. See *Zik. A Selection From the Speeches of Nnamdi Azikiwe* (Cambridge University Press, 1961), 23.

the Anglo-Saxon users of the English language, early usage in West Africa asserted a personality of its own.

It might even be argued that great figures in English literature were now subject to the laws of conversation of indigenous African languages. Conversational wit in many African languages postulates a ready command of diverse proverbs. It is assumed that there is a given number of human situations which keep on recurring. The incidentals vary; the personalities vary – but the essential elements of the situation are supposed to be recurring themes in human experience. Westerners make a similar supposition when they attribute to great plays or great novels the quality of "universality" in the experiences they depict. A set of words about "grief" which was used when Juma lost his first wife, when Rajabu lost his eyesight, and when Maryamu's son betrayed his ancestors, are used again – now that Singida is sent to jail for failing to pay the new poll tax. The situations vary, sometimes in important ways – but the proverb captures the recurrent nature of grief in "the human condition". The brilliant conversationalist is he who can penetrate into the fundamental similarities between types of human experience. The incidentals of each experience might try to disguise the familiarity of the essence – but wisdom consists in capacity to discern that essence. A ready grasp of proverbs, utilized convincingly, is therefore evidence of discernment and wisdom. As a Yoruba proverb has put it, "A wise man who knows proverbs reconciles difficulties." [11]

A similar admiration of elegant speech, and of the place of proverbs in that speech, can be found among the Ibo. Donatus Nwoga tells us that the Ibos have a dictum to the effect that to make a speech without using proverbs is like trying to climb a palm tree without the climbing rope. Nwoga then goes on to make a connection between traditional proverbs and Shakespearean quotations in contemporary Africa. He says:

I suggest that the tendency towards supporting one's statements with proverbs might have carried over into this market literature in the form of using quotations. *In Veronica, My Daughter*, between pages 20 and 23, there are quotations from Richard Whately, William Shakespeare, G. A. Gallock, Rudyard Kipling, Benjamin Harrison, William Ernest Henley and Henry Longfellow; and before the end of the story there are further quotations from Johann Wolfgang Von Goethe and some unknown poet. [12]

Lest it be assumed that it is only the semi-literate who use English quotations with the same abundance as they might use African prov-

---

[11] See *African Proverbs*, compiled by Charlotte and Wolf Leslau (Mt. Vernon, New York: Peter Pauper Press, 1962). Introductory page.
[12] Nwoga, "Onitsha", 31.

erbs, Nwoga warns that 'the mania for quotations is not determined by the standard of education". On the day he started thinking about this matter he happened to pick up a Nigerian newspaper – and the lead article started its second paragraph with a quotation from Edmund Burke. Nwoga observes:

This is impressive where breadth of knowledge of English is not only a prestige factor but also a guide to social and employment status.... But one has to admit that sometimes quotations are used for the genuine purposes of giving to the opinion of the speaker or writer an extra and higher authority.[13]

Capacity to adorn one's speech, and to give it weight by citing great names, was an important factor in the process by which leadership emerged. To be able to make a good speech is an asset for a politician in almost any society, but it is even more crucial in situations where patronage as an alternative way of recruiting influential followers is as yet inadequately established. In the early days of nationalism in Africa the politicians had limited tangible rewards to offer those whose allegiance they were seeking. It was the colonial government and, in some cases, the tribal chiefs that had the more immediate powers of patronage. What the modern politicians in the colonies could best do was precisely what they were often accused of doing — they worked on the vague grievances of the people and made them less vague. And in a competition between the leadership of one politician and that of another, the better speaker had an advantage which was more significant in those early African situations than the same advantage might be in Africa today. The British colonies by the 1940's were nearer to being "open societies" than are some independent African countries today. And precisely because the latter are less "open", the ability to make a good speech has depreciated in value as a qualification for political success. Nkrumah's opponents after independence were not in a position to attribute to oratorical powers the same relevance for one's political destiny that Nkrumah attributed to his own debating abilities in the colonial period. In his autobiography he tells us how he discovered quite early his talents in verbal persuasion:

I discovered that at whatever disadvantage I began, I usually ended up winning the day, frequently converting many of my opponents to the point of view that I had conveniently supported. Although this was only a kind of game with me then, it turned out to be my most valuable discovery. Without this "gift of the gab", my battle would have been lost from the very beginning and the whole struggle would have been in vain.[14]

[13] Nwoga, "Onitsha", 31-32.
[14] *Ghana: The Autobiography of Kwame Nkrumah* (New York & Edinburgh: Nelson, 1957), 19.

But the power of verbal persuasion can sometimes be as effectively used in religion as in politics. In the earlier days of the colonial period the pulpit could be as "seductive" to a talented young man as the political platform. Nkrumah was, as it were, a "near-Jesuit". For a whole year as a young man he played with the idea of joining the Jesuit Order. But in the end his old desire to "further my education and proceed to America in order to do this, got the better of me".[15]

When he got to America he studied subjects like philosophy and sociology – but the old idea of theology kept on recurring. In 1942 he graduated from the seminary at Lincoln University, at the head of his class, with a Bachelor of Theology degree. His oratorical talents were once again tested on this occasion. It fell upon him to deliver the seminary graduation oration. The subject he chose to speak on was "Ethiopia shall stretch forth her hands unto God. . . ." He was inadequately prepared and worried about how the oration was going, but when the warm congratulations ensued later he was, like a true performer, deeply gratified.[16]

In fact, by that time he had already had some practice in preaching. While he was studying theology at Lincoln Seminary Nkrumah spent much of his free time preaching in black churches.[17]

This is where we ought to include the influence of the Bible on the idiom of African rhetoric. In terms of style and language the Bible in English is, in a sense, part of the corpus of English literature. And it had an important place in the kind of literary education to which many of the African leaders were exposed in the formative years. Of Nigeria in those days James Coleman has had this to say:

In literature, Shakespeare and the Bible held the stage. Even today, it is not uncommon to find a semi-educated Nigerian working as a steward who can . . . quote the Bible, and recite Hamlet. . . .[18]

In independent Ghana the influence of the Bible came to result in a language of political adoration for the leader which was strikingly derived from the Holy Book.[19] Nkrumah came to be invested with Messianic attributes and powers of "redemption". As for the idiom of his own political speeches, perhaps the most famous single sentence uttered by Nkrumah was "Seek ye first the political kingdom and all

---

[15] Nkrumah, *Ghana*, 21.
[16] Nkrumah, *Ghana*, 32.
[17] Nkrumah, *Ghana*, 41.
[18] Coleman, *Nigeria*, 114-115.
[19] For a sensitive socio-political analysis of this kind of phenomenon see David E. Apter, "Political Religion in New Nations", in: *Old Societies and New States*, Clifford Geertz (ed.) (London: Free Press of Glencoe, 1964).

things will be added to it."[20] In a neo-biblical imperative Nkrumah thus asserted the primacy of politics as a basic precept of African nationalism in the struggle for independence.

Further south, religious and political sensitivities among Africans have sometimes also converged round a concept of messianism – but this time in a different sense from that attributed to the Osagyefo in Ghana. In an article written in 1953 Georges Balandier urged greater sociological investigation into "Neo-Christian movements" and separatist churches in Black Africa. He said:

Neo-Christian movements must come to the attention of the sociologist insofar as they are reactions against the colonial situation.... These movements lead above all to the study of the origins of nationalism, and, in so doing, confront the sociologist with one of the most important problems of our time.[21]

Balandier saw these messianic movements as being mainly in South and Central Africa. But the influence of Christianity on nationalism in these parts is by no means limited to those who rise as "prophets". One of the striking aspects of nationalistic leadership in English-speaking Central Africa and in South Africa is how often it seems to bear a deep religious impact. In Zambia, Kenneth Kaunda is a son of an African missionary and is himself a devout Christian. Hastings Banda in Malawi is now a more controversial figure, but in his old campaigns for Nyasaland's secession from the Federation of Rhodesia and Nyasaland, Banda's standing among sympathizers in Britain was helped by his position as an elder in the Church of Scotland. In Southern Rhodesia Ndabaningi Sithole, the more militant of the two leaders of African nationalism, is a priest. In South Africa Chief Albert Luthuli, winner of the Nobel Prize for Peace, was a deeply devout Christian.

As for the influence of the Bible in their idiom, Luthuli entitled his book *Let My People Go,* echoing the Mosaic imperative to the Pharoah. Kaunda's response to Ghandi's doctrine of non-violence has Christian echoes and is related to Kaunda's Christian upbringing. And the Reverend Sithole devotes part of his book *African Nationalism* to the role of Christianity in the growth of African militancy.[22]

[20] See, for example, Nkrumah, *I Speak of Freedom, A Statement of African Ideology* (New York: Frederick A. Praeger, 1961), 90-91.
[21] "Messianism and Nationalism in Black Africa", translated by Pierre L. Van den Berghe from an article from *Cahiers Internationaux de Sociologie* 14 (1953), 41-65; See Van den Berghe, *Africa: Social Problems of Change and Conflict* (San Francisco: Chandler Publishing Co., 1965), 460.
[22] See Sithole, *African Nationalism* (London: Oxford University Press, 1959). See also Sithole's article, "African Nationalism and Christianity", *Transition* 4 (10) (September 1963).

What religious fervour, nationalism and poetry have in common is, in the ultimate analysis, the essential emotionality of the three experiences. It is to this factor of emotionality in Africa that we must now turn.

Of all African leaders Léopold Senghor has perhaps gone furthest in discussing with approval the place of emotion in Africa. He has asserted that a highly developed "emotive sensibility" is what distinguishes the genius of Africa from that of the Western world. "Emotion is black . . . reason is Greek", Senghor once claimed.[23]

This interpretation of original Africa exposed Senghor to the charge of depriving the traditional African of the gift of rationality. Senghor defends himself with his usual ingenuity – by asserting that, while European reasoning is purely analytical, African reasoning is intuitive.[24]

Senghor might be overstating his case but his generalizations are not entirely devoid of substance. The extra-emotionalism of Negro Christianity, especially in the New World, is one area of experience which affords some evidence for Senghor's assertion. Among the earliest Church services attended by the youthful Nkrumah on his arrival in the States was a Negro service at the Abyssinian Church in New York. Nkrumah tells us about the minister's "dramatization" of the story of Jesus carrying the cross to Calvary. Before long the women in the congregation were overawed and began to weep and to shout. "It is Jesus! Have mercy! Hallelujah!" The response of the audience as a whole had become loudly emotional.

Nkrumah was embarrassed. But he was embarrassed because he was accompanied by a European friend that he had met on board a ship from Liverpool. With the stereotyped "stiff-upper-lip" British culture for a background, Nkrumah had apparently assumed that all Europeans despised displays of emotions. In a sense, he was accepting Senghor's categories of "Greek reason" and "black emotion" – and was ashamed of that "black emotion" in the Abyssinian Church because there was a white man there to witness it. Nkrumah tells us: "It was very embarrassing. Here was a European witnessing a most undignified Negro service. As we left the Church I tried to apologise . . . ."[25]

But the young Dutchman, who had come back to America to complete his theological studies at the Harvard Divinity School, was apparently taken aback by Nkrumah's apology. He told Nkrumah that the service at the Abyssinian Church was the most beautiful thing he had seen in any church. "It was my turn to be astonished", Nkrumah relates.

Many years later, when he was back in the Gold Coast, a hymn sung at a touching moment in Nkrumah's early political career made

[23]   L. S. Senghor, *Négritude et humanisme* (Paris: Seuil, 1964), 24.
[24]   Senghor, *On African Socialism* (London: Pall Mall, 1964), 74.
[25]   Nkrumah, *Ghana*, 28.

Nkrumah weep in public. He was confronted by an excited crowd which wanted him to resign as General Secretary of the old United Gold Coast Convention, dominated by lawyers, and form a more radical party of his own. "Resign!" the crowd shouted, "resign and lead us. . .!" Nkrumah suddenly felt that they meant it. He made up his mind to resign not only the general-secretaryship but also his membership of the United Gold Coast Convention. Standing on a platform, surrounded by an expectant crowd, he asked for a pen and a piece of paper and, using somebody's back for support, wrote out his official resignation and read it out to the people. Their enthusiasm was deafening. Then one of the women supporters jumped up on the platform and led the singing of the hymn "Lead Kindly Light". Nkrumah relates:

What with the strain of it all and the excitement, the singing of this hymn was as much as I felt I could take. I covered my eyes with my handkerchief, a gesture which was followed by many others. . . . The impact of all this made me suddenly humble and lonely and the tears that came were shed not from sorrow but from a deep sense of gladness and dedication.[26]

From then on that memorable hymn came to be sung at many a rally of the new and dynamic Convention People's Party.

Yet it was not just Christian hymns which captured the mood of the new Africa. Straight English poetry also played its part. Senghor talks about "Greek reason". He might also have mentioned the "gravest charge against poetry" made by the most rational of the Greeks – Plato's charge that poetry had "a terrible power to corrupt even the best characters".[27]

As we have mentioned, Plato himself was in favour of submitting poetry to a censorship which was "designed to expunge everything unsuitable to its educational purposes".[28] But colonial powers in Africa in the Nineteenth and Twentieth Centuries, though sensitive to "sedition" and "subversion", underestimated the political implications of those poetically expressed ideas which were scattered in their own literary classics. Among Nyerere's earliest publications, we recall, was a pamphlet entitled *Barriers to Democracy*. This was in the days when he was still trying to organize Tanganyikans to fight for greater democratization in the territory. Nyerere chose to appeal to his countrymen in Shakespearean terms.

Chief Obafemi Awolowo, the controversial founding father of the

[26] Nkrumah, *Ghana*, 107-108.
[27] This rendering is from the Penguin Classics' edition of *The Republic*, Book X ("The Effects of Poetry and Drama") (London, 1963), 383.
[28] Michael B. Foster, *Masters of Political Thought*, vol. I (London: George G. Harrap, 1961, reprint) 62.

Yoruba wing of Nigerian nationalism, has been specific in his acknowledgments. "Some of the mighty lines of Shakespeare must have influenced my outlook on life", Awolowo confided in his autobiography.[29]

For Nkrumah in his formative years it was not so much Shakespeare as Tennyson who gave an exciting expression to some longing of his. In 1934 Nkrumah applied to the Dean of Lincoln University for admission. As we have noted, in his application he quoted from Tennyson's *In Memoriam:*

> So many worlds, so much to do,
> So little done, such things to be.

In his autobiography Nkrumah said that this verse "was to me then, and it still is today, an inspiration and a spur. It fired within me a determination to equip myself for the service of my country."[30]

But it was not with Tennyson that Nkrumah opened and concluded the longest and "in some respects the most important speech" he made before independence. The speech was made on 12 November 1956. He was asking the National Assembly to approve his Government's Revised Constitutional Proposals for Gold Coast Independence. Nkrumah opened his speech with a reference to Edmund Burke's remark: "We are on a conspicuous stage and the world marks our demeanour." Nkrumah asserted: "Never has this been truer than today. How we conduct ourselves when we become independent will affect not only Ghana but the whole of Africa."[31]

He concluded his speech with Wordsworth's lines about the French revolution. Nkrumah said: "I hope that some day, somewhere, we also may be able to say with William Wordsworth:

> Bliss was it in that dawn to be alive,
> But to be young was very heaven!"[32]

As for the relationship between literature and political parties, it lies in the fact that the genesis of some of the African political parties was some literary or cultural organization in the early days of African political consciousness. Nkrumah's own party, the CPP, is not directly descended from a literary group, but Nkrumah's first exercise in organization on leaving school was in organizing the Nzima Literature So-

---

[29]   "Shakespeare is my favourite. I have read all his plays, and have re-read some of them – like *Julius Caesar, Hamlet, The Tempest, Anthony and Cleopatra* and *Henry V* – more than three times. Some of the mighty lines of Shakespeare must have influenced my outlook on life." See *Awo, The Autobiography of Chief Obafemi Awolowo* (Cambridge: Cambridge University Press, 1960), 70.

[30]   Nkrumah, *Ghana*, p. v.

[31]   Nkrumah, *Freedom*, 71.

[32]   Nkrumah, *Freedom*, 84. The italics are Nkrumah's.

ciety and other literary societies in the Axim area.[33]

Not all the literary groups which gave birth to political organizations were preoccupied with English literature as such. Sometimes the impact of Western culture gave rise to a new possessiveness about the local culture – and associations emerged to serve the interests of a tribal or linguistic heritage of some local group. Thomas Hodgkin reminds us that the Action Group in Nigeria was born out of a Yoruba cultural association, inspired and created by Awolowo. As for the Northern People's Congress, the biggest Nigerian party, it was, on attainment of independence, a recent offspring of a predominantly Hausa cultural society, the *Jami'a*.[34]

We might therefore conclude that, either directly or by kindling a new interest in local culture, English literature is part of the genesis of political consciousness in former British Africa. It afforded quotations for use in those early moments of aggressive African intellectualism. It inspired a paradoxical cultural nationalism among the original "scholars" of West African self-assertion. It afforded a new version of discourse by proverbs. It merged with the Bible and the poetry of Christian hymns to provide an additional stimulant to the emotional sensibilities of the new Africa. And it sometimes provided the rationale for an exercise in organization and oratorical wits in those early formative years of African nationalism.

But it is in the nature of nationalism to be sparing in its acknowledgment of foreign inspiration. If it be asked why nationalism should be so inhibited, the reply might best be given by the Rhodesian nationalist, Ndabaningi Sithole. His answer rests on the premise that nationalism has a strong component of sheer ambition – and his answer is directly Shakespearean. Why are the origins of African nationalism not acknowledged by the nationalists? Sithole quotes:

> But 'tis a common proof,
> That lowliness is young ambition's ladder,
> Whereto the climber upward turns his face;
> But when he once attains the upmost round,
> He then unto the ladder turns his back,
> Looks in the clouds, scorning the base degrees
> By which he did ascend.[35]

---

[33] "The Nzima Literature Society ... is still functioning today", Nkrumah tells us in his autobiography two decades after he formed it. See Nkrumah, *Ghana*, 21.
[34] See Hodgkin, *Nationalism in Colonial Africa* (London: Frederick Muller, 1956), esp. 154-155.
[35] *Julius Caesar*, II, 1. Quoted by Ndabaningi Sithole in his book *African Nationalism*, 57. We have referred to James Coleman's remark that in a colonial school "Shakespeare and the Bible held the stage". What Sithole was concerned with in this particular chapter was the influence of the Bible and the Church on the growth of African nationalism.

9

MEANING VERSUS IMAGERY IN AFRICAN POETRY

INTRODUCTION

In a short article written for the inaugural issue of the new literary magazine *Zuka* I argued that abstract verse of the kind written by some contemporary African poets was a fundamental departure from indigenous modes of poetic expression in Africa.[1] There have been reactions to that article since it was published, and there may be a case for taking the discussion a stage further here.

The word "abstract" is used here – as it was used in the original article – in a sense rather similar to the one it carries when we talk about abstract art at large. Abstract painting is differentiated from representational work. The abstract artist makes no attempt at closely imitating Nature, but feels free to achieve imprecise evocation by the sheer force of shapes and colour. In the case of abstract verse, words are put together to make beautiful pictures and patterns of imagery, but the arrangement of the words carries no special conversational meaning behind it.

Much of the late Christopher Okigbo's poetry was abstract verse in this sense. Okigbo's poem *Transition*, for example, is attractive but in a meaningless kind of way.

> Drop of dew on green bowl fostered
> on leaf green bowl grows under the lamp
> without flesh or colour;

[1] Ali A. Mazrui, "Abstract Verse and African Tradition", *Zuka* (Nairobi: Oxford University Press, 1967) 1 (1).

under the lamp into stream of
song, streamsong,
in flight into the infinite –
a blinded heron
thrown against the infinite –
where solitude
weaves her interminable mystery
under the lamp.
The moonman has gone under the sea:
the singer has gone under the shade.

And Rajat Neogy, the Editor of another *Transition,* has, as I indicated
elsewhere, powerful imagery in lines such as these:

Green biting on glass
red writing on walls
rock cemented with kisses
She was the woman of the stained thigh

Follow the quay
Where the urine hangs on the walls
The lizards are flying
She was the woman of the stained thigh [2]

This is good poetry. But it is not an attempt at being meaningful. It is
at best an achievement of being imageful. On the other hand, I would
argue that much of indigenous poetry in traditional African languages
is an art of meaning rather than an art of mere imagery. To the extent
that traditional African poetry is social, it is conversational. And for
two poets to have a conversation their poetry must transmit more than
just images. A high level of sophisticated communication presupposes
intelligibility. I would therefore maintain that there can be no meaningful conversation between abstract poets. At best there is only minimal
communication of the kind that a human being might find it possible
to have with his pet by making a few strategic noises. But a full conversation in poetry presupposes the making of evocative propositions,
the formulation of statements, addressed to both the mind and the
imagination.

LANGUAGE VERSES WORDS

Great abstract verse demands a gifted command of words but not necessarily of language. A command of language must include sophisticated conversational communication.

[2] *Transition* (Kampala) 3 (8) (March 1963), 29.

That is why abstract verse is not only excessively private; it is also linguistically parochial. In other words, abstract verse refuses completely to be translatable. Since nothing is being intelligibly said, how could one possibly even approximate translation? Word pictures are attached to the specific language used. They refuse to be brought out into the glare of universality and moved from one language to another. Okot p'Bitek could translate *Song of Lawino* into English from Acholi only because it was not a mere pattern of little pictures. And how could Julius Nyerere have conceivably translated Shakespeare's *Julius Caesar* into Swahili if all that Shakespeare had done was to arrange images beautifully? Of course no great poetry is completely translatable. But the measure of ultimate greatness is perhaps the capacity of the poem to have something of itself saved as it moves from the parochialism of its original language into the traumatic experience of being transported into another linguistic universe.

Much of the late Christopher Okigbo's poetry could not step out of the enclosed world of the English language without risking total disintegration. How could anyone translate the following words into Swahili and still retain whatever beauty they might have in the original English?

> The only way to go
> Through the marble archway
> To the catatonic ping pong
> Of the evanescent halo.

But here it is important to emphasize that the purpose of this article is not to argue against the writing of abstract verse. It is to argue simply against letting abstract verse ever be the dominant mode of poetry in Africa. A unilingual country like Britain or France might be able to afford the total untranslatability of its verse, but multilingual African countries cannot endure a situation in which the dominant mode of poetic expression relies so heavily on the unique images of a particular language that nothing can be saved when translated.

Nor is this simply a plea against obscurity in verse. One of the more obscure of the poets of this century was the French writer, Stéphane Mallarmé. The French themselves have apparently been known to comment that Mallarmé's language "is so peculiar that it can be understood only by foreigners".[3]

But there are different forms of obscurity. There is certainly a good deal of obscurity in some of the great epics of Swahili. Indeed, traditional African poets sometimes revelled in sophisticated verbal ob-

---

[3] Charles Norman (ed.), *Poets on Poetry* (New York: The Free Press, 1962), 338.

scurity. Enigmatic expressions, if properly handled, could be evidence of profundity. But in the case of such obscure expressions in Swahili poetry there was indeed such a thing as "the right meaning" of a given passage, and the task of the sophisticated reader was to discover what it was. It was possible for a reader to be wrong. But the obscurity of abstract verse gives too much sovereignty to the reader. "The reader can do no wrong." Virtually any interpretation is defensible. It is true, as T. S. Eliot once observed, that "a poem may be something larger than its author's conscious purpose . . . ." But in the case of an abstract poem, the author's purpose becomes virtually irrelevant. It is what the reader sees in it which decides what the poem signifies.

There are times when obscurity is not evidence of profundity but a substitute for it. In philosophy, Hegel is an interesting example. He is reported to have complained that "there was only one man who understood him, and he misunderstood him".[4]

More recently, Bertrand Russell has described Hegel's thought in the following terms:

Hegel's philosophy is so odd that one would not have expected him to be able to get sane men to accept it, but he did. He set it out with so much obscurity that people thought he must be profound.

Russell was being too severe. Hegel's obscurity was, on the whole, evidence of profundity rather than a substitute for it. But the distinction – however elusive – is worth noting in assessing both obscure philosophy and obscure poetry.

In poetry, another form of obscurity comes with a quest for sound effect. There are critics who are prepared to forgive much in a poet if it can be demonstrated that he is making music.

This kind of reasoning is profoundly unjust to the art of poetry at large. At best, poetry can but be a very poor imitation of music, if all it aspires to is sound effect. The business of the poet is not simply to try to approximate the work of a composer. Poetry is an autonomous art-form in its own right. And the poet need not be acclaimed simply because he has made a brave attempt to imitate a composer.

T. S. Eliot's earlier assessment of Milton's *Paradise Lost* does suggest that it takes more than great music to make good poetry. Eliot argues that Milton's blindness had tended to exaggerate the sensitivity of the ear at the expense of visual detail in his art. Only when Milton talks about a vast expanse of emptiness, or of cosmic visuality, does he attain inspired visual evocation. But for the detail of the eye there is

---

[4]   Cited by R. H. Murray, *Studies in the English Social and Political Thinkers of the 19th Century*, vol. 1 (Cambridge, 1929), 400.

little. And Milton makes up for this by a glorious response of the ear.

One need not agree with Eliot's assessment of Milton in order to accept the point that while musicality is a great adornment for poetry, and must as far as possible always accompany it, it can never be the essence of poetry. To make it so is to reduce poetry to a handmaiden of another art form altogether.

By the same token, we can argue that poetry can only be a poor imitation of visual art if all it seeks is pictorial representation. Beautiful word pictures, exciting patterns of images, do indeed have an aesthetic value. But they constitute an attempt to do what is perhaps best done on the canvas. Abstract verse at its most successful is then simply an imitation of visual art.

The essence of poetry must therefore be that which only verbal language can achieve – and that is the full sophisticated capacity for conversational communication, for making statements, for argument and rebuttal, for attempting to express a truth, for saying something meaningful, man to man.

AN AUTOCRITIQUE

To my article in *Zuka* I appended two very plain poems of my own. The idea was not to demonstrate poetic achievement but to demonstrate versified intelligibility. In the first poem, on deafness, I had this to say:

Deafness

There was an accident at Kilembe –
    He never heard another call.
He took his wage, and left Kilembe;
    And that was it; and that was all.

For a passing moment he did toy
    With the thought of a house career:
But then recalled the shout of 'Boy!'
    Was one he would not hear.

Perhaps the station would engage
    A porter as deaf as he –
When all the world's a miming stage
    What was his cue to be?

A herdsman's job was next in mind –
    But then he thought of cattle thieves:
He would not hear from behind
    The warning of rustling leaves.

There was more to living pain
Than the pure worker distressed.
In the throbbing of his brain
Was a memory suppressed.

Not the thunder would he miss
Nor the tune he once espoused.
It was the hungry nasal hiss –
The sigh of a woman aroused.

There is a plainness in the diction of this poem, partly influenced by Wordsworth's philosophy that "the language of Prose may yet well be adapted to Poetry ... [Indeed] it may safely be affirmed that there neither is, nor can be, any essential difference between the language of prose and metrical composition."[5]

A Nairobi newspaper published a criticism of my views on abstract verse. And the critic accused me of insensitivity to levels of meaning. His suggestion was that abstract verse allowed for variations in levels of meaning for the individual reader.[6]

My objection to abstract verse was not that it did not allow for levels of meaning – but that the number of levels was infinite and undirected. The arbitrary sovereignty of the reader was given unlimited scope. There was no level at all at which the language of poetry and the language of prose converged to give plain intelligibility.

Partly in the face of this criticism of my views, there might now be a case for me to indulge in an autocritique of the two poems which accompanied my original short article in *Zuka*. The poem *Deafness* definitely has a level of convergence in meaning between the language of prose and the language of poetry. This level is, by definition, self-evident. But I would like to demonstrate that the fact that there is this level of literal convergence of meaning need not exhaust the range of levels of interpretation. After the accident at Kilembe the man "took his wage and left Kilembe; / And that was it and that was all".

One level of meaning is that of social criticism in situations where workmen's compensation, insurance policies and safeguards are abysmally inadequate. But another level of meaning is that of finality. He had lost his power to hear. That was the fundamental fact about the accident. And for that there seemed to be no solution. It was it. It was all.

But now that he had lost his power of hearing what alternative job should he seek?

---

[5] "Preface to the Lyrical Ballads", in: *Poetical Works of Wordsworth*, Thomas Hutchinson (ed.) (London: Oxford University Press, 1936), 737.
[6] Ian J. Inglis under "Kazi Moto", *Sunday Nation* (Nairobi), November 26, 1967.

> For a passing moment he did toy
>   With the thought of a house career:
> But then recalled the shout of 'Boy'!
>   Was one he would not hear.

Why did he think of becoming a houseboy? Well, the "house" itself is a symbol of refuge. In moments of crisis, after having worked in a mine, there is a temptation to go home, now that the worst has happened. But a job is still needed. The only kind of job with the comfort of domesticity is that of a houseboy.

Secondly, this is a job with a master/servant relationship. Again, at its best, a master/servant relationship or patron/beneficiary relationship has achieved high levels of personal protectiveness. Even the domestic slave has found a sense of insurance within the home. It makes sense therefore that the man from Kilembe mines should instinctively think first, if only for a passing moment, of the refuge of a house, the comfort of having a master.

But when he gives up that idea, he thinks of a job much less personal. Instead of master/servant, this one is employer/employee, and often at the height of impersonality.

> Perhaps the station would engage
>   A porter as deaf as he –
> When all the world's a miming stage
>   What was his cue to be?

The third kind of occupation he thinks of is that of a herdsman. This need not be a master/servant or even employer/employee relationship, but could demand a good deal of autonomy as one tends the herd, often in the midst of the wide expanse of natural openness. Moreover, being a herdsman does provide comfort in a different direction from that of the protection of a master. In the first case, the man from Kilembe mines needed to be reassured by the warmth of someone protecting him, even if that someone was also dominating him. But were he instead to look after animals, he himself would now become the protector. He would attain self-confidence, not by having a person over him, but by having creatures under him for whom he would have responsibility.

> A herdman's job was next in mind –
>   But then he thought of cattle thieves:
> He would not hear from behind,
>   The warning of rustling leaves.

But this very idea fuses with the notion of a lingering honesty. He thinks of being a herdsman and he thinks of cattle-thieves. But he does not consider himself a cattle-thief, though that is certainly one possible occupation he might have speculated on taking up. The man is deaf. In a significant sense, his physical personality has been drastically changed. But his moral personality has survived the shock. He thinks of cattle-thieves as "they". He could only place himself as a potential herdsman, and not as a potential raider.

> But there was more to living pain
> Than the pure worker distressed.
> In the throbbing of his brain
> Was a memory suppressed.
>
> Not the thunder would he miss
> Nor the tune he once espoused;
> It was the hungry nasal hiss –
> The sigh of a woman aroused.

In the last four lines are compressed a variety of sounds. The thunder – very obvious, loud and God-made. The tune he once espoused – it might in its own way also be obvious and loud, but it is man-made; perhaps a piece of music composed by someone. "The hungry nasal hiss, the sigh of a woman aroused" – this was perhaps at once God-made and man-made. God-made in being a spontaneous physiological reaction in the very being of the woman. Yet also man-made perhaps because it is man-caused – by his touch or lingering caress, or profound verbal suggestion.

The second of the two illustrative poems which accompanied my article in *Zuka* was the following:

The Bed and the Mirror

> All the shadows that night
> Failed to hide that sight
> Of her body, all white,
> As I touched her.
>
> I emerged from my gown
> And she sensed I was brown
> As I pulled her down
> To embrace her.
>
> Through the curtains moonlight
> Came, and the mirror to the right
> Reflected with delight
> As I held her.
>
> Yes, I did: Yes, I saw!
> I saw all – and saw!
> And manhood was my Law
> When I saw her.

This second poem is a useful foil to the first. The first poem was about a great absence of sounds – *deafness*. This second poem emphasizes a great presence of visuality. The "shadows" are being frustrated in their endeavour to cast a blanket of modest darkness over her body. Her body was, in any case, white against the background of the colour of the night. The body of her partner was of a darker hue – and so she sensed he was brown rather than saw him as such. But then compulsive visibility reasserts itself as moonlight defies the curtains and invades the sanctuary of the bedroom in sheer aggressive inquisitiveness. And what is more, this is a case of double revelation – for the mirror, by reflecting reality, adds vision to vision, and delights in doing so.

The final stanza asserts the ultimate supremacy of sight and its control over the man's will in moments of this kind: "Yes, I did: Yes, I saw! / I saw all – and saw! / And manhood was my Law / When I saw her."

The very juxtaposition between the first poem about an absence of sound and the second poem about an omnipresence of sight requires for its effect a sensitivity to levels of meaning. The fact that the two poems have one level which is a literal convergence of meaning between the language of prose and the language of poetry, does not deprive them of other interpretative dimensions.

CONCLUSION

Tradition has it that when Robert Browning was once asked about the meaning of one of his poems, his answer was: "When I wrote the lines only God and Robert Browning knew what they meant. Now only God knows."[7] His poetry is at times quite obscure. But it would never have made sense to ask him such a question if he had been an abstract poet. His obscurity – like the obscurity of the more profound Swahili poets – still presupposed a level of original intelligibility which even the poet himself could be called upon to rediscover.

The bulk of African poetry in this modern phase must continue to have such a level. This is not to suggest that African poetry is the poorer for having had Christopher Okigbo. On the contrary, he remains one of the most gifted poets modern Africa has produced. But, to put it bluntly, Africa cannot afford too many Okigbos. She cannot afford too many versifiers the bulk of whose poems are untranslatable, and whose genius lies in imagery and music rather than conversational meaning. Of course there will be attempts at "translating" Okigbo, but

[7]   One reference to this tradition occurs in Robert H. Murray's book *Studies in the English Social & Political Thinkers of the Nineteenth Century*, vol. 1.

for much of his work the exercise is futile and perhaps basically dishonest. Meaning can be translated, but imagery can only at best be imitated.

Christopher Okigbo has served African literature well. But one can only hope he does not produce too many imitators after him. His was the kind of genius which must remain fundamentally a luxury. A limited amount of it is deeply satisfying and is a great adornment to culture. A massive outpouring of this particular kind of genius could, however, destroy a literary civilization.

10

DRAMATIC DISCOURSE AND THE DIALOGUE
OF POLITICS

The most important single characteristic shared between dramatic art
and political activity lies in the concept of *conflict*. Politics has often
been defined as a constant search for methods of resolving conflicting
interests. When politics was described as a struggle to determine "who
gets what when and how", conflict was placed at the very heart of
political activity in terms of *inputs of demands*, which are processed
within a political system, some of which then emerge as outputs of
policies and services. The demands themselves are inevitably in a tense
relationship of competitiveness, even when they are pulling in the same
direction. The political goods which generate such a scramble may vary
from the issue of where a particular new factory should be situated to
questions of sharing power *per se*.

Drama, too, derives its ultimate animation from the idea of conflict
at work. The conflict may be between people, or between men and
gods, or between great ideas effectively represented on the stage. Great
drama manipulates the emotions of the audience, sometimes in a highly
partisan way, as when the audience knows which side in the conflict it
would like to see victorious. But even greater effect is sometimes
achieved by manipulating the emotions of the audience in a manner
which introduces conflict in those very emotions themselves. The spec-
tator becomes involved in what is happening on the stage, but involved
in a manner where loyalties are ambivalent and sympathy has a tight

This chapter was originally presented as a paper at the International Conference on Cultural Diversity and National Understanding within West African
Countries, held at the University of Ife, in December 1970. I am indebted to
my wife, Molly, for her co-authorship of this paper.

grip on hostility, a breathless deadlock of the passions. Conflict in such situations activates both the action on the stage and the inner response of the onlooker.

When the issues being thrashed out on the stage are big, and there is a human toll exacted in the resolution of those conflicts, the setting is ready for tragedy. High conflict which is resolved on a note of high price in terms of human casualties, provides the playwright with the raw material for tragic drama. For example, great issues of filial love in conflict with great issues of ambition and greed, erupting into grotesque acts of cruelty, provide the setting for Shakespeare's *King Lear*. And in *Hamlet* we have a psychological tragedy – the tragedy of indecision, arising out of conflicting pulls in Hamlet's own mind as suspicion grapples with loyalty. Hamlet had the weakness of intellectual circumspection, tossing up pros and cons, working out an ethical balance sheet before a decision was made. Swift action could have ended his uncle's life quite early, and perhaps even resulted in Hamlet's own death – without necessarily expanding the boundaries of the human toll. By the time Hamlet acquired the necessary decisiveness for action, he had become too impulsive. Polonius behind the curtains did not deserve to die.

But it is not simply in relation to tragic drama that conflict is a relevant animating factor. Even for comic presentation conflict is central. What differentiates tragedy from comedy is not the presence or absence of conflict but the nature of that conflict and its treatment by the playwright. Almost any kind of quarrel can be treated either tragically or comically, and yet certain types of quarrels lend themselves more easily to one kind of treatment than to the other. If what is at stake is trivial, like two romantic rivals scrambling to restore to its owner a handkerchief which their ladylove has dropped, there is potentiality here for relatively conventional comic treatment. It is still possible for a playwright to convert this entire exercise into acute tragic symbolism – but the skills needed to make trivial conflict tragic are greater than those which would be called for to bring out the comic nature of the triviality.

DRAMATIC DIALOGUE AND POLITICAL SCIENCE

A related characteristic shared between politics and drama is *dialogue*. In politics, dialogue is the mechanism by which compromises are sought and the limits of accommodation are defined. When dialogue between contending parties stops altogether, political activity dries up. They may resort to guns or spears. But the very resort to violent weaponry would be an indication that politics as a dialogue to seek areas of compromise has failed.

In drama, dialogue serves a different purpose. It helps to define the plot, completes the picture of experience as it fills in the gaps left by the action on the stage, provides the means of bringing out the characterization, furnishes the framework for human interaction among the personalities in the play, and helps to bring out the issues at stake. Very often, a dialogue requires the presence of more than one person to articulate different positions, but the presence of a second person is not a defining characteristic of a dialogue. A character can be having a dialogue with himself, if there is a conflict of values or argument which he is trying to resolve by articulating both positions. A soliloquy by a character like Hamlet, torn internally by conflicting interpretations of the reality surrounding him, is a dialogue going on within the mind of a single character.

In the history of political science, dialogue constitutes part of the genesis of the scientific method itself. Political science over the centuries has been struggling to achieve scientificity, in the sense of minimizing the bias of individual values and norms in the study of political behaviour. Can the study of human beings interacting with each other in politics ever be as scientific as the study of the human body within the biological sciences? The answer has yet to be finally resolved, though the term political *science* has been gaining increasing acceptance, at least as a label for the discipline.

A major presumption behind the scientific method has sometimes been a free interplay among competing interpretations of reality. Truth is arrived at if a hypothesis is verifiable or falsifiable; and the verifiability of a proposition depends in part on the possibility of triumphing over an alternative or rival proposition.

The scientific method has therefore often been regarded to include within it a residual critical scepticism. There has to be a recognition that a Newtonian paradigm could conceivably one day be replaced by an alternative paradigm from an Einstein.

Propositions in science must therefore at least be exposed to constant testing and potential challenges. It is out of this assumption that the concept of dialogue derives its status within the scientific method.

In the study of politics its earliest form was the Socratic method, with its attempt to arrive at the truth through a purposeful interaction between questions and answers. In political literature the most important beginning came with Plato's *Dialogues*, as Plato utilized the Socratic method to reveal the implications of different interpretations of the political and moral world.

In its original formulation the Socratic method was not value-free, though it did attempt to reveal the implications of different interpretations. The questions series in the Socratic method consisted of posing the sort of questions which would lead to a predetermined kind of answer, but in a manner designed to involve both the questioner and the person who was providing the answer in the reasoning. In fact the questions come not from the person who does not know, seeking information from the knowledgeable, but from the person who knows, guiding the reasoning of the ignorant. Plato writes his *Dialogues*, sometimes having as the central character Socrates, his own teacher. Socrates asked his disciples the sort of questions which the disciples could, in their very answers, gradually be led into resolving.

Socrates: Come then, and let us pass a leisure hour in story telling, and our story shall be the education of our heroes.
Adeimantus: By all means.
Socrates: And what shall be their education? Can we find a better than the traditional sort? And this has two divisions, gymnastic for the body, and music for the soul.
Adeimantus: True.
. . . . . .
Socrates: And when you speak of music, do you include literature or not?
Adeimantus: I do.
Socrates: And literature might be either true or false?
Adeimantus: Yes.
Socrates: And the young should be trained in both kinds and we begin with the false?
Adeimantus: I do not understand your meaning.
Socrates: You know, I said, that we might begin by telling children stories which, though not wholly destitute of truth, are in the main fictitious. . . . You know also that the beginning is the most important part of any work, especially in the case of a young and tender thing; for that is the time at which the character is being formed and the desired impression is most readily taken.
Adeimantus: Quite true.
Socrates: And shall we just carelessly allow children to hear any casual tales which may be devised by casual persons, and to receive into their minds ideas for the most part the very opposite of those which we should wish them to have when they are grown up?
Adeimantus: We cannot.
Socrates: Then the first thing will be to establish a censorship of the writers of fiction, and let the censors receive any tale of fiction which is good, and reject the bad; and we will desire mothers and nurses to tell the children the authorised ones only. Let them fashion the mind with such tales, even more fondly than they mould the body with their hands; but most of those which are now in use must be discarded.

Adeimantus: Of what tales are you speaking?

Socrates: You may find a model of the lesser in the greater; for they are necessarily of the same type, and there is the same spirit in both of them.

Adeimantus: Very likely; but I do not as yet know what you would term the greater.

Socrates: Those which are narrated by Homer and Hesiod, and the rest of the poets, who have been the great story tellers of mankind.

Adeimantus: But which stories do you mean; and what fault do you find with them?

Socrates: A fault which is most serious, the fault of telling a lie, and, what is more, a bad lie.

Adeimantus: But when is this fault committed?

Socrates: Whenever an erroneous representation is made of the nature of gods and heroes. . . .

It is quite clear here that Socrates is being used by Plato from the start to make the case for censorship. Plato was himself a poet and an admirer of the poetic gift. Yet, as we have mentioned, he distrusted the influence of poetry. The poet was a manipulator of emotions, and his craft of manipulation had therefore to be subject to state control. In discussing education, Plato therefore makes Socrates ask the kind of questions which are already biased in the direction of censorship. But the great drama here is of participation in the reasoning between Socrates and his disciples.

Sometimes a simple point is placed in a dialogue of high confidentiality, suggesting the drama of startling revelation.

Socrates: Of the many excellencies which I perceive in the order of our State, there is none which upon reflection pleases me better than the rule about poetry.

Disciple: To what do you refer?

Socrates: To the rejection of imitative poetry; which certainly ought not to be received; as I see far more clearly now that the parts of the soul have been distinguished.

Disciple: What do you mean?

Socrates: Speaking in confidence, for I should not like to have my words repeated to the tragedians and the rest of the imitative tribe – but I do not mind saying to you, that all poetical imitations are ruinous to the understanding of the hearers, and that the knowledge of their true nature is the only antidote to them.

Disciple: Explain the purport of your remark.

Socrates: Well, I will tell you, although I have always from my earliest youth had an awe and love of Homer, which even now makes the words falter on my lips for he is the great captain and teacher of the whole of that charming tragic company, but a man is not to be reverenced more than the truth, therefore I will speak out.

Disciple: Very good.
Socrates: Listen to me then, or rather, answer me.[1]

The imperative "Listen to me then, or rather, answer me" catches the essence of this kind of dialogue. The distinction between being merely a listener to the great sage or answering his questions so that you may learn is blurred. The teacher poses questions as a technique of teaching. The dialogue is indeed part of the scientific method; but in the hands of Plato it is itself used as a skill of dramatized philosophy.

Notwithstanding all this, there is in the Greek notion of the dialectic a special approach to the quest of determining the truth. In Greek terms, the dialectic is indeed the dialogue. It consists of one proposition clashing with a contrary proposition, each partially true, and both adding up to a synthesis which merges the two half truths. The dialectic under Hegel later came to take a different meaning, and it took on a third meaning still under Marx and his successors. But in its inception the dialectic was inseparable from the dialogue, an interaction of ideas revealing in their very conflict new insights on the highroad towards broader human understanding.

Yet it is not simply by bequeathing the Socratic method to education that Plato contributed to scientific approaches. It is also in his capacity to build models and define logical utopias. Plato's republic itself is an ideal world constructed not as an unattainable set of legal prohibitions, but as a paradigm for assessing the implications of human institutions and testing the validity of human aims.[2]

Again, there are in this notion of a utopia some of the elements of drama in Plato's approach to political analysis. Plato lets the imagination go, and develops a set of structures, creating new conditions for human interplay. Both the technique of the dialogue, and the technique of an imaginative utopia have helped to give Plato's approach to political analysis elements of high drama.

THE ACTOR AND THE ORATOR

From dialogue as a shared characteristic of politics and drama we move on to oratory. R. S. Crane put the issue in the following terms when discussing the place of platform skills for drama:

... the whole art of the drama, for the critics who thus take the satisfaction

---

[1] These exchanges are taken from Book 2 and Book 10 respectively of Plato's *Republic*.

[2] This point is also discussed, but in a different context, in Irene Samuel, *Plato and Milton* (Ithaca, N.Y.: Cornell University Press [first published 1947], 1968 edition), 60-62.

of the audience as a first principle rather than merely as a necessary condition of dramatic production, inevitably assumes the character of a kind of rhetoric (the dramatic poet's occupation, said Schlegel, "coincides with that of the orator") all the special problems involved in the making of plays being assimilated to the central problem of how "as promptly as possible to win the attention of the audience" and how "to hold that interest steady, or better, to increase it till the final curtain falls".[3]

Dialogue on the stage is verbal interaction between the characters themselves, whereas oratory from the stage is verbal interaction between the characters, on one side, and the audience, on the other. The critical importance of an audience is present both in politics and in drama. It was Francisque Sarcey who wrote in 1876:

It is an indisputable fact that a dramatic work, whatever it may be, is designed to be listened to by a number of persons united and forming an audience . . . no audience, no play. The audience is the necessary and inevitable condition to which dramatic art must accommodate its means. I emphasise this point because it is the point of departure, because from this simple fact we can derive all the laws of the theatre without a single exception.[4]

Oratory is a less central aspect of politics than it is of drama. There is a lot of politics going on which does not seek the attention of an audience. On the contrary, there may be a good deal of politics which is strictly under the counter, or behind closed doors, as intrigue, bargaining and plotting take place. But there is a side of politics which is, of necessity, public. Indeed, a politician's career is sometimes described as "public life" because of areas of exposure to the attention of the public and to public scrutiny. Within that part of politics which is concerned with direct interaction between politicians or leaders and their followers, oratory and skills of articulation and persuasion assume importance.

The crowd or rally sometimes has a behaviour of its own, almost a mind of its own. In his book entitled *Power*, Bertrand Russell discussed the power derived from the capacity to skilfully manipulate a crowd. He drew attention to the phenomenon of collective excitement. In an enthusiastic public meeting there could be exultation, combined with warmth and safety if the members of the crowd shared a mood. Russell described collective excitement as "a delicious intoxication, in which sanity, humanity, and even self-preservation are easily forgotten, and in which atrocious massacres and heroic martyrdom are equally possible".

[3] R. S. Crane, "Varieties of Dramatic Criticism", in: *The Idea of the Humanities* (Chicago and London: University of Chicago Press, 1967), 231.
[4] Cited by Crane, "Varieties".

This kind of excitement need not be evoked by any specific leader, it could conceivably occur as a result of the crowd witnessing a particular event. But the words of an orator are the easiest and most prevalent means of inducing it. If a leader has the power to arouse collective excitement over an issue, this is an important asset in the great gamble of politics. Russell pointed out that the leader need not share in the feelings which he arouses; he may say to himself, like Shakespeare's Antony after his devastating speech following the assassination of Caesar: "Now let it work; mischief thou are afoot, take thou what course thou wilt!"

On the public platform it may be necessary to act a part, as Mark Antony acted. The leader has sometimes to work himself into some form of excitement in the delivery of his speech, if the spell on his audience is to take effect. The orator then becomes an actor, just as every actor on the stage has to be an orator.

Sometimes what is at stake is the art of repeating something for the fiftieth time and still managing to say it with excited spontaneity. Again it is an art form necessary both for the actor on the stage, repeating his lines after long hours of memorization and indeed after several performances, and the travelling public speaker on an election campaign who repeats his speech from one whistle stop to another without betraying the agonizing boredom behind the utterance.

Both politics and drama are, therefore, fundamentally public exercises. Other forms of art may be profoundly individualistic, as the artists seek to express their inner selves without direct response to their assumed demands from the public. But with drama it is different. In the words of William Archer:

The art of theatrical story-telling is necessarily relative to the audience to whom the story is being told. One must assume an audience of a certain status and characteristics before one can rationally discuss the best methods of appealing to his intelligence and sympathies. . . . The painter may paint, the sculptor may model, the lyric poet may sing, simply to please himself, but the drama has no meaning except in relation to an audience. It is a portrayal of life by means of a mechanism so devised as to bring it home to a considerable number of people assembled in a given place.[5]

PRIVATE ANGUISH AND PUBLIC RESPONSE

But here an important difference has to be noted in African conditions as between the power of the speech of the orator and the effect of

[5] Cited by Crane, "Varieties". The quotations from Bertrand Russell are drawn from Russell, *Power* (London: Unwin Books, [first published 1938], 1962 edition), 19-21.

theatrical representation. When it comes to the more solemn emotions – pity, anger, depression – African audiences are moved more easily by speech-makers than by actors. On this hinges the whole problem of presenting tragedy in such a way to an African audience that the audience does not laugh at moments of high drama. In a report about the early experimental days of the Travelling Theatre in East Africa in 1966, David Cook discussed the preparations which the Travelling Theatre made before setting out, including psychological preparation. The troupe discussed this whole phenomenon of *laughter* in Africa. But in spite of this attempted psychological readiness, the actors were very often put out when dramatic passages "were dissected by laughter". David Cook has his own theory to explain this phenomenon:

East African audiences (and probably any audience not elaborately con- ditioned) laughs not only at things we recognise as "funny", but also whenever it is surprised especially if the surprise is under emotional tension. People also laugh when they are shocked, even when the shock has been carefully prepared for. We all know that a comic fulfilment causes us to laugh even when we foresee what is going to happen; but an expected tragic fulfilment may also demand a release which comes out as "laughter"; at a tragic death, for instance. A writer needs to allow for this by pauses and a sequence of action which enables the actor to quieten his excited hearers before they must hear more words.

Cook refers to an incident in their presentation of Tom Omara's *The Exodus*. The play was a major success, but the actors had to shout the audience down at certain points of high drama.

Interesting examples of unexpected laughter came in the middle of long speeches where producer and actor had decided on a sudden dramatic change of tempo; at several such moments every single audience laughed, though we had not foreseen such a reaction in rehearsal.[6]

In fact, this kind of response is by no means peculiar to East African audiences. In April 1970 I had occasion to visit Ghana, and had ex- tensive discussions with some colleagues there on precisely this phe- nomenon. Apparently even university audiences at Legon burst into laughter in moments of high drama. But the sector of the audience which would respond in this way at Legon was usually the student sector, resembling in its spontaneity some of the audiences which David Cook's Travelling Theatre entertained in East Africa.

There are occasions when the precise form of tragedy represented on the stage might well have had a good deal to do with the particular re-

[6] David Cook, "Theatre Goes to the People!", *Transition*, (Kampala), 25 (1966), 31-32.

sponse evoked. For example, *King Lear* has been known to provoke outbursts of laughter, precisely in relation to the torment of lunacy.

As a form of tragedy lunacy does, as it happens, lie on the borderline between the domain of pity and the domain of amusement. Indeed, it was not so long ago that, as lunatics in cages were being transported through the streets of London, they provided entertainment to the pedestrian public. A man talking aloud to himself in great agitation is betraying a mental imbalance deserving compassion; and yet the mere incongruity of agitated discourse without an audience can provoke amusement. Lunacy, therefore, as a form of tragedy, engulfing Lear, or Ophelia in *Hamlet* has tended to carry all the potentialities of provoking hilarious response from African audiences.

Another form of tragedy which lies on the borderline between the domain of pity and the domain of amusement is sexual impotence. J. P. Clark treats this phenomenon in *Song of a Goat*, and, at the performance of this play in Accra, once again the actors had to confront outbursts of bawdy laughter. It is clear that impotence of this kind reduces an individual's range of experience tragically; and yet it is equally clear that of such stuff jokes are made.

But while there are specialized reasons why African audiences laugh at particular kinds of tragedy, there is evidence to show that tragic drama at large represented on the stage has tended to command amused and even hilarious enjoyment, rather than tense solemnity and inner disturbance.

But put the same African audience in front of a gifted public orator, discoursing on a tragic or otherwise emotive theme, and the impact is transformed into one of earnestness rather than amused reactivation. In the earlier days of nationalistic agitation Nkrumah did sometimes succeed in moving his audiences almost to tears. More often, he succeeded in arousing earnest enthusiasm for specific causes, and occasionally passionate indignation. When he actually broke loose from the Gold Coast Convention, and was urged at a public rally to lead his followers and admirers in a new party, a prophetic sense of destiny seemed almost to descend upon the rally. And, as we will recall, when the crowds burst out with the hymn "Lead, kindly Light" Nkrumah's eyes moistened as he reached for his handkerchief; and many in the audience cried.

The history of African politics in different African countries includes other instances of crowds deeply moved at public rallies. The orator has been able to move the more solemn emotions; if circumstances conspired to help him. But the actor on the stage has had a tougher time in inducing solemnity of response.

In December 1963, Kampala reverberated with the news of a notorious party held in an area known locally as Tank Hill. The party was held on the eve of Kenya's independence. Those attending the party were predominantly European expatriates. It was reported that the occasion was utilized to ridicule and satirize the whole idea of African independence. Games and mimicry, allegedly designed to make fun of the "premature" granting of self-government to African countries, were part of the evening festivities. The party was also a lament for the last days of Empire, and a nostalgic cry for the older days of European supremacy.

Milton Obote, then Prime Minister of Uganda, became aware of these activities, and decided to address Parliament. He succeeded in contriving a sense of drama in the House as he related the events of that evening. He spoke in terms which were deliberately calculated to arouse anger against those who had held the party. With dramatic effect he produced exhibits from the party, robes and garments used for effect within the satire. Obote's own performance in the House succeeded in intimating that the merry-makers on Tank Hill had indulged in ritualistic arrogance and wanton presumption in an African country.

This dramatization in the National Assembly did have an impact. Dr. Obote succeeded in arousing the fury of fellow parliamentarians. There were cries for revenge and retribution against those arrogant merry-makers. There have been few occasions when an African parliament has ever been as angry. The House reverberated with the passion of wounded dignity. Never was an evening party a more momentous national issue.

Obote succeeded in relation to his audience within the House. Would he succeed in arousing the country as a whole? There were indeed repercussions in the country, as might have been expected. The house in which the party took place was set on fire. A member of the editorial staff of a leading English language newspaper, the *Uganda Argus* was "kidnapped" by members of the Youth Wing of the ruling party, and subjected to minor forms of humiliation, like carrying a bunch of *matoke* (local plantain used as a staple food by the Baganda). It is likely that a similar speech made in the Parliament in Nairobi by Kenyatta would have had more widespread consequences, endangering to some extent members of the white community not immediately involved in such a party. It was the kind of speech which, in an inflammable racial situation, could lead to riots in the streets. But it was clear in Uganda that Ugandans were not that easily mobilizable by a single dramatic speech in Parliament. They were significantly less mobilizable in this respect than either Kenyans or Tanzanians. As an audience for the drama in Parliament, Ugandans were, therefore, not to be counted as highly responsive.

But within the more limited scale of the four walls of the House of Parliament in Kampala, Obote's dramatization of the Tank Hill party was masterly in its effect. It could have been the envy of the Makerere Travelling Theatre, which has had a tougher time trying to manipulate the more solemn emotions among rural audiences in Uganda.[7]

But do African audiences respond differently to tragedy on the cinema screen than to tragedy on the live stage? There is some evidence that African school-children in East Africa were *not* moved to laugh at Olivier's *Hamlet* when they saw it on the screen. The same kind of audiences have found it harder to be "disciplined" when Shakespeare has been produced live. Was the difference due to the quality of the acting or did it lie in the medium?

It may well be that in order to engage the emotions of ordinary African audiences, tragedy must be either indisputably real or indisputably artificial. The cinema is indisputably artificial; the live politician is indisputably real. But a group of actors on a live stage are caught in between. They are not larger than life (like a close-up on the screen) nor are they life itself, like a political rally in Africa. It is, perhaps, this ambivalence of theatrical tragedy which ultimately explains the laughing audiences it has encountered.[8]

ON POLITICAL DRAMA

We have so far discussed some of the elements which politics and drama

---

[7] The incident of the Tank Hill party is discussed in relation to questions of leadership in Ali A. Mazrui, "Leadership in Africa: Obote of Uganda", *International Journal* XXV (3) (1970).

[8] On this issue of ambivalence we are indebted for stimulation to Mrs. Anna Gourlay, Secretary to Ali Mazrui, at the time of writing. An alternative view is advanced by an editorial colleague at the Makerere Institute of Social Research (also a woman) whose reactions were as follows:

I happen to think the cinema is much more real than the stage. In films, scenery is more life-like, and the audience can see even minute facial nuances of the actors. Also, with such a big screen, you are completely engulfed by the film (provided the acting is good, of course). On the other hand, in a theatre, especially a large one, the stage is such a small part of the total environment, you are more often aware of where you are (i.e., sitting in a theatre), even in the middle of the proceedings on the stage. In addition, it is more difficult to hear the actors' words in a theatre than at a cinema. And, finally, stage actors, in order to project, must often exaggerate some words or sounds, and this helps to remind the viewer that he is viewing "actors", not real characters.

For these reasons, I would either omit or revise the last paragraph.
P.S. I cry much more often at films than at stage theatres! – perhaps further proof of which is more realistic?

share. In conclusion, let us take a look at a specific type of drama, namely, *political drama* itself.

The range of political drama is wide but, for convenience, it may be divided into four broad categories. These are, first, didactic plays; second, nationalistic plays; third, plays of social commentary; and fourthly, plays of social protest. Political drama which is primarily didactic is that which is specifically intended to teach people their civic duty. In countries where art is subject to governmental control, didacticism in drama is particularly prevalent. Nationalistic plays tend to idealize national qualities or romanticize a nation's past, sometimes combined with a moral judgement upon the enemies of the nation. Often such a play would evolve around the life of a national hero or be based on an epoch of national achievement. "Negritude" plays would fit into this category. The third category of plays encompasses those which serve as a commentary on political events in a country. Such plays need not be specially critical of society or didactic towards the citizen; they simply use political life as material for drama. Finally, there is the drama of social protest, sharply censorious of prevailing conditions, often implying a commitment to social reform. While didactic plays preach to citizens, plays of social protest preach to society.

The elements of the different categories of political drama may, of course, be combined in one play. *La Mort de Chaka* by Badian comes to mind as an example of this.

A further point to bear in mind is that a play may have a political framework and yet not, itself, be a political drama. *Antigone*, by Jean Anouilh, is one example. The reverse is also true, political drama may be found within a non-political framework, as in Soyinka's play *A Dance of the Forest*.

The historical theme as the basic framework for a play has appealed to many playwrights of all nationalities and all ages. The historical theme may be used to illustrate the glories of the past (glories perhaps denied by colonial rulers in Africa, for example), and thus instil pride into the present generation, and perhaps facilitate the task of nation-building. But great historical drama also contains within it both a commentary on certain universal values and a commentary on contemporary events, which may include criticism and warning.

We discussed earlier the centrality of conflict in both politics and drama. Ndao's *L'Exil d'Albouri* shows the problems faced from within and without by an African king confronted with colonialism. Here indeed is conflict at different levels. There is conflict between the King and the Prince, Laobe Penda, over the correct course of action to be taken when faced with the superior armed might of the colonial invader. The Prince seems over-anxious to preserve the throne, whatever the cost. There is conflict between the King's sister and his wife, the Queen, over their respective interpretation of the role of a royal woman. There is conflict within the Prince himself, under pressure from the Diarafs, as to how best to preserve the throne – by battle or by treaty. There is conflict between the supporters of the King and the supporters of the Prince. And within the characters themselves there is conflict between the motives which form the mainsprings of their action, often self-preservation, and what they know to be in the nation's interest. The King, for example, seems to put the nation first; the Diaraf de Thingue is concerned only with saving himself and his material possessions; the Prince and the other Diarafs and Ardo are themselves motivated by a mixture of loyalty, emotions and desires.

In a brief preface to the play, the author, Cheik Ndao tells us that he has used history in a literary manner to illustrate and interpret some of the noteworthy elements in the African past in order to encourage the present generation to strive towards greater things and to be worthy of their past.

Badian's *La Mort de Chaka* and Dervain's *La Reine Scelerate* also use historical themes but have also, more implicitly, a more modern theme than we find in *L'Exil d'Albouri*. Robert Bolt's *A Man for All Seasons* is a political play even within its own historical setting, and yet no one watching that play today could ever imagine that Bolt merely intended to write a historical play as a record of the past. The play's contemporary relevance is so striking.

In his introduction to his English translation of Badian's *La Mort de Chaka* Clive Wake makes the point that he believes Badian himself had Kwame Nkrumah in mind when he was creating the character of Chaka within his play:

Badian wrote his play in the post-independence period, and it reflects the common preoccupation at this time with two major inter-related problems: the need to create national unity once political freedom had been obtained, and the role of the all-powerful almost messianic leader. In Badian's play, Chaka's violent methods of uniting the Zulu and of absorbing the conquered tribes are condoned by his supporters on the grounds of their necessity. Badian wrote his play at a time when Nkrumah's rule of Ghana and his status as national and pan-African leader were already the centre of considerable controversy. It seems obvious that Badian had Nkrumah in mind when he wrote his play since no other contemporary African leader has had quite the same charismatic appeal that would allow him to be equated with Chaka. One cannot help reading the play on two closely related levels: historical and modern.

In 1970 an essay on Badian's play was assigned to a group of eighteen students at Makerere University. They had a choice of three subjects.

In some ways, the most difficult of the three asked for their comments on the comparison made by Wake between Chaka and Nkrumah, and yet eighty per cent chose to tackle this subject – another instance of the fascination of the past as a compelling foil to the present.

CONCLUSION

The future of political drama in Africa seems well assured. So indeed is the future of both politics and drama at large. This is a continent at once highly politicized and potentially responsive to the arts of make-believe. Those elements which politics as an activity shares with the theatre as an art-form seem, at times, to be at their most inflated in Africa. The agonies of *conflict*, the ancestral tradition of palaver and dialogue, the skills of persuasion and oratory, the interplay between laughter and pain, the soft integration between faith and acceptance, the eternal interaction between reality and make-believe – in these elements we have the dynamics of both politics and drama. But in the ultimate analysis they seem even larger than life on the stage of Africa's own experience.

11

THE IMPACT OF ENGLISH ON AFRICAN
INTERNATIONAL RELATIONS

"I myself am a product of French culture, but we also look to the United States for help." This statement was made by President François Tombalbaye of Chad early in 1966.[1] The President seemed to be suggesting that his cultural background had to be conquered before he could comfortably turn to the United States. How important a factor is the cultural background of African countries in shaping their international relations?

This question is part of the broad theoretical context of this chapter. But this chapter selects one single aspect of culture in Africa – one particular metropolitan language inherited from a former colonial power. In some cases it becomes artificial to isolate language from the total cultural impact of the colonial power. However, language is so central to culture that even this isolation is defensible in spite of its artificiality. One cannot adequately learn about French culture, for example, through the medium of Hindi or Arabic. Complete access to French culture must itself be through the French language. The ways of thought of a people are inseparable from the language they use. A whole complex of attitudes and ideological orientations might be influenced, modified, or sometimes transformed by the impact of a given language.

The first inter-continental role that the English language played in African affairs in this century was perhaps the role of making Pan-Negroism possible. We have defined Pan-Negroism as that movement,

I am again indebted to my wife, Molly, for her co-authorship.
[1] See Drew Middleton, "Chad's Ties Bind; They Also Pinch: Traditions are French but Need is U.S. Assistance", *New York Times*, April 19, 1966.

ideology or collection of attitudes which is primarily concerned with the black people wherever they might be. The banner of Pan-Negroism brought sub-Saharan Africans and Afro-Americans together. But racial affinity alone could not have converted these feelings of distant fellow-ship between Africans and Afro-Americans into an international move-ment. Race alone could not have brought these black fighters together in those early pan-African conferences. After all, there has never been much political intercourse between black Brazilians and nationalists in English-speaking or French-speaking Africa. Given the limitations of those early years, it was a matter of direct significance for African nationalism that American blacks were English-speakers.

This is not to deny the importance of a Francophone influence from the Americas. The fountain head of negritude as a literary movement is perhaps Aimé Césaire of Martinique. His new theme of "the Noble Savage" captured the defiant mood of the literary radicals:

> Hurray for those who never invented anything,
> For those who never explored anything,
> For those who never conquered anything!
> Hurray for joy,
> Hurray for love,
> Hurray for the pain of incarnate tears!

These famous lines of Césaire's defiance, first published in a Parisian review in 1939, launched a new form of black assertiveness. The word "negritude" entered the vocabulary of African agitation. Césaire vir-tually coined it in his line:

> My negritude is no tower and no cathedral:
> It dives into the red flesh of the soil.[2]

Within the African continent itself the leading proponent of negritude has remained Léopold Senghor, the poet-President of Senegal. There is no doubt that the whole movement of negritude has manifested a deeply nationalistic attachment to the heritage of black peoples. And the movement has been predominantly French-speaking.

Yet that is precisely the difference between Francophone assertiveness and Anglophone militancy. On the whole the French impact has been on *literary* nationalism rather than on concrete political strategy. Struc-tured nationalism as an organized movement agitating for self-govern-

---

[2] For this rendering see Gerald Moore, *Seven African Writers* (London: Three Crowns Book, Oxford University Press, 1962), p. viii. See also the chapter "Africa and the Third World", in: Ali A. Mazrui, *On Heroes and Uhuru Wor-ship* (London: Longmans, 1967), and Mazrui, "The Caribbean Impact on African Nationalism", *East Africa Journal* III (3) (June 1966).

ment was led by English-speakers. So was Pan-Africanism. The Anglo-phone leadership of the latter was facilitated by the fact that English-speaking blacks in the Americas in any case far outnumbered the French-speakers.

All these factors help to explain the basic Anglo-American orienta-tion of those pan-African conferences in the early part of this century. The fifth conference was held in Manchester in 1945. The towering figures of that conference were overwhelmingly English-speakers. Two of the most famous became presidents of their countries – Jomo Keny-atta and Kwame Nkrumah.

But, in this generation, what is left of the political importance of the English language within Africa now that independence has been sub-stantially achieved? One useful approach is to divide the answer into three categories. We might first examine the role of English in national integration. We could then assess its impact on pan-African politics. We shall conclude with an analysis of the implications of English for African diplomatic behaviour at large.

NATIONAL VERSUS REGIONAL INTEGRATION

On the issue of nation-building in each individual country, the first thing which needs to be noted is the integrative function of political activity itself. Let us illustrate by reference to the experience of Zaïre. One of the reasons why the Congo (now Zaïre) emerged into independence in such a state of fragmentation was because Belgian rule had not allowed political activity to take place earlier. The nature of pre-independence nationalistic activity elsewhere was such that it had a propensity to involve more and more of the general populace of a given territory. Anti-colonial sentiments fostered by a few "agitators" in the capital city gradually spread outwards and increased a conscious-ness of the territorial unit in the population as a whole. To that extent political activity in British Africa was an important contributory factor towards national integration in each colony. Zaïre was kept in a state of depoliticization – and the consciousness of territorial identity was retarded for that very reason.

If then the very phenomenon of national politics is, over a period of time, a factor which further integrates a society, anything which helps to make national politics possible is a contribution to the greater inte-gration of that society. It is partly this factor which retains for English a continuing role in nation-building in much of former British Africa. There are some areas of political activity in some of these countries which would come to a standstill if the use of English were suddenly withdrawn. Nkrumah saw from the outset both the political necessity of the English language and its relative incongruity in an independent Ghana. Speaking to his fellow parliamentarians in Ghana on the eve of independence, Nkrumah said:

Everyone of us in this Assembly today has to conduct his parliamentary business in a language which is not his own. I sometimes wonder how well the House of Commons in the United Kingdom, or the Senate in the United States, would manage if they suddenly found that they had to conduct their affairs in French or Spanish. Nevertheless we welcome English ... a common medium for exchange between ourselves ... .[3]

But English is not merely a medium for *political* exchange in the narrow sense. In those countries which lack a common indigenous language, English has other integrative functions as well. India is a multi-lingual country which, in February 1965, was confronted with riots against replacing English with Hindi. A Nigerian Minister, Mr. J. M. Johnson, had visited India only some weeks before the anti-Hindi riots. In the course of his visit Mr. Johnson had told his Indian hosts about his country's own linguistic diversity. He went on to say: "We are not keen on developing our own languages with a view to replacing English. We regard the English language as a unifying force."[4]

A few weeks later Uganda in turn announced measures to increase the proportion of the time in the syllabus of primary schools devoted to the teaching of English. In explaining the reasons for the increased effort in the teaching of English, Uganda's Minister of Education drew attention to Uganda's lack of an indigenous national language. He said: "Whether we like it or not this does emphasize what a great task we have of building up a nation."[5] The Minister envisaged the English language as one instrument in that task of nation-building. In January 1965 the Uganda Teachers' Association followed this up with a call for the establishment of a language institute to train Ugandan teachers to teach more effectively in the English language "from Primary One".[6] All these are indications of an increased possessiveness about the English language, particularly in those areas which need it for purposes of creating greater national cohesion.

And yet it is precisely such purposes which indirectly militate against Pan-Africanism as a movement for greater *inter-territorial* integration. For as long as Africa was colonized national consciousness in Africa

[3] Kwame Nkrumah: *I Speak of Freedom* (New York: Frederick A. Praeger, 1961), 102-103.
[4] Reported in *Uganda Argus*, November 13, 1963.
[5] *Uganda Argus*, December 16, 1963.
[6] *Uganda Argus*, January 11, 1965.

took a continental or broadly racial dimension. But now that Africa has been substantially decolonized, national consciousness is taking a narrower territorial form in some respects. If it therefore be asked whether English is a unifying force, the answer must be that it depends upon the unit that one is examining. If, for example, one takes Uganda as the unit, then the English language does serve an integrative purpose. But if one takes East Africa as the unit of study, then the very effectiveness English might have in fostering a sense of Uganda nationhood is making it harder for Ugandans to relinquish their sovereignty for the sake of an East African union in the days ahead.

PAN-AFRICANISM IN FRENCH AND ENGLISH

In some ways Pan-Africanism today is better served by the French language than by the English language. Francophone Africans are more sentimental about their French than English speakers are about their English. This is partly the consequence of the assimilationist component in the old French educational policy in the colonies, as contrasted with the more pragmatic British educational experiments. The French romanticized their language and passed it on with patriotic eulogies, while the British made compromises with local vernaculars and set up special committees to improve the effectiveness of African languages as educational media. The "price" that British Africa paid was an imperfect command of their metropolitan language; the "price" that Africans in French colonies paid was, in some cases, so good a command of French that their nationalistic rebellion against France became the more ambivalent.

What must not be overlooked are the pan-African implications of this. It is a matter of direct relevance for Pan-Africanism that the process of mastering the French language tends to foster a sentimental attachment to that language. The result of this attachment is that there is a greater cultural identification between former French colonies and France than there is between former British colonies and Britain. But the very cultural affinity which binds Francophone states to France also helps to bind the Francophone states themselves together. A shared affinity to France is a factor for unity at the vertical level. A shared affinity to the French language unites the Francophone African states both vertically with France and horizontally with each other.

But it goes further than that. Not all French-speaking African states are, in fact, former French colonies. There are the former Belgian colonies, too, to be taken into account – Zaïre, Rwanda and Burundi. In spite of having had different colonial powers to rule them, the French language after independence once helped to bring former French and former Belgian countries in Africa together into the single organization of OCAM. In spite of the controversy which accompanied the admission of Moise Tshombe in 1965, the criteria of membership in this organization seems to include an unmistakeable French-language requirement. There is no English equivalent of this kind of linguistic bond in Africa. The only English-speaking African country which is not formerly British is Liberia. And Liberia has had a much longer period of intercourse with Nigeria, Sierra Leone and Ghana than the former French colonies have had with the former Belgian colonies. Yet there has been no strong tendency towards functional co-operation in English-speaking West Africa. East Africa has actually experienced closer economic integration, while Malawi and Zambia were formerly a part of the same federation. Yet the tendency in relations among English-speaking states has been towards a loosening up of former ties. The English language is too emotionally neutral to slow down the disintegration. There is no English equivalent of the apparent sentiment of "Pan-Francophonia" which one sometimes observes between former Belgian and former French Africa.

It is these factors which indicate that the French language has served Pan-Africanism better than the English language has. Yet, paradoxically enough, the Pan-Africanism which French is helping to bring about is a *non-nationalistic* Pan-Africanism. It is not even particularly anti-colonialist. The closest states in Africa are those which least resent being dependent on their former colonial rulers. It is as if the most unifying factor in Africa is the psychology of neo-dependency. And outside Guinea and Mali, a sentimental attachment to French language and culture is one factor which has fostered a sense of cultural neo-dependency in so much of former French Africa. On the other hand, the English language, by fostering a greater sense of independence, has helped to reduce the chances of effective Pan-Africanism in former British Africa. There is still more militant attachment to racial dignity and greater objection to colonialism in former British than in former French or Belgian Africa. But Pan-Africanism as a closer relationship between African states themselves is inadequately realized by the very English-speakers who launched Pan-Africanism onto the world stage in the first place.

As for the relationship between the English language and African diplomatic activity at large, here again we might divide the subject up into, first, the English language and the Commonwealth; secondly, the English language and non-alignment; and thirdly, the English language and the politics of the United Nations.

THE WEAKNESS OF NUMBERS

As regards the place of English in Commonwealth relations, it is sometimes taken too readily for granted that a common language is one of the factors which keep the Commonwealth together. Among the functions of the English language in the Commonwealth must indeed be included a function which is unifying. What are often overlooked are some of the *anti*-Commonwealth tendencies which are also part of the English language. One of these tendencies is implicit precisely in the incapacity of English to produce a sentiment of "Pan-Anglophonia" to compare with what the French language has achieved in Africa. By helping to foster a greater sense of nationalistic self-assertion in British Africa than is found in French-speaking Africa, the impact of English on Africans has had an anti-Commonwealth component.

A related factor to this concerns the type of Pan-Africanism which English has tended to foster. We have already argued that Pan-Africanism as a quest for African unity has, on the whole, been better served by the French language than by the English. But this is not to say that there is no Pan-Africanism in the English sector of Africa. On the contrary, it is more in former British Africa than elsewhere that Pan-Africanism as a nationalistic commitment to the liberation of the continent has best been exemplified. Commonwealth Africans respond more readily to a defence of racial dignity than to the creation of a functional union among themselves. The latter type of Pan-Africanism could preserve fairly close ties with the former colonial power – as Francophone Africa has preserved. The former dignitarian Pan-Africanism has a propensity to loosen ties with the old "mother-country". This is what gives it a certain anti-Commonwealth tendency.

Another characteristic of the English language which has implications for the Commonwealth concerns the number of countries which speak English. We might here recall Léopold Senghor's observation that French was "a language of fewer countries than English".[7] That is one reason for the greater degree of integration which has remained between Francophone Africa and France. English suffers from its very dispersal in the world. After all, the more widely a language is spoken the looser are the ties it forges.

An alternative way of framing this factor is to argue that the British Commonwealth is weak today precisely because the British Empire had the strength of massive size. A large empire when liberated is less likely

---

[7] "Negritude and the Concept of Universal Civilization", *Présence Africaine* 18 (26) (Second Quarter 1963), 10. In the same article Senghor says: "if we had a choice we would choose French".

to retain intimacy between its parts than a smaller empire would have managed to do. Yet the very size of former British hegemony was what has made the English language so widespread. There is something emotively neutral about internationality. English is the most international of the world languages today. It has therefore lost some of the defensive emotional militancy that a more exclusive and less widespread language commands.

This is illustrated not only by the recurrent attempts in France to "purge" the French language of English expressions but also by visions of solidarity between French-speakers on a global scale. De Gaulle himself seemed to be more inspired by the broader vision of Pan-Latinism than by the more limited one of Pan-Francophonia. Something approaching this broader vision manifested itself during de Gaulle's Latin American tour. But the friends of France in Africa have more immediate ambitions. At the Tananarive conference of OCAM in June 1966, President Senghor of Senegal outlined some of the steps which could gradually be taken towards creating *francophonie*, or a French-speaking "Commonwealth". He envisaged meetings of African educational and cultural ministers leading to a council for higher education, and later inter-parliamentary meetings and economic action based on existing institutions in Africa and the franc zone. These stages were gradually to mature into "a freely accepted solidarity in the cultural, economic, financial, and monetary fields". The OCAM conference then authorized President Diori Hamani of Niger to travel through the Maghreb, other French-speaking areas in Africa not represented on OCAM, as well as France, to sound feelings on the issue.

Even within sub-Saharan Francophone Africa on its own there is significant disagreement as to the desirability of having a French-speaking fellowship of such ambitious intimacy. But that such a proposal has at all been made by distinguished French-speaking Africans is itself an indication of the greater unifying potential of the French language as contrasted with English.[8] It is hard to imagine a meeting of English-speaking African leaders seriously considering the formation of a community of all English-speakers of the world, including the United States. The larger size of the English-speaking world has weakened the bonds of linguistic sentiment among those who share this language. Even within the British Commonwealth the consciousness of a shared language has declined in emotive force as a result of expanding Commonwealth membership in the last decade or so.

---

[8] For a brief report of the Tananarive conference of OCAM and its main resolutions, see *Africa Report* II (7) (October 1966), 25-26.

THE COLD WAR OF LANGUAGES

Let us now turn to examine the English language in relation to non-alignment. In an article in a British weekly in August 1965, John Hatch made the following observation:

> It is not sufficiently recognised in the West that, after independence, African leaders have to take deliberate steps to attain a non-aligned position. Throughout their colonial era these countries have been firmly fixed within the anti-communist camp. . . . Their lines of communication are drawn to Western Europe, the language and literature is that of their ex-imperialists. The first need, therefore, is to establish new links with the communist countries.[9]

It is true that both English and French are, in a cold war sense, "Western" languages. This does have implications for non-alignment, though John Hatch is perhaps oversimplifying those implications. There is no inclination in any African country to balance the presence of a "Western" language in the school curriculum with an introduction of Russian or Chinese. On the contrary, pan-African considerations are making English-speaking Africans more interested in French and Francophone Africans more interested in English. Each African country might therefore end up adding another "Western" language to the one she inherited from her own former colonial ruler.

But is this really a matter of cold war implications? How many of Africa's best students are educated in the West is partly determined by language considerations. For certain types of technical assistance too, it is indeed a matter of relevance to the cold war that African countries share languages with Western Powers. Given that African countries attach great importance to the teaching of English, for example, it is to Britain and the United States rather than to Russia and China that they would turn for this kind of service. Even for other categories of technical assistance, linguistic competence is a matter of importance. There are more Western economists, for example, who can communicate with African governments without the need of an interpreter than there are communist economists. This is a factor which influences the choice of expertise to which African governments might turn. Some English-speaking African leaders might in any case feel more at ease with Britons and Americans than they might with Chinese and Russians. As John Hatch pointed out, in August 1965 there were still less than two hundred people from Communist China in Tanzania, in spite of a calculated policy to diversify the personnel of technical assistance in the

<hr>

[9] "The Kaunda-Nyerere Axis", *New Statesman*, August 20, 1965.

country. "The country still relies almost exclusively on Western European and American helpers", Hatch asserted.[10]

But in this general context of the cold war is there no difference between the English and French languages themselves? Or does the quality of their both being "Western" languages disguise important variations in their implications for African non-alignment?

It is the latter question which is to be answered in the affirmative. The English language is not merely a language of a member of the Western bloc. It is the language of the *leader* of the bloc. And American commitment to anti-communism is more total than that of almost any of the lesser members of the Western alliance. It is certainly more total than the French commitment. In part, it is precisely because former British Africa shares a language with the United States that it has tended to attract more interest from the Americans than the French-speaking sector of the continent has so far. This is not to suggest that areas of the world which are not English-speaking are necessarily low on the list of American priorities. On the contrary, there are often other factors in America's relations with the rest of the world which outweigh the linguistic consideration. Geographical contiguity with Latin America is one type of factor which has outweighed linguistic differences. Direct strategic needs in Asia sometimes constitute another type of factor for greater American interest and involvement. But where, as in the African continent, other considerations tend to even out, the linguistic factor assumes effective significance. The balance of Peace Corps volunteers is affected. How many American scholars have worked in British Africa or how many teachers and other personnel find their way there is partly determined by the relative familiarity of a shared language. How many students from former British Africa go to the United States for further studies is also influenced by language.

Another implication for African non-alignment in this comparison between French and English hinges on the attitude of France under General de Gaulle and immediately following. A number of French-speaking African countries continue to have some kind of military pact with France. In a sense this is a compromise of their non-alignment. But in general it is a greater compromise of non-alignment to have a military pact with Britain than with France. The difference arises because Britain is a more loyal follower of America's leadership in the cold war than France has been. In fact, General de Gaulle's conception of his role in the cold war had become virtually a kind of non-alignment. If then French-speaking Africans had a pact with de Gaulle, it was al-

---

[10] Hatch, "Axis", See also report of Nyerere's angry press conference on the subject of balance of personnel in Tanzania in *East African Standard*, September 1, 1964.

most like having a pact with a fellow non-aligned country. And a pact with such a country is less of a compromise in cold war terms than a pact with the more committed Britain.

The relevance of the English language partly lies in the reasons as to why Britain is closer to the United States than France is, even after de Gaulle. The Anglo-American *entente* in the post-war period is sometimes traced back to Winston Churchill's Fulton speech of 1946. Churchill said:

Nobody knows what Soviet Russia and its Communist international organization intends to do ... what are the limits, if any, to their expansive and proselytizing tactics ... from Stettin in the Baltic to Trieste in the Adriatic, an iron curtain has descended across the Continent ... neither the sure prevention of war, nor the continuous rise of world organization will be gained without ... a special relationship between the British Commonwealth and Empire and the United States.[11]

The whole idea of a special relationship as enunciated by Churchill in that speech was, we might note, partly inspired by considerations of cold-war strategy. That special relationship has had its moments of acute trial ever since then, never more so than during the Anglo-French Suez adventure. But in 1959 it was still possible for a distinguished student of Commonwealth affairs to make a sweeping generalization that "all roads in the Commonwealth now lead to Washington".[12] Since then the Commonwealth has admitted eleven more African states. In foreign policy these states are among the least susceptible of the Commonwealth group to American influence. But the following observation by J. D. B. Miller continues to retain some validity:

... future Commonwealth relations with the United States ... will be governed by two things over which the Commonwealth countries have no control: the increasing productivity of American industry and the fact that Americans speak English.[13]

A large number of former British countries have established their own versions of a "special relationship" with the United States. They have felt more directly the American cultural as well as economic presence in the world than their Francophone counterparts have.

Another difference between English and French which is of relevance for non-alignment concerns the more abstract intellectuality of the

---

[11] Winston S. Churchill, "Alliance of the English-Speaking Peoples", *Vital Speeches of the Day* 12 (March 15, 1946), 329-332.
[12] Cited with approval by Zolman Cowan, "The Contemporary Commonwealth", *International Organization* XIII (2) (Spring 1959), 211.
[13] J. D. B. Miller, *The Commonwealth in the World* 2 (London: Duckworth Press, 1960), 295.

French language when compared with English. Marxism seems to have a greater intellectual fascination for the French turn of mind than for the Anglo-Saxon. At any rate the Marxist idiom of reasoning, and the use of literary paradox to echo a dialectical process of reasoning, is much more in evidence among French-speaking African intellectuals than among English-speaking. We might also remind ourselves that the very size of the French Communist Party and its historical involvement in African affairs contributed to the general exposure to Marxism which French Africa experienced.

In practice, however, there is more anti-Russianism in French-speaking Africa than one is likely to find in English-speaking Africa. There is also a considerable anti-Chinese feeling in the old Brazzaville group of African states. Some Francophone leaders even publicly speak of the "yellow peril". The meeting of French-speakers which created the OCAM in February 1965 was reported to be passionately hostile to the Chinese presence in Africa. By the middle of May, Kwame Nkrumah of Ghana was driven to say to a correspondent of a Nigerian newspaper:

The stand of OCAM on Africa is indistinguishable from that of US imperialism – support for Tshombe, opposition to China and disruption of the OAU.[14]

After making allowances for Nkrumah's rhetoric, and for the expulsion of the Chinese from Ghana after Nkrumah was overthrown, the fact still remains that Francophone Africa has so far tended to take positions which have been more frankly anti-communist than English-speaking Africa generally has. Dr. Banda of Malawi took an anti-Chinese stand from the start. Kenya politics since 1964 have included heated debates on foreign policy issues, but the debates themselves have indicated that the communist countries have a strong lobby of supporters among prominent Kenyans at home. In any case, the strong reluctance of many French-speaking African countries on attainment of independence to recognize Red China had, in its generality, no real equivalent in English-speaking Africa. The majority of Francophone states attained sovereign status with a diplomatic posture of hostility to the East at large.

As for comparative attitudes to capitalism, the Ivory Coast still remains the nearest case of a *laissez-faire* country in black Africa. In the words of the President of the Ivory Coast to his countrymen in 1962:

We have no factories to nationalize, only to create; we have no commerce to take over, only to reorganize better; no land to distribute, only to bring

14 *The Sunday Express* (Lagos), May 16, 1965. See also Drew Middleton, "Chad's Ties Bind".

into production ... neither in the agricultural, commercial, industrial or social fields does revolution accord with Ivorian reality.[15]

The government does indeed participate in the economy – but more often than not government participation is with a view to maximizing private investment and enterprise. As an official of the Ivory Coast Chamber of Industries is reported to have put it: "No industry is started or run here without private participation.... [This] is an economy of private enterprise."[16]

What all this indicates is that although Francophone Africa was exposed to greater Marxist intellectualism than English-speaking Africa ever was, in concrete policies after independence there is more anticommunism and anti-revolution among Francophone elites than among English-speaking leaders.

Yet just as Francophone Africa includes the most anti-Communist of African countries, it also includes the most Marxist. Guinea and Mali come nearest to being communist countries in Africa. Algeria under Ben Bella also had a strong Marxist orientation. In all three cases theoretical Marxism probably came as much from the French heritage as from any other source.[17]

FRENCH AND ENGLISH IN THE UN

Finally let us compare English and French in relation to the policies of the United Nations. There is, first, the very location of UN headquarters in New York. It is safe to assume that English-speaking African delegates at the UN tend to fit more easily into the surrounding environment than their Francophone counterparts do. If we presumed that neither group was fluent in the other group's language – a presumption by no means unreasonable at the present stage of African linguistic competence – the location of the world body might have a marginal influence on general African orientation towards it. African diplomats from English-speaking areas often have other platforms in the United States apart from the General Assembly from which to air the views of their countries. The English-speakers can more easily be invited to address meetings in other parts of the United States or to participate on

---

[15] Cited in "Foreign Aid for the Ivory Coast", *West Africa* 2508 (June 26, 1965).
[16] Cited in "Industry in the Ivory Coast", *West Africa* 2507 (June 19, 1965).
[17] Needless to say, communism in an African country could grow as a result of other causes, too. The communist movement in South Africa is one movement which has, of course, little to do with a French intellectual tradition. In Zanzibar, Abeid Karume was not a Marxist, but Abdulrahman Babu was. And Babu's initial exposure to Marxism was perhaps through British socialism.

American television programmes on topics of international interest. French-speaking African missions at the world body probably have as much access to the American government as their English-speaking counterparts, but they have less access to the American public at large. But is this important? Since the propogandist element is so much a part of national representation at the United Nations, a reduced access to the public of the most influential country in the world must be a loss of some significance in that kind of exercise. It is conceivable that French-speaking Africans feel that they get less "propaganda value" out of their participation at the world body than do their fellow Africans from the other linguistic sector.

Any such feelings have their analogue in the attitude of France herself to the world body. Although American control of the UN has slackened a little in recent times, the United States still remains a factor of vast importance in the politics and fortunes of the world body. Further, the special relationship that the United States has with Britain might at times give the United Nations the image of being yet another arena for "Anglo-Saxon" diplomatic manoeuvres. Of the five Powers with a veto in the Security Council, two are English-speaking. The balance of influence within the non-communist world continues to be heavily tilted on the side of an English-speaking leadership. And nowhere else is this illustrated better than within the United Nations itself.

As for the kind of issues which agitate the Africans in the world body, the problem of *apartheid*, for one, has a more immediate effect on English-speakers than on the French-speakers. Malawi and Zambia especially sense an immediacy of the South African problem which has no equivalent in Francophone Africa though the reactions of Malawi and Zambia to that immediacy differ radically. A number of Africans from former British East and Central Africa were actually educated in South Africa. Economically South Africa established ties with British colonies which again had no equivalent in French Africa. When the policy of boycotting South Africa captured the imagination of the new African states, it had a more tangible meaning to countries like Kenya, Zambia and Ghana which had been trading with South Africa in the colonial period than to countries in the French orbit of influence.

Another factor which makes South Africa of greater immediacy to English-speaking Africa is the very fact that the African nationalists in South Africa are themselves English-speaking. Rebels and refugees from South Africa choose to go to Tanzania and Ghana partly for linguistic reasons. And one can more readily find black South Africans in London than in Paris.

Yet another factor which gives South Africa this sense of nearness to English-speakers is, indirectly, the problem of Rhodesia. Rhodesia is of course, a distinct problem from that of *apartheid*, but the nearness of Rhodesia to South Africa, the economic intercourse that the two countries have had, and the clear evidence that white Rhodesians might, in the ultimate show-down, prefer the successors of Malan and Vorster to Joshua Nkomo, have all helped to link Rhodesia and South Africa together in the minds of many English-speaking African nationalists.

This, then, is the general role that the English language has played in the political fortunes of the African continent. It initially helped to foster African national consciousness. Out of that consciousness grew notions of pigmentational self-determination and continental identity. Further factors in the world, partly using English as a medium of transmission, then increasingly helped to give shape and direction to African political thought. The birth of the United Nations, the independence of India, the competitive militancy of the cold war, all played their part in the emergence of political and diplomatic attitudes in the new generations of Africans. The English language as an initiator of an intellectual revolution was joined by a number of other factors. The proportion of its impact on the minds of African leaders in the English-speaking Africa was reduced. But new African roles have also emerged for English since the early days of its impact, including its part in the latest phases of Pan-Africanism, in Commonwealth relations, in relations between Africa and the United States, in Africa's participation in the United Nations, and in world politics at large. Sometimes English serves no greater purpose than that of a label of identity between one set of Africans and another. Yet the very fact that it serves as a basis of classification has important implications for the identity of those Africans that are so classified.

In the final analysis it might even be English, rather than French, that will ultimately emerge as "the Latin" of Africa's own intellectual history. But that is a long-term speculation. What is evident already is the decisive contribution that the English language has made to the whole movement for African statehood and to the emergence of a sovereign African factor in international politics at large.

Conclusion

TOWARDS THE DECOLONIZATION OF RUDYARD KIPLING

One could look at Rudyard Kipling's poem, "The White Man's Burden" as symbolic of that massive historical phenomenon, Euro-American imperialism. There is no doubt that Kipling was the poet of militant expansionist patriotism, and was, in some sense, a hero of both the British and the American wings of Anglo-Saxon militancy. He married an American woman, Caroline Balestier and lived for a few years in Vermont. As Louis Untermeyer has observed:[1] "It is probable that Kipling would have remained in America, where he wrote several of his most popular works, if a quarrel with his brother-in-law had not driven him back to England."

Kipling's poem, "The White Man's Burden", first appeared in *The Times* of London, on February 4, 1899. This was on the occasion when the United States emerged triumphant out of the Spanish-American war. In May 1898, Commodore Dewey defeated a Spanish fleet in Manila Bay. The annexation of the Philippines followed, in the face of some significant opposition in the Congress of the United States. The imperial mission, which had already been under way for quite a while among Europeans, was now manifesting itself more blatantly among Americans. Kipling's poem, "The White Man's Burden" was in part addressed to white Americans as they stood on the threshold of becoming – like their European parent nations – an imperial power.

> Take up the White Man's Burden –
> Send forth the best ye breed –

---

[1] Untermeyer (ed.), *A Treasury of Great Poems: English and American* (New York: Simon and Schuster, 1955 Edition), 1046-1047.

Go bind your sons to exile
To serve your captives' need;
To wait in heavy harness,
On fluttered folk and wild –
Your new caught sullen people,
Half-devil and half-child.

The American Government was certainly entering into this mood of legitimation in terms of civilizing the natives and raising their moral stature and material standards. President McKinley denied emphatically any colonial mission in the Philippines – and salved his conscience by affirming that:

... there was nothing else for us to do but to take them all, and to educate the Filipinos, and uplift and civilize and Christianize them, and by God's grace do the very best we could by them, as our fellowmen for whom Christ also died.[2]

Partly because "The White Man's Burden" was composed on the eve of the American colonization of the Philippines, we might say that Rudyard Kipling was not only the voice of the British empire but the voice of the "Anglo-Saxon Destiny". In this chapter we shall attempt to place him in that wider context, touch upon other symbols of this line of imperial thinking, and then indicate the degree to which Kipling and his language were diffused to other societies as part of the emergence of a world culture.

In sentiment Rudyard Kipling belonged to the second half of the nineteenth century and the first decade of the twentieth. The Anglo-Saxons were deemed both a "race" and a linguistic group. There was optimism that the race would dominate the world. This prediction has not been borne out by history. But there was also optimism that the English language would conquer the world. This latter prediction continues on the road towards fulfilment. The militancy of Rudyard Kipling's rhetoric and poetry was animated by the forces of enthusiasm implicit in both those prophecies. In 1868 Sir Charles Wentworth Dilke published his two volume study, *Greater Britain*, after his travels in the United States, New Zealand, Australia, Ceylon, India and Egypt. "Everywhere I was in English-speaking or in English-governed land." He detected the resilience of "the essentials of the race" and the power of both the English language and English laws. He was particularly impressed by the potentialities of America as a field for the dissemination of English values. To use a more recent metaphor, Sir Charles Dilke saw the United States as the microphone and loudspeaker for the

---

[2] Cited by Michael Edwardes, *Asia in the European Age, 1498-1955* (New York: Frederick A. Praeger, 1962), 162.

British heritage. In his own words: "Through America, England is speaking to the world . . . Alfred's laws and Chaucer's tongue are theirs whether they would or no."

Sir Charles shared the view that Britain could claim the glory of "having planted greater Englands across the seas" and here he was capturing a sentiment made even more immortal by Kipling's lines:

> Winds of the World, give answer! They are
> whimpering to and fro –
> And what should they know of England who only
> England know?[3]

Across the Atlantic in the United States Josiah Strong, a Congregationalist minister, even more explicitly associated the destiny of the Anglo-Saxon "race" with the destiny of the English language, and saw the latter as the carrier of Christian ideas and as the medium of "Anglo-Saxonizing mankind". Strong heartily quoted the German philologist Jacob Grimm's predictions about the English language.

> . . . the English language, saturated with Christian ideas, gathering up into itself the best thoughts of all the ages, is the great agent of Christian civilization throughout the world; at this moment affecting the destinies and moulding the character of half the human race. . . . It seems chosen, like its people, to rule in future times in still greater degree in all the corners of the earth.[4]

Strong took up this solemn prophecy about the infinite conquering power of the English language. The racial chauvinism detracts from what would otherwise be a prediction still very far from being invalidated. In his own exaggerated way, Strong saw the potentialities of the English language as a factor in world order problems. And he tied this issue to Tennyson's vision of a future "Federation of the World". Half-chauvinist and half-genuine prophet, this Congregationalist minister in the United States asserted that "the language of Shakespeare would eventually become the language of mankind". He then asked whether Tennyson's noble prophecy about the end of war and the beginning of world federalism would not find its fulfilment.

> in Anglo Saxondom's extending its dominion and influence –
> 'Til the war-drum throbs no longer, and the battle-flags are furl'd
> In the Parliament of man, the Federation of the world.[5]

---

[3] Kipling, "The English Flag". For the quotations from Dilke see Sir Charles Wentworth Dilke, *Greater Britain: A Record of Travel in English Speaking Countries* (two volumes, London 1868), vol. I, vi-viii.

[4] Cited by Josiah Strong, *Our Country* (New York: 1885), 178-179.

[5] Strong, *Our Country*. The lines from Tennyson are from his poem "Locksley Hall" (1842), Lines 1-7, 8.

The British certainly extended their sway across much of the globe as an imperial power; and the United States rose as the most powerful nation in the history of mankind. But then other forces in the world began to conspire against the political domination or hegemony of both the British and the Americans. With the Americans it took longer for the hegemony to be fully on the defensive, and to start beating a retreat to some limited extent following challenges which ranged from the war in Vietnam to the nationalism of Charles de Gaulle. In fact the American decline in world stature is still in its initial stages, but the British decline is more firmly demonstrable.

Africa was among the last sectors of the British empire to be liberated. 1966 marked the virtual end of British colonialism in Africa, except for the continuing legal fiction of British power over rebellious Rhodesia. But while 1966 marked the end of the British empire, it witnessed at the same time newer reports about the expansion of the English language. We mentioned earlier the African magazine which was reporting to its readers in East Africa in December 1966 that the English language had already become the primary language of science in the world, and of aviation, sports, and increasingly of literature and the theatre. As the magazine put it in a delightfully pungent if journalistic style: "When a Russian pilot seeks to land at an airfield in Athens, Cairo, or New Delhi, he talks to the control tower in English."[6]

As we indicated, that same weekly magazine drew from a recently established report estimates to the effect that 70% of the world's mail was by 1966 written in English and an even bigger percentage of cable and wireless transmissions. Sixty per cent of the world's broadcasts were already in English. And more and more countries were introducing English as a compulsory second language in schools.

What the world picture as a whole does indicate is not only the significance of French and English as the two most important languages of international politics, but also the simple fact that English continues to outstrip French even in diplomatic importance.

Even within the European Economic Community there is anxiety among champions of French now that Britain has been admitted to the Community. The British themselves, far less nationalistic about their language than the French, have indicated a readiness to let French continue to hold a special position in the councils of Europe. But English has often spread and conquered in spite of Britain's own lack of interest in that spread. The European Economic Community may fall under the spell of the English language, whatever reassurances Mr. Heath may have given to President Pompidou.

---

[6] See section on "Education", *Reporter* (Nairobi), Dec. 30, 1966, p. 13.

In May 1971 President Pompidou was asked why he insisted on the importance of the French language. His answer, which became more elaborate as the time of British entry approached, conceded first the idea of equality of languages, but then intimated that French had to remain the first among equals in Europe. President Pompidou wanted to safeguard the special role of French within the bodies of the European Economic Community and the working parties of experts. Why did he want to do so? "Because the language reflects a certain way of looking at the world."[7]

In some ways the conquest of continental Europe by the English language would be an even more dramatic victory for the language than its triumphs in Asia and Africa. After all, within Europe the overpowering rivalry of French and German as adequate languages of science and culture for so many years would normally have been expected to present an intractable obstacle to the new hegemony of a language from outside the continent. English has indeed been replacing German as the second language in places like the Scandinavian countries. But French has continued to resist the encroachment of English. President Pompidou's worry about the linguistic implications for the European Economic Community of the British entry is an illustration of a continuing vigilance by France to protect the interests of French.

Edward Heath's reassurances to President Pompidou on the linguistic question are by no means an adequate safeguard for French. After all, English has been known to extend its frontiers in spite of lukewarm support from England. English may push back French in Europe in one sweeping invasion, and beat French into a retreat behind the Maginot line of France herself. Such an event would be even more impressive than the acquisition of English by Indians and Nigerians, who were colonized and were also more vulnerable because their languages had not as yet acquired the kind of scientific and modern technological capability which French and German had already imbibed prior to the English challenge on the continent.

And yet English, even at its most victorious, can only be a foreign language in Europe. Great Britain and Ireland are destined to be the only European countries that have English as the official language. Everywhere else English will be playing a secondary role within the European continent.

In Africa, however, the position is different. As we indicated earlier, Dr. Tom Soper, Deputy Director of the Overseas Development Institute in London at the time, once estimated that two-thirds of black Africa was English-speaking and one-third was French-speaking. What Dr.

[7] See *The Daily Telegraph* (London) May 27, 1971, p. 4.

Soper meant was that two-thirds of the population of black Africa was under a system of Government which had adopted English as the official language, or one of the official languages, whereas about one third or less was under systems of Government which had adopted French for that purpose. In terms of the number of independent states in sub-Saharan Africa, there are indeed about as many French-speaking Governments as there are English-speaking. But in terms of population the picture is different. Nigeria alone has more than the population of former French Africa put together. But then out of the hundred-million Commonwealth Africans, or so, about half are Nigerians in any case.

Against this must be balanced two factors. First, French-speaking Africa does not consist merely of former French Africa. It includes former Belgian Africa – Zaïre, Rwanda and Burundi. And the population of this former Belgian part of the continent is over twenty million.

A second factor to bear in mind is the calculation that there may be more people who actually speak French in French-speaking Africa than there are people who speak English in English-speaking Africa. But this calculation is impressionistic, based partly on observations in major centres of population, and partly on the sophistication in the command of French maintained by the French-speaking elite. It is certainly true that many African users of French have a more sophisticated command than African users of English have.

Calculating the population as a whole it is not really certain that the number of people who speak French in French-speaking Africa is greater than the number of people who speak English in English-speaking Africa. And even if it were certain, another difference has to be borne in mind. The schools in English-speaking Africa are producing educated Africans more rapidly than the schools in French-speaking Africa are. There is a greater commitment towards promoting education in Commonwealth Africa, and towards disseminating it widely. Former French Africa still inclines towards an elitist conception of education, and the expansion of the primary and secondary sectors of education in even such a rich francophone country as the Ivory Coast does not compare with the expansion of pre-University education in, say, Kenya and Ghana. Again all these are impressionistic assessments, but at least they do add up to the phenomenon of a dual Franco-English cultural and linguistic penetration into the African continent. And of the two languages there is no doubt at all that English is the more dominant in the affairs of the continent.

What all this means is that Strong's prediction concerning the conquest of the world by the English language is coming into conflict with another prediction made famous by Rudyard Kipling himself. We had indicated before that Kipling belonged to that school of militant Anglo-

Saxon patriotism which saw the world falling under the influence of those that spoke "the tongue that Shakespeare spake". But it was also Kipling who bequeathed to human thought the witticism captured in the verse:

> Oh, East is East, and West is West, and
> never the twain shall meet,
> Till Earth and Sky stand presently at God's
> great Judgment Seat.[8]

What this means is that the English language itself is helping to contradict the prediction that "never the twain shall meet". The language of Shakespeare, even more so the language of Kipling, has established points of contact, avenues of meeting, between Americans and Pakistanis, Australians and Nigerians, Jamaicans and New Zealanders. Thanks to Kipling's own language, East may still be East and West may still be West, but it is harder than ever to predict that "never the twain shall meet".

Kipling himself can be regarded as a symbol of the language in some ways more up-to-date than Shakespeare. When we look at the history of English as a whole, it is true that among the poets it was Shakespeare and Alexander Pope who contributed most to the phraseological heritage of English. But Kipling was the nearest modern equivalent to Shakespeare and Pope as a contributor to popular English. In the words of George Orwell:

Kipling is the only English writer of our time who has added phrases to the English language. The phrases and neologisms which we take over and use without remembering their origin do not always come from writers we admire.[9]

Orwell refers to phrases coined by Kipling which "one sees quoted in leaderettes in the gutter press or overhears in saloon bars from people who have barely heard his name". Orwell mentions phrases like "East is East, and West is West", "The female of the species is more deadly than the male", "Paying the Dane-Geld" and of course "The white man's burden".

Orwell sees in Kipling's capability to enrich the language a capacity to capture the urgency of things. One did not have to agree with the

---

[8] *The Ballad of East and West.* The rest of the stanza goes thus:
But there is neither East nor West, Border, nor Breed, nor Birth,
When two strong men stand face to face, though they come from the ends of the earth!
[9] Orwell, "Rudyard Kipling", in: *Decline of the English Murder and other Essays* (Penguin Books in association with Secker & Warburg, 1965 edition), 56-57.

philosophy put forward by Kipling, but a phrase may capture an area of importance, even if there is a divergence of values. " 'White man's burden' instantly conjures up a real problem, even if one feels that it ought to be altered to 'Black man's burden'." [10]

Even Orwell's modification of the concept in the direction of the oppressed, the black man, was already echoed earlier by other users of English. Edmund D. Morel, founder of the newspaper *West African Mail*, and founder of the Congo Reform Association in defence of the rise of the Congolese against the King of the Belgians, wrote a book entitled *The Black Man's Burden*. This was in 1920. Taking a point of view diametrically opposed to that of Kipling, Morel nevertheless echoed the rhetoric of his more nationalistic colleague.

It is [the peoples of Africa] who carry the "Black Man's Burden". They have not whithered away before the white Man's *occupation*. . . . The African has survived, and it is well for the white settlers that he has. . . . [But] in fine, to kill the soul in a people – this is a crime which transcends physical murder. [11]

We are taking Orwell's analysis of Kipling a little further, to illustrate the importance of linguistic dissemination and the power of words. Orwell asks "But how true is it that Kipling was a vulgar flag waver, a sort of publicity agent for Cecil Rhodes?" Orwell, himself basically an anti-imperialist, conceded that it was true that Kipling provided rhythmic legitimation to British jingoism and British imperialism. Kipling also helped to romanticize the values popular with the ruling classes of Britain.

In the stupid early years of this century, the blimps, having at last discovered someone who could be called a poet and who was on their side, set Kipling on a pedestal, and some of his more sententious poems, such as "If", were given almost biblical status. [12]

What Orwell did not realise was that the very poem "If" captured the imagination not simply of the blimps and jingo imperialists, but of African nationalists far away from Britain. On the eve of an election in Nairobi, before a massive crowd waiting to hear his last speech before the great day, Kenya's Tom Mboya stood there and recited to that African audience the whole of Rudyard Kipling's poem "If". The whole concept of leadership unflappable in the face of adversity, unwilling to pass the buck ("Here the buck stops"), unwilling to collapse under the weight of pressures, and characterized by the supreme British virtue of

---

[10] Orwell, "Kipling".
[11] E. D. Morel, *The Black Man's Burden* (London, 1920), 7-11.
[12] Orwell, "Rudyard Kipling", 50-51.

the "stiff upper lip", seemed captured in those lines from a supreme British patriot.

> If you can keep your head when all about you
> Are losing theirs and blaming it on you,
> If you can meet with Triumph and Disaster
> And treat those two imposters just the same,
> If you can talk with crowds and keep your virtue,
> Or walk with kings – nor lose the common touch,
> If you can fill the unforgiving minute
> With sixty seconds' worth of distance run,
> Yours is the Earth and everything that's in it,
> And – which is more – you'll be a Man, my son.[13]

There in Nairobi was this immortal son of Kenya, worn out by the exertions of campaigning, nervous about the election the next day, confronting an eager audience of fellow black people listening to his words of wisdom. Mboya was later to communicate to posterity the following paragraph:

...I read out to the great crowd the whole of Rudyard Kipling's poem *If*. When facing the challenge of nation-building, nobody can claim to have played a manly part if he (or she) has not

> ". . . filled the unforgiving minute
> With sixty seconds' worth of distance run."[14]

Across the border in Uganda, Rudyard Kipling had had a similar impact. Mr. J. W. Lwamafa, Minister and Member of Parliament, commemorated President A. Milton Obote's ten years in Parliament with the observation:

He is essentially a man of crisis – he has a unique flair for solving them, but once solved, he will never wait for applause, he simply moves on to the next problem as if nothing had happened. No one reminds me more than President Obote of Rudyard Kipling's poem (which, by the way, I have got framed and hangs in my office) and more particularly the verse, "If you can keep your head when all about you are losing theirs. . . ."[15]

Kipling, the poet of "The White Man's Burden", had turned out also to be the poet of "The Black Man's Leader". The man who had contributed significantly to the phraseological heritage of the English language was also serving inspirational purposes for African politicians

---

[13]   Kipling, "If" (1903).
[14]   Tom Mboya, *Freedom and After* (London: Andre Deutsch, 1963), 114.
[15]   *Thoughts of an African Leader*, compiled by the editorial department of the Uganda Argus (Kampala: Longmans Uganda Ltd. 1970), 68.

within their own domestic systems. The cultural penetration of the English language was manifesting its comprehensiveness. That was in part a form of colonization of the African mind. But when Rudyard Kipling is being called upon to serve purposes of the Africans themselves, the phenomenon we are witnessing may also amount to a decolonization of Rudyard Kipling. It was Kipling himself who said in 1923: "Words are, of course, the most powerful drug used by mankind."[16]

The drug of words may hypnotize men away from rationality. But there are times when drugs are used for medicinal and curative purposes. And there are times when one drug is used to neutralize the hypnotic effects of another. In these latter two cases the story of the English language and its role in the world may include the remedial functions of mitigating man's inclinations towards cultural autarky.

[16] Speech, Feb. 14, 1923. See *The Times* (London) Feb. 16, 1923.

Appendix A

A. Milton Obote

LANGUAGE AND NATIONAL IDENTIFICATION

The task of opening Seminars insofar as I am concerned very often gets me in trouble. When I received your letter to open the Seminar, I had to take a quick decision and I had to consider carefully whether to come here and discuss with you in the Opening Address what I consider to be important in respect to the issues you are going to discuss and from the viewpoint of the administration of Uganda.

I came to the conclusion that I should not at the Opening Address say too much that might create an artificial atmosphere in the Seminar. I agreed to come to open this Seminar not only because of my association with one of the organizations co-sponsoring it but also because of my interest in the subject matter of the Conference. I have a personal interest in the subject matter and at the same time in an official capacity I have a very big interest in what you will be discussing here for the next four days.

I want to say briefly that Uganda finds difficulties in identifying herself, and that Uganda has a serious language problem. Our present policy as a Government is to teach more and more English in schools. We are not unmindful of disadvantages inherent in this policy. We know that English, before Independence, was the language of the administrator. It was the language of the people who were rulers and by which Uganda was ruled. We also know that many of our people learned English in order to serve in the Administration, at least to serve our

This opening address was delivered by the Hon. Milton Obote, President of Uganda, before a Seminar on Mass Media and Linguistic Communications in East Africa, meeting in Kampala from March 31 to April 3, 1967. Reprinted with permission from *East Africa Journal* (Nairobi) 4 (1) (April, 1967).

former masters. It would appear that we are doing exactly the same; our policy to teach more English could in the long run just develop more power in the hands of those who speak English, and better economic status for those who know English. We say this because we do not see any possibility of our being able to get English known by half the population of Uganda within the next fifteen years. English, therefore, remains the national language in Uganda when at the same time it is a language that the minority of our people can use for political purposes to improve their own political positions. Some of our people can use it in order to improve their economic status.

In spite of this reasoning, we find no alternative to English in Uganda's present position. We have, therefore, adopted English as our national language – in fact it is the political language. No Member of Parliament, for instance, is unable to speak English and indeed it is a qualification for membership to Parliament. Those in the Seminar will understand the challenge facing us. The Uganda National Assembly should be a place where Uganda problems are discussed by those best able to discuss them, and in our situation it would appear that those best able to discuss our problems are those who speak English. This is a reasoning which cannot be defended anywhere; there is no alternative at the present moment. We do also see that those amongst us in Uganda who speak English and have obtained important positions because of the power of the English language, are liable to be regarded by a section of our society as perpetrators of colonialism and imperialism; or at least as potential imperialists. This, fortunately, has not yet become a public issue in Uganda. Nevertheless there is a real possibility that as long as English is maintained as the official language, spoken by a minority, a charge against its use could be made on the ground that it is the language of the privileged group.

But the Government and the people of Uganda do realise that there are certain advantages in our learning English. We could not, for instance, adopt Lugbara – one of our Northern languages – as our national language. It is clear that the task of teaching Lugbara itself would be beyond our capacity and ability and since language has an economic power in that whoever in a country of this kind knows the official language is likely to get higher and higher in the Government service, the task of teaching Lugbara or adopting it could result in serious riots and instability.

I suggest that the same applies practically to every other language in Uganda. It is probably safe to say that Luganda and Lunyoro are spoken by the greatest number of our people but immediately we adopt either of them as the official language for administrative purposes or legislation, some of us will have to go out of the Government. I, for instance, would not be able to speak in Parliament in Luganda, neither could I do so in Lunyoro, and I think more than half the present National Assembly members would have to quit. The areas we now represent would not like to have just any person who speaks Luganda to represent them. They would feel unrepresented. So, there again, we find no alternative to English.

Then comes culture. The problem of culture is slightly different from the political problem and this is essentially a problem of how best we can maintain and develop the various cultural forms in Uganda through a common language. I have no answer to this. I am well aware that English cannot be the media to express Dingidingi songs. I have my doubts whether Lwo language can express in all its fineness Lusoga songs, and yet I consider that Uganda's policy to teach more and more English should be matched with the teaching of some other African language.

Currently we are thinking of what this African language should be. Already, of course, in Primary schools children learn in their own mother tongues but then it means that we have to find Primary School teachers and post them to each tribal area. This does not allow for the movement of teachers which may be a great disadvantage to the teachers themselves. The practical effect is that, having been to a Teacher Training College, teachers have no other place to go to except the tribal district. I consider this as something an Independent Uganda should not encourage.

There can be no doubt that time will come when some of these languages will lose meaning. We may today think that a tribe will lose very much if it loses its tribal language. I do not think so. Not at least two thousand years from now. I find it, therefore, easy to suggest that the teaching of an African language in Uganda schools today is difficult because of the lack of teachers. Someone may suggest that there are some two million people who speak Luganda and ask: "Why not recruit some fifty thousand to teach Luganda throughout Uganda?" I think the problem posed by languages like Runyoro/Rutoro and Luganda in the context of Uganda's geographical position is a different problem from that posed, for instance, by Swahili. The teaching of Runyoro/Rutoro or Luganda will assist Uganda in the years to come in that people of Uganda will be able to communicate with one another in one common language. But it will not assist Uganda in communicating with her neighbours. It would be difficult for the Congolese who already, by the way, speak some kind of Swahili to bother to learn our new national language when they know that across the borders of Uganda there are millions of people who speak a language they already know – which is Swahili.

So the adoption of any one of our present languages in Uganda may just go to endorse our isolation; we cannot afford any kind of isolation. We are surrounded by five countries. We can easily talk with them, and as they say here, walk across Rwanda village, walk across Congo village, walk across Sudan village, walk across Kenya and Tanzania and drink water by the simple words *mpa maji* "give me water". It is possible today for the people of Uganda to communicate with the people in the neighbouring countries in broken Swahili but it is not possible today for the people of Uganda to communicate with the neighbouring countries in broken Luganda. If we cannot communicate with our neighbours in broken Luganda today, how much more difficult would it be to try and communicate in first class Luganda.

I do think also that Swahili has its own problems within the context of Uganda. It is possible that one can learn a language without taking the culture that that language expresses. But the real question as I see it here is: Why should Uganda learn Swahili? or: Why should Kenya adopt Swahili as a national language, or for that matter, why has the Government of Tanzania announced the policy of the adoption of Swahili as a national language? I ask this question because I am not quite convinced that having adopted an African language as a national language, a tendency would not develop to discourage all other languages around the country. If that tendency developed and became the official policy, are we satisfied that my remarks regarding the inability of Luganda to express Dingidingi songs would be satisfied by Swahili? I am not satisfied, and here we are trying to think about a possible answer to the question of why we need an African language as a national language? Do we need it merely for political purposes, for addressing public meetings, for talking in Councils? Do we need it as the language of the workers, to enable them to talk and argue their terms with their employers? Do we need an African language for intellectual purposes? Do we need such a language to cover every aspect of our lives intellectually, politically, economically?

I would not attempt to answer that question but it appears to me that Uganda at least is faced with a difficult future on this matter and the future might confirm that a decision is necessary to push some language deliberately and to discourage the use of some other languages also deliberately.

Swahili was taken out of schools in the past for political reasons but I think there were also strong cultural reasons.

When Independence came, Radio Uganda was broadcasting in English, Luganda, Runyoro/Rutoro, Ateso and Lwo. Today we have added another ten languages on the Radio and this is a subject that interests me a great deal. Perhaps in this Seminar you will find an answer as to what is the objective in having a National Radio. I am in Government and I have to take political feelings of the people into account in formulating policies. I would not say that all our fourteen languages on the Radio are in every case necessary but I would not also go as far as to say that they are there merely because of political reasons. I think to some extent – much as we would like to have one language – there is advantage in broadcasting in these various languages as things stand today. Our policy on Radio Uganda is to inform the public and that is our first task, first objective. We want to inform the people of Uganda. We find it exceedingly difficult to inform the Karamojong in Luganda or in any other language except their own, so we have Karamojong broadcast on the Radio. Then we use the Radio for educational purposes and we find that to assist those who never went to school at all, we must broadcast in their own mother tongues.

Then there is what is called entertainment which should actually be development of culture. Since the Radio began broadcasting these various languages, there has been a new spirit in Uganda, simple composition of songs, dance teams and various competitions around the countryside. Every village is eager to surpass the other in its cultural activities with a view that one day Radio Uganda recording vans will pass around the village and record the songs and the poems of a particular group. We find this useful although we are creating a problem of how to co-ordinate these activities in future.

The only aspect which I do not like on our Radio but which I cannot do anything about, is the "Pop Song". But I understand that there are people who like pop, so that too has to stay.

When it comes to news, our National Radio is in the same weak position as many national radios in Africa. I will perhaps illustrate this, by telling you that I know of a Minister in the Government of Uganda who followed the Sierra Leone trouble by tuning to the B.B.C. and to the Voice of America. Certainly there was more news on the B.B.C. and the Voice of America about Sierra Leone – more than Radio Uganda could give. What news was it? And in any case what is news?

Well, we struggled for Independence. We have got it. There remains a problem in this context as to whom we should listen [sic] and what we want to hear. I find it extremely difficult here in Uganda to give the people of Uganda what I consider news. I find it difficult because, first, we do not have enough trained manpower to collect what we consider news throughout Uganda every day and to present that news to the people of Uganda. Secondly, we have tremendous difficulties in broadcasting what is news in Kenya, or what is news in Tanzania – the happenings in Kenya or the happenings in Tanzania, or the happenings in any part of Africa. What comes to us as news very often turns out to be ideas of those they call "informed observers" and if you go to investigate as to who are the "informed observers" you will find their position extremely interesting and disturbing. So we are not giving the right type of news to our people first because of our own inability to collect the news within our territory.

This is because of lack of contact and lack of communication channels between one African capital and another. The O.A.U. has been talking about an African News Agency. This is the age of talking. We find it easier to talk about Union Government and to write the Constitution of that Government, than to talk about African News Agency or to talk about how to finance it, and yet the struggle goes on as to who should control the minds and the ears of Africa.

Today I have to, like all my colleagues in Africa, think in a foreign language in order to express myself to Africans on problems affecting Africans. When I move out of Kampala to talk to the people, I have to talk in English. Obviously I have no alternative but I lose a lot especially as far as the Party is concerned. The Party welcomes everybody and some of the greatest and most dedicated workers are those who do not speak English and yet the Party Leader cannot call this great dedicated worker alone and say "Thank you" in a language the man will understand. It has to be translated. There must always be a third party, and that is why it is said there are no secrets in Africa. This is our challenge. We are a young country and the vitality of youth should be able to lead us to greater days. I urge particularly the people of Uganda to turn the weaknesses of today into the strength of tomorrow.

Appendix B

Chinua Achebe

ENGLISH AND THE AFRICAN WRITER

In June, 1962, there was a writers' gathering at Makerere, impressively styled: "A Conference of African Writers of English Expression". Despite this sonorous and rather solemn title it turned out to be a very lively affair and a very exciting and useful experience for many of us. But there was something which we tried to do and failed – that was to define "African Literature" satisfactorily.

Was it literature produced *in* Africa or *about* Africa? Could African literature be on any subject, or must it have an African theme? Should it embrace the whole continent or South of the Sahara, or just *Black* Africa? And then the question of language. Should it be in indigenous African languages or should it include Arabic, English, French, Portuguese, Afrikaans, etc.?

In the end we gave up trying to find an answer partly – I should admit – on my own instigation. Perhaps we should not have given up so easily. It seems to me from some of the things I have since heard and read that we may have given the impression of not knowing what we were doing, or worse, not daring to look too closely at it.

A Nigerian critic, Obi Wali, writing in *Transition* 10 said: "Perhaps the most important achievement of the conference ... is that African literature as now defined and understood leads nowhere."

I am sure that Obi Wali must have felt triumphantly vindicated when he saw the report of a different kind of conference held later at Fourah Bay to discuss African literature and the University curriculum. This conference produced a tentative definition of African literature as fol-

Reprinted with permission, from *Transition* (Kampala) 4 (18) (1965).

lows: "Creative writing in which an African setting is authentically handled or to which experiences originating in Africa are integral." We are told specifically that Conrad's *Heart of Darkness* qualifies as African literature while Graham Greene's *Heart of the Matter* fails because it could have been set anywhere outside Africa.

A number of interesting speculations issue from this definition which admittedly is only an interim formulation designed to produce a certain desirable end, namely, to introduce African students to literature set in their environment. But I could not help being amused by the curious circumstances in which Conrad, a Pole, writing in English produced African literature! On the other hand if Peter Abrahams were to write a good novel based on his experiences in the West Indies it would not be accepted as African literature.

What all this suggests to me is that you cannot cram African literature into a small, neat definition. I do not see African literature as one unit but as a group of associated units – in fact the sum total of all the *national* and *ethnic* literatures of Africa.

A national literature is one that takes the whole nation for its province, and has a realised or potential audience throughout its territory. In other words a literature that is written in the *national* language. An ethnic literature is one which is available only to one ethnic group within the nation. If you take Nigeria as an example, the national literature, as I see it, is the literature written in English; and the ethnic literatures are in Hausa, Ibo, Yoruba, Effik, Edo, Ijaw, etc., etc.

Any attempt to define African literature in terms which overlook the complexities of the African scene and the material of time is doomed to failure. After the elimination of white rule shall have been completed, the single most important fact in Africa in the second half of the twentieth century will appear to be the rise of individual nation states. I believe that African literature will follow the same pattern.

What we tend to do today is to think of African literature as a new-born infant. But in fact what we have is a whole generation of new-born infants. Of course if you only look cursorily one infant looks very much like another; but each is already set on its own journey. Of course, you may group them together on the basis of the language they will speak or the religion of their fathers. Those would all be valid distinctions; but they could not begin to account fully for each individual person carrying, as it were, his own little lodestar of genes.

Those who in talking about African literature want to exclude North Africa because it belongs to a different tradition surely do not suggest that Black Africa is anything like homogenous. What does Shabaan Robert have in common with Christopher Okigbo or Awoonor-Williams? Mongo Béti of Cameroun and Paris with Nzekwu of Nigeria; or what does the champagne-drinking upper-class Creole society described by Easmon of Sierra Leone have in common with the rural folk and fishermen of J. P. Clark's plays? Of course, some of these differences could be accounted for on individual rather than national grounds but a good deal of it is also environmental.

I have indicated somewhat off-handedly that the national literature of Nigeria and of many other countries of Africa is, or will be, written in English. This may sound like a controversial statement, but it isn't. All I have done has been to look at the reality of present-day Africa. This "reality" may change as a result of deliberate, e.g. political, action. If it does an entirely new situation will arise, and there will be plenty of time to examine it. At present it may be more profitable to look at the scene as it is.

What are the factors which have conspired to place English in the position of national language in many parts of Africa? Quite simply the reason is that these nations were created in the first place by the intervention of the British which, I hasten to add, is not saying, that the peoples comprising these nations were invented by the British.

The country which we know as Nigeria today began not so very long ago as the arbitrary creation of the British. It is true, as William Fagg says in his excellent new book *Nigerian Images*, that this arbitrary action has proved as lucky in terms of African art history as any enterprise of the fortunate Princess of Serendip. And I believe that in political and economic terms too this arbitrary creation called Nigeria holds out wonderful prospects. Yet the fact remains that Nigeria was created by the British – for their own ends. Let us give the devil his due: colonialism in Africa disrupted many things, but it did create big political units where there were small, scattered ones before. Nigeria had hundreds of autonomous communities ranging in size from the vast Fulani Empire founded by Usman dan Fodio in the North to tiny village entities in the East. Today it is one country.

Of course there are areas of Africa where colonialism divided a single ethnic group among two or even three powers. But on the whole it did bring together many peoples that had hitherto gone their several ways. And it gave them a language with which to talk to one another. If it failed to give them a song, it at least gave them a tongue, for sighing. There are not many countries in Africa today where you could abolish the language of the erstwhile colonial powers and still retain the facility for mutual communication. Therefore those African writers who have chosen to write in English or French are not unpatriotic smart alecs with an eye on the main chance – outside their own countries. They are by-products of the same processes that made the new nation-states of Africa.

You can take this argument a stage further to include other countries of Africa. The only reason why we can even talk about African unity is that when we get together we can have a manageable number of languages to talk in – English, French, Arabic.

The other day I had a visit from Joseph Kariuki of Kenya. Although I had read some of his poems and he had read my novels we had not met before. But it didn't seem to matter. In fact I had met him through his poems, especially through his love poem "Come Away My Love", in which he captures in so few words the trials and tensions of an African in love with a white girl in Britain.

> Come away, my love, from streets
> Where unkind eyes divide
> And shop windows reflect our difference.

By contrast, when in 1960 I was travelling in East Africa and went to the home of the late Shabaan Robert, the Swahili poet of Tanganyika, things had been different. We spent some time talking about writing, but there was no real contact. I knew from all accounts that I was talking to an important writer, but just how important I had no idea. He gave me two books of his poems which I treasure but cannot read – until I have learnt Swahili.

And there are scores of languages I would want to learn if it were possible. Where am I to find the time to learn the half-a-dozen or so Nigerian languages each of which can sustain a literature? I am afraid it cannot be done. These languages will just have to develop as tributaries to feed the one central language enjoying nation-wide currency. Today, for good or ill, that language is English. Tomorrow it may be something else, although I very much doubt it.

Those of us who have inherited the English language may not be in a position to appreciate the value of the inheritance. Or we may go on resenting it because it came as part of a package deal which included many other items of doubtful value and the positive atrocity of racial arrogance and prejudice which may yet set the world on fire. But let us not in rejecting the evil throw out the good with it.

Some time last year I was travelling in Brazil meeting Brazilian writers and artists. A number of the writers I spoke to were concerned about the restrictions imposed on them by their use of the Portuguese language. I remember a woman poet saying she had given serious thought to writing in French! And yet their problem is not half as difficult as ours. Portuguese may not have the universal currency of English or French but at least it is the national language of Brazil with her eighty million or so people, to say nothing of the people of Portugal, Angola, Mozambique etc.

Of Brazilian authors I have only read, in translation, one novel by Jorge Amado who is not only Brazil's leading novelist but one of the most important writers in the world. From that one novel *Gabriella* I was able to glimpse something of the exciting Afro-Latin culture which is the pride of Brazil, and is quite unlike any other culture. Jorge Amado is only one of the many writers Brazil has produced. At their national writers' festival there were literally hundreds of them. But the work of the vast majority will be closed to the rest of the world for ever, including no doubt the work of some excellent writers. There is certainly a great advantage in writing in a world language.

I think I have said enough to give an indication of my thinking on the importance of the world language which history has forced down our throats. Now let us look at some of the most serious handicaps. And let me say straight away that one of the most serious handicaps is *not* the one people talk about most often, namely, that it is impossible for anyone ever to use a second language as effectively as his first. This assertion is compounded of half-truth and half bogus mystique. Of course, it is true that the vast majority of people are happier with their first language than with any other. But then the majority of people are not writers. We do have enough examples of writers who have performed the feat of writing effectively in a second language. And I am not thinking of the obvious names like Conrad. It would be more germane to our subject to choose African examples.

The first name that comes to my mind is Equiano Clauda, better known as Gustavus Vassa, the African. Equiano was an Ibo – (I believe from the village of Iseke in the Orlu division of Eastern Nigeria). He was sold as a slave at a very early age and transported to America. Later he bought his freedom and lived in England. In 1789 he published his life story, a beautifully written document which, among other things, set down for the Europe of his time something of the life and habit of his people in Africa, in an attempt to counteract the lies and slander invented by some Europeans to justify the slave trade.

Coming nearer to our times we may recall the attempts in the first quarter of this century by West African nationalists to come together and press for a greater say in the management of their own affairs. One of the most eloquent of that band was the Hon. Casely Hayford of the Gold Coast. His Presidential Address to the National Congress of British West Africa in 1925 was memorable not only for its sound common sense but as a fine example of elegant prose. The Governor of Nigeria at the time was compelled to take notice and he did so in characteristic style: he called Hayford's Congress "a self-selected, and self-appointed congregation of educated African gentlemen". We may derive some wry amusement from the fact that British Colonial administrators learnt very little in the following quarter of a century. But at least they *did* learn in the end – which is more than one can say for some others.

It is when we come to what is commonly called creative literature that doubts seem to arise. Obi Wali whose article "Dead End of African Literature" I referred to, has this to say:

... until these writers and their Western midwives accept the fact that any true African literature must be written in African languages, they would be merely pursuing a dead end, which can only lead to sterility, uncreativity and frustration.

But far from leading to sterility the work of many new African writers is full of the most exciting possibilities.

Take this from Christopher Okigbo's "Limits":

Suddenly becoming talkative
    like weaverbird
Summoned at offside of
    dream remembered
Between sleep and waking.
I hang up my egg-shells
To you of palm grove,
Upon whose bamboo towers hang
Dripping with yesterupwine
A tiger mask and nude spear ...
    Queen of the damp half light,
I have had my cleansing,
Emigrant with air-borne nose,
    The he-goat-on-heat.

Or take the poem "Night Rain" in which J. P. Clark captures so well the fear and wonder felt by a child as rain clamours on the thatch-roof at night and his mother walking about in the dark, moves her simple belongings.

Out of the run of water
That like ants filing out of the wood
Will scatter and gain possession
Of the floor ...

I think that the picture of water spreading on the floor "like ants filing out of the wood" is beautiful. Of course if you have never made fire with faggots you may miss it. But Clark's inspiration derives from the same source which gave birth to the saying that a man who brings home ant-ridden faggots must be ready for the visit of lizards.

I do not see any signs of sterility anywhere here. What I do see is a new voice coming out of Africa, speaking of African experience in a world-wide language. So my answer to the question, "Can an African ever learn English well enough to be able to use it effectively in creative writing?" is certainly "yes". If on the other hand you ask: "Can he ever learn to use it like a native speaker?" I should say, "I hope not". It is neither necessary nor desirable for him to be able to do so. The price a world language must be prepared to pay is submission to many different kinds of use. The African writer should aim to use English in a way that brings out his message best without altering the language to the extent that its value as a medium of international exchange will be lost. He should aim at fashioning out an English which is at once universal and able to carry his peculiar experience. I have in mind here the writer who has something new, something different to say. The nondescript writer has little to tell us, anyway, so he might as well tell it in conventional language and get it over with. If I may use an extravagant simile, he is like a man offering a small, nondescript routine sacrifice for which a chick or less will do. A serious writer must look for an animal whose blood can match the power of his offering.

In this respect Amos Tutuola is a natural. A good instinct has turned his apparent limitation in language into a weapon of great strength – a half-strange dialect that serves him perfectly in the evocation of his bizarre world. His last book, and to my mind, his finest, is proof enough that one can make even an imperfectly learnt second language do amazing things. In this book *The Feather Woman of the Jungle* Tutuola's superb story-telling is at last cast in the episodic form which he handles best instead of being painfully stretched on the rack of the novel.

From a natural to a conscious artist: myself, in fact. Allow me to quote a small example, from *Arrow of God* which may give some idea of how I approach the use of English. The Chief Priest is telling one of his sons why it is necessary to send him to church:

I want one of my sons to join these people and be my eyes there. If there is nothing in it you will come back. But if there is something there you will bring home my share. The world is like a Mask, dancing. If you want to see it well you do not stand in one place. My spirit tells me that those who do not befriend the white man today will be saying *had we known* tomorrow.

Now supposing I had put in another way. Like this for instance:

I am sending you as my representative among those people – just to be on the safe side in case the new religion develops. One has to move with the times or else one is left behind. I have a hunch that those who fail to come to terms with the white man may well regret their lack of foresight.

The material is the same. But the form of the one is *in character* and the other is not. It is largely a matter of instinct, but judgement comes into it too.

You read quite often nowadays of the problems of the African writer having first to think of his mother tongue and then to translate what he has thought into English. If it were such a simple, mechanical process I would agree that it was pointless – the kind of eccentric pursuit you might expect to see in a modern Academy of Lagado; and such a process could not possibly produce some of the exciting poetry and prose which is already appearing.

One final point remains for me to make. The real question is not whether Africans *could* write in English but whether they *ought to*. Is it right that a man should abandon his mother-tongue for someone else's? It looks like a dreadful betrayal and produces a guilty feeling.

But for me there is no other choice. I have been given this language and I intend to use it. I hope, though, that there always will be men, like the late Chief Fagunwa, who will choose to write in their native tongue and ensure that our ethnic literature will flourish side by side with the national ones. For those of us who opt for English there is much work ahead and much excitement.

Writing in the London *Observer* recently, James Baldwin said:

My quarrel with English language has been that the language reflected none of my experience. But now I began to see the matter in quite another way ... Perhaps the language was not my own because I had never attempted to use it, had only learned to imitate it. If this were so, then it might be made to bear the burden of my experience if I could find the stamina to challenge it, and me, to such a test.

I recognise, of course, that Baldwin's problem is not exactly mine, but I feel that the English language will be able to carry the weight of my African experience. But it will have to be a new English, still in full communion with its ancestral home but altered to suit its new African surroundings.

Appendix C

ORIGINAL REFERENCES

The following are the original essays on which the chapters in this book are based.

1. "The King, The King's English and I", *Transition* (Accra) 38 (1971).

2. "The English Language and the Origins of African Nationalism", *Mawazo* (Kampala) 1 (1) (June 1967).

3. "Islam and the English Language in East and West Africa", chapter in: *Language Use and Social Change*, edited by W. H. Whiteley (published on behalf of the International African Institute by Oxford University Press, 1971).

4. "The Racial Boundaries of the English Language", paper presented at the Round Table of the International Political Science Association, and the International Center for Research on Bilingualism, Laval University, Quebec City, on the theme "Politics in Multi-Lingual Societies", March 1972.

5. "The English Language and Political Consciousness in British Colonial Africa", *Journal of Modern African Studies* (Cambridge, U.K.) 4 (3) (1968).

6. "Obote's Milton and Nyerere's Shakespeare: The Ideological Consequences of an English Literary Education", background paper for conference on "Indigenous and Imported Systems of Education in Africa",

London School of Oriental and African Studies, March 1973.

7. "Language in Military History: Command and Communication in East Africa", written for this collection.

8. "Some Socio-Political Functions of English Literature in Africa", in J. A. Fishman, C. A. Ferguson and J. Das Gupta (eds.), *Language Problems of Developing Nations* (New York, Wiley, 1968), 183-198.

9. "Meaning versus Imagery in African Poetry", *Présence Africaine* (Paris) (3) (1968).

10. "Politics and Drama: Some African Perspectives" (co-author Molly Mazrui), presented at conference on "National Unity and Cultural Diversity in West Africa", held at the University of Ife, Nigeria, December 1970.

11. "The Impact of the English Language on African International Relations" (co-author Molly Mazrui), *Political Quarterly* (London) 38 (2) (April 1967).

FURTHER REFERENCES

(i) The Introduction and Conclusion contain ideas which are discussed in a wider context in a future book by the same author concerning the emergence of a world culture. Research for this latter book was under the African Section of the World Order Models Project, supported by the World Law Fund and the Carnegie Endowment for International Peace.

(ii) President Obote's essay, "Language and National Identification" was the Opening Address of the Seminar on Mass Media and Linguistic Communications in East Africa, organized by the East African Academy and the East African Institute of Social and Cultural Affairs held at Makerere University College, Kampala, in 1967. The Address was first published in *East Africa Journal* IV (1) (April 1967).

(iii) Chinua Achebe's essay "English and the African Writer" is reprinted here from *Transition* (Kampala) 4 (18) (1965).

Index of Names

Subject Index